EQUIPPING FOR SERVICE

A HISTORICAL ACCOUNT OF THE
BIBLE COLLEGE MOVEMENT
IN NORTH AMERICA

D1713713

EQUIPPING FOR SERVICE

A HISTORICAL ACCOUNT OF THE BIBLE COLLEGE MOVEMENT IN NORTH AMERICA

LARRY J. MCKINNEY

ACCREDITING ASSOCIATION OF BIBLE COLLEGES

Accrediting Association of Bible Colleges
130-F North College
Fayetteville, AR 72701

McKinney, Larry J.
    Equipping for Service

    1. History. I. AABC. II. Title.

ISBN 1-890273-01-5 $17.95

CONTENTS

FOREWORD

Several years ago, as I contemplated our forthcoming fiftieth anniversary celebration, I envisioned a book on the history of the Bible college movement to commemorate this historic milestone. When Dr. McKinney expressed interest in such a project, I eagerly encouraged him to proceed. Frankly, the result has exceeded my expectations.

It has been suggested that Bible college educators have been too busy doing the work of the kingdom to write much about it. I was startled to discover that so little has been written on the movement, especially in light of its contributions to world missions and church leadership. McKinney's work provides a major contribution to the literature of the movement along with *Education with Dimension* by Safari Witmer and the *AABC Story* by John Mostert.

Even with more than 27 years of involvement in the movement as a student and as an employee, this manuscript was very informative. I believe readers will gain a new appreciation for those who committed themselves to passing on the treasure and heritage of faith.

The subject of this book has been researched from two directions. First, the AABC board of directors has been studying the movement in terms of structure and future direction for the association. McKinney pursued his research from a historical viewpoint. Yet, the conclusions drawn from both sources are strikingly similar. If we can read McKinney's concluding chapter perhaps ten or fifteen years from now, it will be interesting to see how his projections will have been fulfilled.

My hope is that readers will be challenged, motivated, and encouraged by this historical work. May we responsibly and courageously accept the baton to continue the work already started, pressing toward maximum effectiveness of service to Christ's kingdom.

Randall E. Bell
AABC Executive Director

PREFACE

The year 1997 marks the one-hundred and fifteenth anniversary of the Bible college movement in North America. From its tiny and unpromising beginning in New York City in 1882, it grew to 248 schools by 1960 and today numbers over 400. This year also marks the fiftieth anniversary of the Accrediting Association of Bible Colleges. Starting with a small group of educational leaders in Winona Lake, Indiana, in 1947, this association has become the primary accrediting body in North America for undergraduate biblical education, providing standardization and accountability for many of the leading Bible colleges.

Besides these historical milestones, Bible institutes and colleges have provided the largest percentage of all evangelical missionaries serving in cross-cultural ministries. These colleges have served as a major source of leadership for thousands of churches and parachurch organizations in North America. As an important, yet neglected, educational and religious phenomenon, it deserves careful attention.

This same educational movement is at a strategic point in its history. It now faces decisions about mission statements, programs, curricula, and even recruitment strategies; its relationship to higher education agencies; and its commitment to Bible-centered education that focuses on equipping students for life and ministry. The timing for this study makes it all the more intriguing.

These facts about today's Bible colleges lead one to consider why this educational movement came into being, why it has grown, and how it has related to the church and higher education over these 115 years.

Larry J. McKinney
December 1996

ACKNOWLEDGMENTS

The many students and leaders, known and unknown, who have been involved in Bible schools and colleges across North America over the last 115 years, and who have given of themselves to the Lord and to the people whom they serve, are the heroes and heroines of this book. These individuals, and many others who have shared in the success of these institutions, have been part of an educational movement rarely recognized for its significance in the equipping of men and women for Christian service. This book is in honor of these students as well as the committed faculty and staff who have helped to shape their lives.

I wish to express a similar word of appreciation to the Accrediting Association of Bible Colleges for allowing me the opportunity to engage in this research and writing project. Your publishing support is appreciated. I must also say a special thank you to Dr. David Smith, Vice President for Academics at Providence Theological Seminary, and Ms. Joniva Mondragon, Administrative Assistant of AABC, for their careful attention to this project as my editors. Because of their efforts, I am able to submit a document that is far more polished than I could have ever produced myself.

Finally, a special word of appreciation to my wife, Debbie, and our two children, who supported me in some of my earlier research and have stood behind me in seeing this project brought to completion in book form. To the three of you, your confidence and love have been a source of encouragement.

CHAPTER ONE

INTRODUCTION:
A STORY THAT DEMANDS TELLING

What is history? There are two definitions that come to mind. First, it is commonly referred to "as a past event or happening." In one sense, history is everything that has occurred, or has been thought, from the beginning of time through the last elapsed instant. It could generally be referred to as all that has taken place at some point in the past.

Second, history is a record of the past—something important enough to be written down. In actuality only a small proportion of all that happens leaves any permanent record. Fortunately, people have long made conscious efforts to preserve the evidence of what they believe to be important occurrences, not only of their own times, but of previous periods. It is this type of systematic study relative to the past that gives us written records. With faithful assistance from librarians and archivists, historians will spend much of their time searching for new evidence and making it freely available for others to study.

In conducting this research on the history of Bible schools/ colleges in North America, a combination of these two meanings is most appropriate. First, the Bible college movement is a significant happening, a religious and educational phenomenon. But it is also a happening that demands an accurate and articulate record. Thus, a historical examination of the Bible college movement in North America is in order.

SIGNIFICANCE OF THIS STUDY

In the late nineteenth century, a movement began that has had a profound influence on evangelical Protestantism. Its impact has been felt in every part of the world, producing a large percentage of North American evangelical missionaries and serving as a primary training center for local church leadership. This religious development was the Bible institute movement, which has evolved into the Bible college movement.

From the humble beginnings of the Missionary Training Institute (Nyack College) in New York City in 1882 to the launching of such schools as Moody Bible Institute in Chicago in 1886 and Toronto Bible School (Ontario Bible College) in 1894, the Bible college movement has proliferated throughout North America over the last century. There are now over 400 Bible schools or colleges in the United States and Canada. Ninety-two of these institutions are recognized by the Accrediting Association of Bible colleges, representing over 31,000 students.[1]

Even though considerable numbers of Bible colleges provide quality education for thousands of young people and adults, the Bible college movement has failed to receive the attention commensurate with its influence. Histories of education afford the Bible college scarcely any notice, encyclopedias make no mention of it, libraries have few volumes on the subject, and even magazine articles provide woefully inadequate material.

Why so little has been written on this movement is difficult to explain. Certainly educators, inside and outside the movement, have become aware that there is a lapse in the field of educational literature. Fifty years ago, Lenice F. Reed made the following statement in a master's thesis entitled, "The Bible Institute Movement in America."

In spite of the fact that so many Bible institutes dot the country from shore to shore, no mention of the movement can be found in an encyclopedia. Even the founders such as D. L. Moody are afforded little space or notice. Though the mission fields are manned by hundreds of Bible school graduates, and though a sizable proportion of Christian

work in the homeland is carried on by those who received
their training in Bible institutes, yet authentic information
seems to be very scant. Many libraries are unable to furnish even a magazine article on the subject.[2]

The most likely explanation is that Bible college educators
have been too preoccupied with the mission and responsibilities
of their own institutions to give much attention to the
description and analysis of their practices. Unfortunately, only
very limited gains have been made since the assessment of Ms.
Reed in 1947. There have been several survey books on the
history of Christian education that have given limited treatment
to Bible colleges and other institutions of Christian higher
education, but nothing of a more detailed nature. There were a
few magazine articles written in the early 1980s, centering
around the one-hundredth anniversary of the movement, but
they did not provide any detail relative to historical influences
or contextual considerations. The topic did not receive the type
of written attention it deserved.

Even the Accrediting Association of Bible Colleges lists few
publications on the topic. The association's list of theses and
dissertations on a wide range of Bible college topics contained
only a small number that were of a historical nature, the majority
of them relating to the development of specific institutions as
opposed to a broader study on the whole movement. With
respect to published books on the subject, S. A. Witmer authored
The Bible College Story: Education with Dimension (Channel Press,
1962), with part of the content dedicated to the history of the
movement. As helpful as Witmer's book has been, over thirty
years have passed since someone from within Bible college
ranks has written any type of comprehensive work. There are
obviously chapters to be added to the story. John Mostert did a
fine job in tracing the forty-year history of the Accrediting
Association of Bible Colleges under the title *The AABC Story*
(AABC, 1986), but his book dealt specifically with the work of
AABC and not the larger Bible college movement.

A more recent book was completed by Virginia Lieson
Brereton entitled *Training God's Army: The American Bible School:
1880-1940* (Indiana University Press, 1990). This scholarly work,

written by one outside the Bible college movement, addresses only the fundamentalist Bible schools in the United States between 1880 and 1940. Her book does not deal with the past 55 years and makes no mention of Canadian institutions.

For a more compelling reason than just adding another book to library shelves, the history of the Bible college movement needs to become articulate for its own benefit. As critical questions are asked about the distinctive role and the future direction of Bible colleges, there is a need to look at the history of the movement. S. A. Witmer, former executive director of AABC, summed it up capably:

> There is a need for Bible college educators to look at the "pit from whence" Bible institutes have been dug; to appreciate the hardships and efforts expended on their founding; the uniqueness and power of biblical education; to see its relevance to the contemporary crisis and the un-precedented vastness of human need for an abiding truth.[3]

OVERVIEW OF THE BOOK

This book traces the history of the Bible college movement in North America from its official beginning in 1882 to the present day. Although there were many church-related colleges and seminaries started in the United States and Canada prior to 1882, most of the institutions commonly recognized as evangelical, and particularly those that are part of the Bible college movement, were started in the later part of the nineteenth century and the twentieth century. Chapters two and three examine the early theological and educational backgrounds of the movement because these were the milieu out of which many of the early Bible schools or colleges developed.

Chapters four through six are dedicated to the Bible school/ college movement during its formative years from 1882 to 1920. Chapter four focuses on many of the early institutions that grew out of the changing patterns of Protestant revivalism in the late nineteenth and early twentieth centuries. Chapter five looks at a number of the leading personalities who provided the leadership for these early schools. Chapter six identifies certain key theological themes that characterized these institutions.

A primary focus of the book is on church and educational developments that have helped to shape the Bible college movement since those early years. Two of these key factors, addressed in chapters seven and eight, include the faith mission movement and the fundamentalist-modernist controversy. Chapter nine examines the growth of Canadian Bible colleges while Chapter ten looks at the growth pattern in the United States and the founding of the Accrediting Association of Bible Colleges. Chapter eleven carefully studies the changes that have taken place in the Bible college movement, particularly from 1960 to the present. Chapter twelve addresses the future direction of Bible colleges given the many changes that are taking place in our world as we look to the twenty-first century.

In summary, this study will seek to shed new light on Bible college education in North America, provide historical perspective for current issues, and provide further inspiration for those involved in theological education. It is a story that demands telling to those who are involved in this unique educational ministry, and even to those who are not.

DEFINITIONS

What is a Bible college? To start with, it is a Christian college, an institution of Christian higher education preparing students for life and ministry. But it is a distinct type of Christian college. It is not a Christian liberal arts college or university, nor is it a theological seminary. It is a Bible college. Perhaps the following definitions will add clearer understanding to the study:

Bible college. According to the Accrediting Association of Bible Colleges, there are three basic distinctives: First, a Bible college requires a core of biblical/theological subjects. Second, a Bible college requires hands-on experience in student ministry or Christian service. Third, the numerous professional options at a Bible college emphasize training that specializes in human services, both in the church and society.[4]

The preceding distinctives represent a broader paradigm than the more traditional model used in the past. In 1969 John Mostert, former Executive Director of AABC, classified Bible colleges as "professional or specialized institutions with the primary purpose of preparing students for Christian ministries or church vocations through a program of biblical, professional and general studies."[5]

While the arguments surrounding the mission of Bible colleges continue, the broader paradigm is consistent with the reasons why today's students select a Bible college: (1) those desiring pastoral training (looking to the Bible college as terminal or pre-seminary training); (2) those looking for quality professional training for a broad array of Christian ministries; (3) those who desire preparation for lay service in the local church; and (4) those seeking preparation for marketplace service in areas such as business, education, teaching English as a second language, social work, sports/recreational ministries, and the performing arts.

Bible institute. The purpose of the Bible institute and of the traditional Bible college are essentially the same. They are both focused on training their students for religious vocations. A major difference between the two types of institution is that the Bible college provides one to two years of liberal arts or general education, while the Bible institute provides very limited offerings in this area. Consequently, the college awards a bachelor's degree, while the institute awards some type of diploma.[6]

Christian liberal arts college/university. The Christian liberal arts college and university, though Christocentric in philosophy, has a foundation of general education in the humanities and sciences to prepare students for a wider variety of vocations than the Bible college. The emphasis is on liberal arts education.[7] A number of the original Bible schools that will be discussed in this study have evolved into Christian liberal arts institutions.

Theological seminary. The theological seminary may be similar in mission to the Bible college in that it prepares students for church-related vocations. An obvious difference, however, is that the seminary provides graduate education. With the bachelor's degree serving as a prerequisite for admission, most seminary programs are at the master's or doctorate level.

In the past, the training received in a Bible college was often recognized as quite adequate for those pursuing a church-related vocation. However, the expectations of churches and parachurch organizations have often changed. Many pastors and church leaders are now expected to have a seminary degree. The Bible college is becoming less of a terminal training institution and more of a foundational step in theological education and career preparation.

LIMITATIONS

A review of historical literature does have certain limitations that are endemic to students of history. Although I will attempt to be scientifically objective, I cannot help but be somewhat subjective, particularly with my personal involvement in the topic. I am a graduate of a Bible college and have also worked for many years as a Bible college professor and administrator. I am a strong proponent of Bible college education.

Writers of history come to the process of selection, emphasis, and arrangement complete with their own values; they cannot and should not prevent the intrusion of these values. In the writing of history, science and art complement each other.[8]

The limitations of unavoidable subjectivity must not, however, be accepted as a disclaimer. Serious writers of history will acknowledge their obligations to be accurate and to present the past with verisimilitude.

Whenever historians defend the scientific objectivity of history, they are most likely to have in mind the historian's ability to prove single facts or sequences of facts. Unless they insist that their interpretations are the only possible correct ones, they cannot maintain that there can be much more than a sweet reasonableness in their evaluation, selection, and arrangement of those facts or sequences.[9]

It is in this spirit of "sweet reasonableness" that I have conducted my research and written this book.

CHAPTER TWO

NORTH AMERICAN PROTESTANTISM: 1882-1920

Throughout its history, the Christian church has attempted, with varying degrees of commitment and success, to relate itself and its message to the world about it. Certainly, one of the most significant challenges of the church within a changing world took place in the last decades of the nineteenth century and the early part of the twentieth century leading up to World War I. Religious historian Sydney E. Ahlstrom stated, "No aspect of American church history is more in need of summary and yet so difficult to summarize as the movements of dissent and reaction that occurred between the Civil War and World War I."[1]

It was a period of unprecedented change, which produced a threat and challenge to biblical Christianity. For the first time in American religious history, the self-confident and aggressive Protestant majority started to lose its strong foundation. "After 1865 the problems of reconstruction, urbanization, natural science, and modern culture destroyed the great evangelical concerns, leaving a situation where dissenters were merely angry and frustrated."[2] In considering this time period, Arthur M. Schlesinger, Sr., purported, "Perhaps at no time in its American development has the path of Christianity been so surely beset with pitfalls and perils."[3] As a result of this significant challenge to Protestant Christianity, patterns of institutional religion were altered.

Canada, in contrast to the United States, was a very young nation at the end of the nineteenth century. It was not until two years after the Civil War had ended in the United States that the Dominion of Canada was formed through the British North America Act of 1867. Yet, only four of Canada's ten provinces were part of the original Confederation. Most of the other provinces would join by the turn of the century. Though larger in area than the United States, Canada was much smaller in population. By 1901 the young nation had a population of about five and a third million, compared to seventy-six million for its southern neighbor.[4]

Canada's long history of English-French tension is another characteristic that separates its church history from that of the United States. Tension between French Catholics and English Protestants provided one of the main external props for Quebec's distinct French-Catholic culture, an issue that is still very alive today. By far the largest single denomination in Canada at the turn of the century was the Roman Catholic Church, which made up 41 percent of the population. The largest bloc of Catholics were French Canadians, who composed about 31 percent of the Canadian people.[5]

Yet, in spite of the many differences between the two countries, Christian development in late nineteenth century Canada showed striking similarities to what was happening at the same time in the United States. Like American evangelicals, Canadian believers were committed to spreading the gospel over a vast frontier. Similarly, they had to respond to the disintegrating affects of liberal ideas on the belief system of conservative Protestantism. Canadian church historian John Webster Grant pointed out that "new intellectual movements were beginning to affect Canadian Protestants in the latter part of the nineteenth century, although the impact on Roman Catholicism would be delayed for several decades."[6]

It was during this same period of tension between the church and the newly emerging patterns of North American life that the Bible college movement was born and experienced its formative growth. How did the intellectual, theological, and social changes in North America in the late nineteenth century and the early twentieth century affect the state of Protestantism during this time period? What were the emerging trends within

North American Protestantism that related to the early Bible schools?

According to historian Louis Gaspar, Protestantism in the late nineteenth and early twentieth centuries, experienced intellectual change.

Various discoveries in experimental sciences not only revealed the potential capacity of men's minds, but they also began to change men's views regarding biblical cosmology, because the new scientific outlook had challenged the place of revelation as a source of knowledge. Churchmen were shocked when colleges eliminated many religious courses, while adding secular subjects in their curricula. They became alarmed when evolution became a working hypothesis in almost every discipline, including religion.[7]

It was, second, a period of theological change. George W. Dollar, an outspoken fundamentalist historian, described the theological change as follows:

The war between the states was over and thousands of war-weary and wounded soldiers of both sides returned to shattered homes and farms. But another war was soon to break out, one which has not yet ended. A war over the Bible, one destined to do more damage, wreck more churches, erode more theological centers, and mislead more people than all our wars. The first chapter in this conflict might be dated accurately as the twenty-five years from 1875 to 1900. A massive attack was raised against the verbal, plenary, and infallible authority of the Word of God. Scholars, teachers, denominational executives, and educators joined to reject the essential truths of historical Christianity.[8]

Gaspar described how this attack upon fundamentalist theology was initiated:

"The higher critics, most of whom had studied in Germany, began to employ the empirical method to the study of the Bible, thereby striking at the roots of evangelical

Christianity, which depended for its epistemology upon an infallible revelation."[9]

Third, it was a period of social and economic change. The population began to shift from the small community to the urban industrial center. According to religious historian Stewart C. Cole,

The small self-sufficient community gave way to the cosmopolitan area interdependent with a national chain of other such trade areas. People were massed to large armies to furnish "hands" for factories. European and Negro immigration was accelerated. Problems of adequate housing, employment, markets, profits and lawlessness accompanied this industrial expansion. The modern city emerged as a new phenomenon with the machine age.[10]

The sources of foreign immigration to the United States changed significantly after the Civil War, particularly among those of European descent. In 1860 immigrants from southern and eastern Europe comprised one percent of the foreign born population; but in 1910, they made up 38 percent.[11] The predominantly Protestant immigration gave way to larger numbers of Roman Catholic, Greek Orthodox, and Jewish people in a new wave of immigration that increased the heterogeneity of the population. This presented a challenge to those of a conservative Protestant persuasion.

As was previously cited, the demographics of Canada were quite different from the United States in the late nineteenth and early twentieth centuries. Although the eastern cities, such as Montreal and Toronto, would experience large numbers of immigrants from southern and eastern Europe, the polarization between Roman Catholicism and Protestantism already existed because of the early influences from France and Great Britain. The western provinces were still in their formative stages of development, but the influences of various ethnic groups from Europe were already being seen.

In the late nineteenth and early twentieth centuries, intellectual and theological as well as social and economic changes affected society as a whole and presented a new set of challenges to Protestant Christianity. Protestant churches, which had wielded significant influence on the development of the North American society, began to be tested as never before. The first major challenge was the influence of Darwinism.

THE INFLUENCE OF DARWINISM

The Civil War has generally been viewed as a watershed in American history, standing at a point of demarcation between the old and the new. Winthrop Hudson suggested that a major difference between pre- and post-Civil War America was a shift in the intellectual climate due in large part to developments in modern science. The symbol of that change was Charles Darwin's *Origin of Species* (1859).[12]

Although the concept of biological evolution is often attributed to Charles Darwin (1809-1882), he historically advanced the speculations and scientific research of previous scholars. Erasmus Darwin, his own grandfather in England, and such French naturalists as Lamarck, Buffon, and Geoffrey Saint-Hicaire taught authoritative systems of evolution in the first half of the nineteenth century.[13] Robert Chambers, a Scotsman, wrote anonymously *Vestiges of the Natural History of Creation* in 1844. This was the first printed work on biological evolution to be circulated in the United States (first American edition, 1845). While the book was denounced for its atheistic presuppositions, it paved the way for Darwin's *Origin of Species* which would soon appear.

The post-Civil War era witnessed changes in denominational attitudes toward Darwin. With the exception of the *Princeton Review*, religious periodicals contained few articles denouncing Darwinism, and some even called for a synthesis. The gradual acceptance of Darwinism is obvious by the lack of antagonism caused by the publication of *The Descent of Man* in 1871, which explicitly taught that man's moral sense developed from the social instinct of animals.[14] Through the efforts of such educators as Alexander Winchell, Josephus Rook, Lyman Abbot, John Fiske, and particularly Henry Ward Beecher, significant steps were taken in winning acceptance of evolution. The synthesis that resulted between the teachings of the Bible and biological evolution became known as Christian or theistic evolution.[15] Pfiefer noted the way in which reconciliation between the two seemingly opposite concepts was possible.

In summary, the doctrine based its proof for God's existence either on design, which evolutionary processes were thought to display, or on a final cause behind evolution. It surrendered the Mosaic version of creation as literal truth and interpreted it allegorically. . . . The Christian evolutionist was then faced with the new difficulty of accounting for the doctrine of man's fall. . . . The Christian evolutionist explained this difficulty by holding that man required a savior because he was sinful, whether or not Adam fell. Thus Christian evolution modified the doctrine of biblical inspiration, explained the creation of God's implanting an immortal soul into a body produced by evolution, and placed atonement upon a new basis.[16]

On the Canadian scene, simultaneously with the Confederation of 1867, the new nation started to show a shift in thinking because of the influence of modern science. The initial impact was primarily in the universities. George Munro Grant, a Presbyterian minister who became principal of Queen's University in 1877 urged the hearers of his inaugural address to cultivate both criticism and science. Darwinism, he said, could do no harm to theology. The true believer in God was never upset by discoveries of the scientists. Darwin denied that the Bible is "an inspired scientific textbook."[17]

Darwinism was well received in the United States and Canada in the late nineteenth century. At that time, interest in the natural sciences started to increase. Articles in religious journals and popular magazines showed that readers were becoming absorbed in the evolutionary controversy.[18] It is not surprising that Darwinism was conceived as "the newest pronouncement of the high priesthood of the microscope and the test tube which spoke with a positive infallibility which for many could neither be denied nor ignored."[19] Darwinism, however, was more than just a scientific theory concerning the origin of life. It was gradually becoming an accepted world view among intellectuals. Richard Hofstadter described this growing world view as follows:

> Darwinism established a new approach to nature and gave fresh impetus to the conception of development; it compelled men to try to exploit its findings and methods for the understanding of society through schemes of evolutionary development and organic analogies.[20]

The impact of Darwinism was felt in the late nineteenth century. Darwin's concepts stood in sharp contrast to the teaching of Scripture. In fact, it was a repudiation of the biblical outlook, and led many intellectuals to make a determined effort to replace the biblical foundation with one that was naturalistic. C. Greg Singer wrote:

> The acceptance of Darwinism not only reshaped American constitutional and political thought in the narrower sense of the word, but it also wrought a veritable revolution in every aspect of American thought and practice.... Thus, there came into being an evolutionary concept of economics, an evolutionary concept of education, an evolutionary concept of human history and all of these, in turn, were the result of the fact that a whole new evolutionary concept of man replaced the biblical doctrine.... It was this new conception which furnished the mainspring for the new philosophies of history, education, economics, and literature. Man, rather than God, was now the center of reference, and neither theism nor deism, had much to say to the Darwinian mind.... The God of the Scriptures was being banished from the affairs of men in much the same way as he had already been banished from any control over the laws of nature.[21]

Needless to say, in the theological realm Darwinism brought a new understanding of the nature and fall of man, sin and depravity, and Christ and salvation. Hofstadter summed it up rather succinctly in the following statement:

> Religion had been forced to share its traditional authority with science, and American thought had been greatly

secularized. Evolution had made its way into the churches themselves, and there remained not a single figure of outstanding proportions in Protestant theology who still ventured to dispute it. But the evolution had been translated into divine purpose, and in the hands of skillful preachers, religion was livened and refreshed by the infusion of an authoritative idea from the field of science.[22]

Although many of the remaining religious citadels, particularly among mainline Protestant denominations, were broken down as chief victories were won for Darwinism, there was strong resistance from the conservative element of the church. The most noted clerical objection of the late nineteenth century came from Charles Hodge in his statement of anti-Darwinian views, *What is Darwinism?* (1874). An old-school clergyman, author of numerous theological works, and editor of the *Princeton Review*, Hodge spoke with authority for a large body of churchmen. In his polemical volume, he reminded his readers that "the Bible has little charity for those who reject it. It pronounces them to be either derationalized or demoralized, or both."[23] "The perilous paths of atheism threaten all who trifle with evolution," he stated, citing a formidable list of alleged materialists and atheists, including Darwin, Haeckel, Huxley, Buchner, and Voght.[24] Hodge charged that Darwin had carefully excluded any suggestion of design for nature, and closed with the assertion that Darwinism and atheism were synonymous.[25]

Probably the most popular religious leader of the later nineteenth century was Dwight L. Moody, a noted evangelist. When Moody began his revivalistic activities in the mid-1870s, churchmen were just starting to worry about the impact of Darwinism. Some of his supporters did attempt to reconcile evolution and theology, but the largest percentage of his ardent backers rejected it entirely from the outset and accepted Charles Hodge's conclusion that Darwinism was atheism.[26] Moody himself rejected evolution and found it advantageous to invite college students to his summer Bible conference at Northfield, Massachusetts, so that those who were troubled by the threat posed to their faith by science could be reassured.[27]

Moody's own view of evolution was, "It is easier to believe that man was made after the image of God than to believe, as some young men and women are being taught now, that he is an offspring of a monkey."[28] However, his biblical literalism was not as bitterly defensive as that of later fundamentalists.

Although the conservative contingent continued to hold to the biblical position of creation as opposed to evolution, Darwinism had made a major impact on Protestant Christianity by the end of the nineteenth century. According to Hofstadter, the impact of Darwinism was evident:

> Periodically in modern history scientists have set forth new theories whose consequences go far beyond the internal development of science as a system of knowledge and far beyond such practical applications as they may happen to have. Discoveries of this magnitude shatter old beliefs and philosophies; they suggest (indeed often impose) the necessity of building new ones.[29]

This growing influence of Darwinism proved to be a significant challenge to conservative Protestants as they attempted to respond to a changing culture in the early twentieth century.

THE INFLUENCE OF HIGHER CRITICISM

The second major challenge presented to conservative Protestantism was a theological one, the development of a critical view of Scripture. It was a major factor in producing in North America "the system of naturalism called liberalism."[30] As Gaspar wrote, most of those higher critics who had "studied in Germany, began to employ the empirical method to the study of the Bible, thereby striking at the roots of evangelical Christianity, which depended for its epistemology upon an infallible revelation."[31]

Modern rationalism or the Age of Enlightenment had its birth in Germany under Immanual Kant (1724-1814). Followers of his school of thought include such prominent figures as Johann Gottfried Eichhorn (1752-1827), Julius Wellhausen (1844-

1918), and Ferdinand C. Baur (1792-1860). The profound impact of this system of thought can only be briefly summarized here.[32]

The Bible came to be viewed only as a subjective record of man's religious experience that could be understood by reason and sensation. Thus, any type of literal approach to the Scriptures was rejected. The subjective, rational approach to the study of the Scriptures had serious and far reaching ramifications. Higher criticism in essence challenged traditional assumptions and opinions, attacked the text of the Bible, contested the genuineness of the biblical books, and removed the foundations for the church and historical doctrines.[33]

It was 1850 when the first impulses of higher criticism were felt in the United States through two New England Unitarian scholars, John Palfrey and Andrew Horton. Their books questioned traditional views of the Pentateuch.[34] By the close of the century every major denomination had teachers in their schools who were teaching higher criticism. In the Presbyterian church, Charles A. Briggs of Union Theological Seminary, Henry P. Smith of Lane Theological Seminary, and A. C. McGiffert of both Lane and Union were brought to trial for denying verbal plenary inspiration.[35] In the Northern Baptist Church, William Rainey Harper, the president of the University of Chicago, William Newton Clarke of Colgate Seminary, and A. H. Strong, the president of Rochester Theological Seminary, held certain critical views.[36] In the Methodist Church, Alexander Winchell of Vanderbilt was dismissed for teaching that man descended from pre-Adamic stock, and H. G. Mitchell of Boston University School of Theology was accused of teaching higher criticism.[37]

The pattern was quite the same in Canada with higher criticism gaining a foothold in many of the denominational colleges and seminaries. In 1893 John Campbell, a professor at the Presbyterian College in Montreal, was accused of heresy by his colleagues on the faculty.[38] Similarly, George Workman, a Methodist who had done graduate studies in Germany, was forced from teaching posts at Victoria University and Wesleyan College at Montreal.[39] Anglican F. J. Steen was forced to resign from his post of the Montreal Diocesan College in 1901 because of his liberal views.[40] At McMaster University, I. G. Matthews was under attack for his critical interpretations of the Old Testament. Scholars at the Baptist University, however, were granted the right to pursue their investigations freely.[41] The rising educational level and the growing sophistication of the times seemed to favor the spread of liberal thought within Canadian Protestantism.

In summary, higher criticism eroded the bulwarks of North American Christianity. Along with the attack on the validity of the Scriptures, the epistemological foundation for biblical education was shaken.

Fundamentalism, a reaction of Bible institutes to liberal views stemming from Darwinism and higher criticism, emerged in the last two decades of the nineteenth century.[42] One of its purposes was to counter liberal theology, which had made inroads into theological seminaries. Conservative groups recognized potential problems if like-minded graduates of these more liberal schools would be positioned in their churches and missions. They also discerned the impossibility of depending on such schools for the training of religious workers. Frank E. Gaebelein wrote,

> The evangelical revivals in the nineteenth century cre-
> ated both a thirst for knowledge and a demand for trained
> laymen. The awakening of the church to its world-wide
> mission called for many more missionary recruits than
> seminaries were producing. . . . Furthermore, the reaction
> to rationalism in denominational colleges and seminaries
> called for schools that were unquestionably evangelical.
> It is not a coincidence that the Bible institute movement
> grew up during this period.[43]

The place of Bible schools as a reaction to theological change will be dealt with more specifically in future chapters of this book.

THE INFLUENCE OF THE SOCIAL GOSPEL MOVEMENT

The social gospel movement is usually regarded as conservative Protestantism's antithesis in social reform. It was born amid the urban and industrial problems near the end of the nineteenth century, and it reached full maturity in the first two decades of the twentieth century. The primary intent of this movement was to respond to the increased social and economic problems that were seeping from society into the churches. The exploited labor force had begun to look upon the churches as benefactors of business with little interest in the social and economic problems of the poor.

Known as the 'Social Gospel,' the movement was essentially the response of certain American Christians to the industrial revolution and the civilization that was produced by this revolution. Traditional Christianity was no longer sufficient for the demands of the day. In an industrial civilization, it was necessary to return to the teachings of Jesus and bring forth a socialized Christianity and a Christianized society.[44]

The rise of this manifestation of social consciousness did not develop in a vacuum; its roots extended back to German Idealism and Friedrich Schleiermacher (1768-1834), the fountainhead of modern theology.[45] Schleiermacher challenged the idea of objective religious authority and plummeted Germany theology into subjectivism.[46] The influence of Kant and Schleiermacher is particularly evident in Albrecht Ritschl (1822-1889), who closely identified religion and morality.[47] Ritschl's understanding of the gospel helps to explain his strong support for the social gospel movement. He saw the gospel as having two different foci: 1) Redemption, and 2) God's establishment of His kingdom. According to Ritschl, God did not take the initiative in redeeming man; rather, man took the first step toward his own salvation by redeeming society through environmental change. Ritschl viewed the kingdom of God as ethical rather than spiritual, coming about through the elimination of social injustice and the establishment of social harmony.[48] Such concepts prompted Dillenberger and Welch to add that Ritschl "gave powerful impetus to the development of the social gospel in Protestantism."[49]

As part of this climate, C. Howard Hopkins, in his study of the social gospel movement in North America, cites four specific groups with varying social outlooks. First, orthodox Protestantism with its pietistically-oriented view of life, reacted to significant social difficulties by emphasizing individual transformation that would in turn respond to social problems. Second, there were the so-called enlightened conservatives, or those who would fit within the framework of what has been called progressive orthodoxy. Henry Ward Beecher and Phillips Brooks were representative leaders in this movement. They were willing to help reconcile their faith to the new development in science and thought and were also willing to combine, in varying ways, the work of the spiritual and social aspects of the kingdom of God. With the third group, Hopkins gave credit to what he calls the "Heritage of Evangelicalism." This group believed that the kingdom of God needed to be active in the world to resolve the traditional dualism between "heavenly" and "earthly" matters, a dichotomy which the revivalists created by falsely separating this world from the other.[50] Finally, there was Unitarianism, which was even further along the road of social concern than the other groups. Unitarians stressed the dignity and divine possibilities of man. They believed that salvation could be attained through character culture, and they greatly strengthened the idealogical roots of social Christianity.[51]

Another source of the social gospel movement was the systematic decline of Calvinism in New England through the so-called "New Divinity" men, particularly Nathaniel Taylor and Horace Bushnell, the Congregationalist pastor of Hartford, Connecticut. Bushnell rejected the traditional "conversion experience" theology and maintained that "the child can grow up as a Christian and never know himself to be otherwise."[52] He contended that conversion is not a onetime experience but the result of the inculcation of Christian ideals through culture and education. Bushnell's rejction of the biblical doctrine of salvation, the belief that man is a sinner and cannot be saved apart from God's grace and initiative, led to an environmental salvation dispensed by social virtue. The ideas embryonic in Bushnell became dominant themes in the writings of Washington Gladden and Walter Rauschenbusch, the primary leaders of the social gospel movement in America.[53]

The most mature, systematic expression of the theology of the social gospel movement is contained in Rauschenbusch's last major work, A Theology of the Social Gospel (1917). Having rejected the biblical account and any concept of original sin, Rauschenbusch defined sin within the context of its social ramifications. Sin, he said, is selfishness. Salvation is the opposite of selfishness, or love for one's fellow man. Sin becomes societal, not individual, and the way to redeem men is to preach a gospel of environmental reform. Salvation, then, is basically a change of attitude toward society. In death Christ bore the sins of society so that society could be redeemed. He wrote, "The fundamental terms and ideas—'sanctification, imputation, substitution, and merit'—are post-biblical ideas, and are alien from the spirit of the gospel."[54]

Out of this theological climate, an increasing social consciousness arose. Many of the clergymen who were increasingly uneasy with social problems and the conservative response to them, were themselves men who had much experience in urban areas. They knew firsthand the always difficult and often unbearable circumstances of working people. They were distressed by social conditions and disturbed by the great gulf between the church and the working class. Their concern was directed toward the myriad of problems facing a fast developing industrial society. These problems included the plight of the worker and the potential violence from such a plight. As Hofstadter commented, ministers were learning about socialism and were generally apprehensive concerning it. What they sought, therefore, was a compromise between the harsh individualism of the competitive order and possible dangers of socialism.[55]

According to Rudnick, the impact of the social gospel movement in America prompted many major denominations to create departments of labor or social action to apply the gospel to social needs.

The impact of the social gospel and its wide acceptance among Protestants can be measured in terms of the many social resolutions and programs which were adopted by denominations and interchurch groups. Most significant of these was the issuance in 1908 by the newly organized Federal Council of Churches of a 'Social Creed of the Churches' which called for significant action on many social problems of the day.[56]

Robert T. Handy, in *The Social Gospel Movement in America, 1870-1920*, contended that the social gospel movement, with its liberal foundations, started to disintegrate after 1932 with the coming of the great economic depression in the United States and Canada, reaching the point of extinction by 1940. He concluded, however, that "the social gospel has left a lasting impression on American church life."[57]

The leading Canadian interpreter of social gospel thought was Salem G. Bland (1859-1950), a Methodist who joined the faculty of Wesley College in Winnipeg in 1903. Although there were radical, progressive, and conservative strands of the social gospel movement in Canada, for much of its early history the movement remained more evangelical than it did in the United States.[58] A driving force in the practical application of the movement was J. S. Woodsworth, superintendent of the All Peoples' Mission in Winnipeg. He worked among newcomers to Canada who were facing unemployment, poor housing and health services, and public neglect. Accounts of his experiences in *Strangers Within Our Gates* (1909) and *My Neighbor* (1911) helped to popularize the growing social movement. University settlement houses, promoted by Sara Libby Carson, a Presbyterian who had experience in settlement houses in the United States, were important in the spread of reform sentiment. Youth fellowships sponsored by the churches and the YMCA and the YWCA also contributed to the growth of the social gospel movement.[59]

Overall, efforts of Canadian Protestants to respond to the changing social needs in the decades before World War I were not any more successful than similar attempts in the United

States. By the turn of the century, with the growth of the urban centers and an increase in immigrants who were not of British ancestry, Canada experienced many of the same difficulties that faced churches and social agencies in the United States.[60]

Those in the more conservative Protestant tradition, including many of the revivalists who led the way in the founding of the early Bible schools, did not support the social gospel movement. If social reform meant direct involvement in institutional efforts to improve society, few conservatives were interested. This element of Christianity ministered in many social realms, such as orphanages, alcoholic rehabilitation centers, prostitute recovery missions, and YMCAs, but their main thrust was the salvation of the soul. They were preachers who saw as their primary duty the conversion of individual souls to Christ rather than the improvement of society. They rejected the notion that the environment made the individual. For them the opposite was nearer to the truth; until individuals were made new by conversion, they believed society would remain seriously flawed.[61]

This does not mean that conservative Christians were indifferent to contemporary social inequities. Their writing evidenced a concern that social gospellers could hardly improve upon with respect to personal morality and also in opposition to political and economic abuses. They did not believe that institutional reforms were wrong. A few strong revivalists, to be sure, considered them a waste of the Christian's time; they believed only Jesus could accomplish complete social regeneration. But the majority, including prominent Bible school founders and leaders, such as A. B. Simpson, D. L. Moody, and A. J. Gordon, believed collective efforts were necessary to curtail, if not to eliminate, the social products of sin. Social concern in the progressive tradition ran deep among fundamentalists, but their theological views about human nature and the roots of sin prevented them from becoming full-fledged social reformers.[62]

D. L. Moody's attitude toward the social gospel movement was marked by an unwillingness to let fresh ideas alter his view of spiritual ministry. To begin with, the social gospel doctrine of the Fatherhood of God and the brotherhood of man was contrary to Moody's theology. Moody stated,

> I want to say very emphatically that I have no sympathy with the doctrine of universal brotherhood and universal fatherhood. . . . Show me a man that will lie and steal and get drunk and ruin a woman—Do you tell me that he is my brother? Not a bit of it. He must be born again in the household of faith before he becomes my brother in Christ.[63]

Moody was involved in the YMCA, YWCA, temperance, city missions, orphanages, and prison ministry. In his work among the poor of Chicago, he often gave coal, food, and clothing to the needy, rescued erring sons of his parishioners from the hands of the law, and found jobs for deserving young men. But his charity was always secondary to this soul winning. The following statement expresses the essence of his attitude toward the social problems of his day:

> A heart that is right with God and man seldom constitutes a social problem and by seeking first the kingdom of God and His righteousness nine-tenths of the social betterment is affected by the convert himself and the other tenth by Christian sympathy.[64]

Conservative Protestants believed that social concern was a natural consequence and proof of conversion. Hence, they were led by this line of reasoning to a final conclusion. If the basic human needs were spiritual and individual, and if a new birth was essential to personal and social improvement, they must devote the bulk of their time and resources to evangelism. "As an ambassador for Christ the Christian minister would not be indifferent to politics, economics, or other aspects of the social order," declared James M. Gray, longtime president of Moody Bible Institute. "But first, last and all the time he will be seeking to reconcile men to God."[65] The primary motive behind evangelism was not the improvement of society but the eternal welfare of the individual. If social improvement followed the gospel, Christians rejoiced, but it was regarded as a secondary motive.

In summary, between 1882 and 1920, unparalleled intellectual, theological, and social change occurred, which greatly altered the state of North American Protestantism. How was this challenge to be met? An answer for some seemed to be a modification of method and a surrender of the old message. For others, however, it was viewed as a time to stand for the truths of the Bible and a time to check the rising tide of irreverent change. According to Dollar, "God raised up able men who would not accommodate, men highly trained and deeply and irrevocably dedicated to the Word of God."[66]

What methods did these religious leaders use to achieve their objectives? Rudnick lists three methods—polemical literature, Bible and prophetic conferences, and Bible institutes.[67] To these could be added vigorous doctrinal and evangelistic preaching from pulpits and an emphasis upon missions. As Carroll Harrington observed,

> A first generation of fundamentalists, led by Dwight L. Moody, the greatest revivalists of the era, began to appear in the Protestant churches after the Civil War. A. B. Simpson, A. J. Gordon, C. I. Scofield, and lesser leaders worked closely with Moody as institution builders and experts in doctrine. Dwight L. Moody and this group of patriarchs labored from 1870 to 1920 to solidify the new movement. . . . By 1900 they had succeeded in planting and expanding the movement within Protestant churches.[68]

These individuals were the visionaries and leaders of the early Bible schools that were started in the late nineteenth and early twentieth centuries. It was an age when North American Protestantism underwent significant change.

CHAPTER THREE

NORTH AMERICAN HIGHER EDUCATION:
1882-1920

The late nineteenth and early twentieth centuries were times of unparalleled change for North American Protestantism and for North American higher education. Traditional values and customs were challenged within the frameworks of the church and academia. This change was so significant that historian Walter Metzger referred to it as an "educational revolution."[1] Both he and Laurence Veysey have contended that this major change, within one generation, was reflected in the early development of the modern university.[2] Prior to this educational revolution, the church or denominational college dominated higher education.

In 1867 Ralph Waldo Emerson observed in his journal that higher education, in the years after the Civil War, would differ from what it had been during the era of the church-related colleges. "The treatises that are written on university reform may be acute or not," suggested Emerson, "but their chief value to the observer is the showing that a cleavage is occurring in the hitherto granite of the past and a new era is nearly arrived."[3] Emerson's observation happened to be prophetic, as a new epoch in higher education was dawning that would bypass the old-time, church-related college or convert it into a defiant outpost of denominationalism. One thing was certain—higher education would never be the same again.

Within this context, how did the emergence of the university relate to the decline of religion within North American colleges?

How did the decline of religion within North American colleges relate to the emerging Bible schools?

EARLY ROOTS

Prior to the Civil War, religion and higher education were practically synonymous in the United States. Most of the early colleges in America were established by Protestant denominations. "Education in colonial America," said Myron Wicke, "was the child of religion; it could hardly have been otherwise."[4] From the founding of Harvard, America's first college, in 1636 until the late nineteenth century, the church remained the controlling influence in American higher education, ministering to the religious needs of students, partly through the parish but primarily through schools and colleges.[5]

Of the first nine colleges (see Table III-1) founded between 1636 and 1769, all but one were religious in nature and represented a particular Protestant denomination. Their primary purpose was to train ministers and to give Christian education to young people.

TABLE III-1

RELIGIOUS AFFILIATION OF THE FIRST NINE COLLEGES IN AMERICA[6]

Year	Institution	Founding Group	Motto
1636	Harvard	Puritan/ Congregational	"For Christ and the Church"
1693	William and Mary	Anglican	
1701	Yale	Congregational	"Light and Truth"
1746	Princeton	Presbyterian	"Under God's Guidance It Flourishes"
1753-55	University of Pennsylvania	Nondenominational	

1755	King's College	Anglican (Columbia)	"In Thy Light Shall We See Light"
1764	Brown	Baptist	"In God We Trust"
1766	Rutgers	Dutch Reformed	"Son of Righteousness, Shine Upon the West"
1769	Dartmouth	Congregational	"Virtue Rejoices in Trials"

Elwood Cubberley, in referring to these first nine institutions, stated,

> The religious purpose had been dominant in the founding of each institution. There was a general shading-off in the strict denominational control and insistence upon religious conformity in the foundations after 1750. Still the prime purpose in the founding of each was to train up a learned and godly body of ministers, the earlier congregations at least dreading to leave an illiterate ministry to the churches when our present ministers lie in the dust.[7]

Harvard was founded in 1636 to train the clergy. Until 1700, more than half of its graduates went into the ministry.[8] An early booklet, *New England's First Fruits*, was distributed in England in 1643 to raise funds for the new college. It stated that the purpose was to lead a student "to know God and Jesus Christ which is eternal life (John 17:3), and therefore to lay Christ in the bottom as the only foundation of all sound knowledge and learning."[9] Harvard, in its first code of laws, stated that a student was expected to "pray in secret" and "exercise himself in reading the Scriptures twice a day."[10]

William and Mary was founded in 1693 to the end "that the church of Virginia may be furnished with a seminary of ministers of the gospel, and that the youth may be piously educated in good letters and manners."[11]

Yale, from its inception in 1701, was more conservative than its New England counterpart, Harvard. In a pamphlet published in 1754, President Clapp declared that "colleges are

societies of ministers, for training up persons for the work of
the ministry," and that "the great design of founding this school
(Yale) was to educate ministers in our own way." Later in 1795
its president wrote about the Bible as "the Word of God." In
1825 an evangelistic group from Yale travelled about the
country.[12]

In a published newspaper announcement in 1754, King's
College (Columbia University) declared:

> The chief thing that is aimed at in this college is to teach
> and engage the children to know God in Jesus Christ, and
> to love and serve Him in all sobriety, godliness, and righ-
> teousness of life, with a perfect heart, and a willing mind;
> and to train them up in all virtuous habits and all such
> useful knowledge as may render them credible to their
> families and friends, ornaments to their country, and use-
> ful to the public weal in their generation.[13]

Brown University was founded by the Baptists to train
clergy. The charter stipulated that twenty-two of its thirty-six
trustees must be Baptist and its president "forever a member
of the Baptist church." Dartmouth College was founded to train
men as ministers to work with the American Indians. Princeton,
in its early days, insisted that the faculty be convinced of the
necessity of religious experience for salvation.[14]

Greek and Hebrew, natural philosophy and science, and
theology formed the curricula of these colleges. These subjects
were rigidly prescribed for all students and presented as truth
to be learned rather than debated. Attendance at religious
services was required, and discipline in moral matters was
expected and enforced. The Bible served as the authority for
life and godliness.

The religious awakening in the early part of the nineteenth
century, along with the vast westward expansion of the country,
had a notable impact on higher education. With a zealous
missionary purpose, the churches established many small
colleges, making it possible for young men who wished to study
for the ministry to obtain the needed education nearer to home
and at a much lower cost than if they were to attend a larger

eastern college. There was considerable competition among the churches in establishing these institutions in the newly settled territory. Many denominations felt the need to have at least one college in every state. Because of this sense of urgency, many small colleges were founded hurriedly with no plan for adequate support and little attention to a desirable location. The result of these and other errors was that "of five-hundred colleges founded in sixteen representative states before the Civil War, only a little more than one-hundred survived as permanent institutions. This was a mortality rate of eighty percent."[15] However, in spite of the large number of schools founded in the early and mid-nineteenth century that did not survive, the religious influence was quite pronounced and continued to prevail in American colleges.[16]

Canadian Christian higher education before the later part of the nineteenth century was almost exclusively church-controlled. A distinguishing quality of Canadian higher education, however, was the major role that the Roman Catholic Church played in the formation of a number of colleges in the early years, largely because of the French influence. For example, the birth of higher education in Canada is usually pinpointed as 1663 when the Jesuits founded the "Seminaire de Quebec," offering the classical college course and instruction in theology.[17]

Most of the colleges were governed by a particular denomination or congregation. Even those institutions that were classified as nondenominational had a strong religious influence in the early years. Since Canadian society was influenced by Christian values and traditions, it was not surprising to find such an orientation at work in higher education. Nor was this situation uniquely Canadian: education in Western civilization was a function of the church, and the vocation of professor was handled by the clergy well into the nineteenth century.[18]

Educational historians Robin S. Harris and D. C. Master identified Canadian colleges founded between 1663 and 1867 (Confederation) along with their denominational affiliation (see Table III-2).

TABLE III-2

RELIGIOUS AFFILIATION OF THE EARLY
CANADIAN COLLEGES[19]

Year	Institution	Founding Group
1663	"Seminaire de Quebec" (Laval)	Roman Catholic
1802	King's (NS) (Dalhousie)	Presbyterian
1802	St. Mary's	Roman Catholic
1821	McGill	Anglican
1828	King's (NB)	Anglican
1836	Victoria	Methodist
1838	Acadia	Baptist
1840	Queen's (ON)	Presbyterian
1843	King's (ON)	Anglican
1843	Bishop's	Anglican
1844	Knox	Presbyterian
1850	Queen's (NF)	Anglican
1852	Trinity	Anglican
1853	St. Francis Xavier	Roman Catholic
1857	Albert	Methodist
1861	Morrin	Presbyterian
1863	Huron	Anglican
1866	St. John's	Anglican

At the time of the Confederation (1867), there were eighteen degree-granting institutions in Canada for 3.5 million persons, compared with four colleges/universities in England and Wales for 22 million people and four institutions of higher education in Scotland for 3.3 million people.[20]

The establishment of these institutions reflected several broad social purposes: 1) to educate the clergy, 2) to instruct the next generation of social and political leaders, and 3) to preserve a tradition, whether British or French.[21]

Although these were church-controlled institutions, they offered broad instruction in the liberal arts and in professions, such as law and medicine, in addition to theology. The preparation of clergy was generally understood to involve a grounding in the liberal arts, and so even institutions adopting the nomenclature of the seminary included such offerings.[22] There was little dispute about the place of "true religion" in a curriculum, but denominational exclusiveness remained an issue. Egerton Ryerson, first president of Victoria College, wrote in 1846, "To be zealous for a sect and conscientious in morals are widely different. To inculcate the peculiarities of a sect, and to teach fundamental principles of religion and morality, are equally different."[23]

THE DECLINING IMPACT OF RELIGION

The religious foundation of American higher education began to change rather significantly after the Civil War as the church became less and less influential. Jencks and Riesman addressed this issue of religious decline succinctly:

A century ago this (religion) would have been chapter one of any book on American colleges, but while the Protestant clergy dominated American higher education from the founding of Harvard to the end of the Civil War, their role has diminished steadily since then and is hardly consequential for the system as a whole though it remained important in some colleges.[24]

After the Civil War, Christian theology started to decline as a central focus in higher education. It did not necessarily mean that religion was no longer an important element of culture, yet it did signify that it was losing its place of prominence within academia. In the decade after the publication of the *Origin of Species*, Darwinism made subtle inroads into American thought. Its impact was greatest among the best educated.[25]

Science became a strong adversary of religion. Knowledge derived from scholarship gained steadily in prestige, and the claims for its validity quickly spread from the physical and natural realms to the social and personal ones. The latter two had formerly been the exclusive domain of religion. The development of sociology, economics, law, politics, and psychology as sciences created new standards for behavior that sometimes clashed with the ethical norms derived from religious sources.[26]

The position of the colleges became ambiguous. As institutions, they were heirs of the old religious traditions, yet their faculties increasingly expounded a new set of truths. President James McCosh, travelling to take up his post at Princeton in 1886, felt the weight of the dilemma resulting from that ambiguity as he pondered whether or not to declare his receptivity to Darwinism. He did speak out, at the cost of having his orthodoxy impugned, and thus began the process of "inevitable compromise" between the old and the new beliefs.[27] Although the battle between the old traditions of religion and the new scientific thought would ensue for several decades, one thing was certain—Protestant influence, which had controlled American colleges for over two centuries, would experience precipitous decline.

The impact of religion in Canadian colleges followed a similar pattern. In the years after the Confederation (1867), church colleges were influenced by significant adjustments in Protestant thought. Educational historian D. C. Master described the situation aptly:

> The impact of new ideas in science and biblical criticism began to weaken the hold of the older faith. The new ideas were chiefly British in immediate origin. The conception of man as a sinner who could only be redeemed by divine grace was partially abandoned. It was coming

to be replaced by the humanist conception of man as essentially good and capable of improvement, largely through his own efforts.[28]

Darwin's *Origin of Species* (1859) and *Essays and Reviews* (1860) influenced the development of this humanistic attitude, which led to a growing skepticism toward the supernatural aspects of Christianity.[29]

These changes in theological thinking in the later nineteenth century affected the whole tone of thought in the Canadian church colleges. The nature of these institutions prior to 1867 was dependent upon orthodoxy, and this orthodoxy characterized the theological teaching and also provided the atmosphere in which secular teaching was conducted.[30]

THE EMERGENCE OF THE UNIVERSITY

After the Civil War, the American university came of age. "So rapid was the transformation of the American university between the 1860s and the end of the century that teachers and administrators with a strong sense of tradition were almost overwhelmed."[31]

Prompting the emergence of the university were the technical needs of agriculture and business. In 1862 the United States Congress passed the Morrill Act, which gave substantial land grants, and money grants later, for the endowment of public institutions of agriculture and mechanical arts. "The act itself provided for the support in every state of at least one college where the leading object shall be, without exceeding other scientific or classical studies, to teach the branches of learning related to agriculture and the mechanical arts."[32] Much of the funds set aside for education were used for the small, struggling vocational schools. In states like Wisconsin, Minnesota, Missouri, Georgia, North Carolina, Tennessee, and Iowa, existing institutions were enlarged.[33]

Besides creating land-grant colleges, the Morrill Act of 1862 also gave impetus to the development of state universities. Land-grant funds were added to an already existing state university endowment. The land-grant colleges, which did thrive under the original Morrill Act endowment, were strengthened more significantly by the second Morrill Act of 1890, providing annual federal appropriations for those institutions and stimulating state legislatures to do the same.[34] The Bankhead-Jones Act of 1905 and the Nelson Act of 1907 provided for additional financial support to land-grant institutions. This federal legislation made the public college or university an established fact.

The Morrill Act and subsequent legislation that assisted land-grant colleges and state universities were also significant because they coincided with the growth of industrialism, urbanism, agricultural commercialism, and corporate enterprise. The growing industrial society needed technical skill to run it, scientific knowledge to improve it, and engineering competence to give it cost advantages. The land-grant colleges and state universities were a key product of this industrial movement.[35] As educational institutions, the new colleges and universities communicated the "know-how" that American industry increasingly required. As research centers, they emphasized the applied sciences that American culture was starting to accept. The combination of technical and intellectual interests was a marriage of two emphases that were supposedly incompatible, yet this eclectic pattern was characteristic of the emerging university that served the growing industrial society.

The emerging university, with its growing emphasis on science and research, stood in stark contrast to the antebellum[36] college that had dominated American higher education before the Civil War. While the university stressed the advancement of new knowledge, the antebellum college was steeped in tradition. While the university was providing greater academic freedom for students and faculties, the denominational college was narrow and prescribed. The traditional college was fittingly described by Walter Metzger:

It looked to antiquity for the tools of thought, to Christianity for the by-laws of living; it supplied furniture and discipline for the mind, but constrained intellectual adventure. Like most institutions anchored to tradition, the antebellum college was also paternalistic and authoritarian. In honoring the past and depreciating the present, it drew doubtful conclusion that age best imparts its wisdom when youth surrenders its style. Students took prescribed courses and recited their lessons by rote; professors acted like school-masters, drill masters, and prisonkeepers.[37]

The pattern of the traditional denominational college included the perceptive imperative of religion, the disciplinary advantage of the classics, and the apparent immaturity of youth that called for precepts and discipline.

The most important single consequence of the emergence of the university was that undergraduate students were able to exercise a larger amount of choice in their studies as opposed to the old required curriculum.[38] The elective principle saw the rise of more course offerings in science, language, social science, and other areas of expanding knowledge as a clear indication that no one person could know everything that was worth knowing. The elective principle also moved students to the center of the educational arena where they made choices based on their needs, interests, and motives, recognizing that all educated people do not know the same things. This new system showed, furthermore, that it was no longer possible to cover all subjects in a four-year curriculum.

The rise of the elective system also had religious implications. It was a move away from the Puritan tradition that had made itself known in American higher education for more than 200 years. "One more link with precise religious tradition had been snapped. Another field of endeavor had been modernized and secularized; only the churches themselves remained to be affected, more or less, by the same process."[39]

In summary, the state of American higher education changed in the late nineteenth and early twentieth centuries with the emergence of the university. This change was affected by the technical needs of agriculture and business, which prompted federal legislation favoring land-grant colleges and universities. This shift was further encouraged by a shift in higher education from traditional religion to scientific knowledge and from a prescribed curriculum to an elective system. The emergence of the university was also coupled with the changing state of the church-related college, which was part of the character of American higher education between 1882 and 1920.

In the later nineteenth century, Canada also saw the birth of the university model of education. The motivational factors behind the formation of the Canadian universities were often quite different from their American counterparts. In the decades following the Confederation (1867), western provinces began to establish nondenominational provincial universities, reflecting a wish to avoid the denominational conflicts that were being experienced in higher education in eastern Canada as well as a desire to avoid squandering limited resources by duplicating institutions.[40] It also demonstrated a shift in control for higher education. Universities were viewed as part of the public domain because they served public interests and were supported by public funding. Essential to the development of the fledgling western provinces, universities were not brought under sectarian control. "The transition of the university from a matter of private interests to public interests was paralleled by a movement toward institutional secularization."[41]

This transition did not mean that the interests of the church were excluded from higher education. For example, the first of these western universities, Manitoba (1877), was started as a non-teaching entity, granting degrees by examination, with constituent colleges (St. Boniface, St. John's, Manitoba, and Wesley) performing the teaching function. Even when the University of Manitoba assumed the primary responsibility of teaching, these colleges remained an integral part of the institution under affiliation agreements, and other colleges (St. Andrew's and St. Paul's) established such agreements.[42]

The pattern of affiliation was established in each western university, and it became a national approach to the "denominational issue" in higher education. Provinces became less inclined to give degree-granting privileges to denominational institutions in non-theological disciplines. Instead, these schools were encouraged to operate under the auspices of public universities. This "distinctive Canadian solution to affiliation" provided an avenue for legitimate denominational interests to be addressed while ensuring that "the central core of the university was built on a secular base."[43] According to Peter Rae, the adoption of this broad affiliation approach is "the watermark of Canadian church-related higher education."[44]

The Canadian paradigm of broad affiliation was quite different from the model used in the United States. It reflected the different ideologies within the two countries relative to the role of public and private institutions. While separation of church and state was an underlying principle in the formation of American colleges and universities, Canadians demonstrated a greater support for church-state cooperation. Evidence of such support was the development of the affiliate universities, private religious interests working in tandem with public universities. What was considered unthinkable in the United States proved to be an acceptable liaison in Canada.[45]

CHURCH-RELATED COLLEGES

In addition to the emergence of the university, its counterpart, the denominational or church-affiliated college, also underwent transformation. As Veysey pointed out, from the inception of the early colleges in the seventeenth century until the end of the nineteenth century, most educators believed that educational and theological orthodoxy went together.

> Orthodox Christianity, as the college president usually understood the term, meant a diluted Calvinism. Man, besides possessing the faculties which education was supposed to develop, ought to undergo a definite experience of conversion.[46]

This was the fundamental idea of the universe embraced by traditional college leaders until the late nineteenth century.

Perhaps the commitment to the integration of faith and learning is best characterized in a speech given by President Noah Porter of Yale in 1870:

> To Christ belongs the supreme authority in heaven and earth and. . . . the goings on of nature and the events of human history, including the developments of science and letters, of culture and art, are all in the interest of Christ's kingdom.[47]

A similar correlation between orthodoxy and education was expressed by President John Mockrett Cramp in his inaugural address at Acadia College (Nova Scotia) in 1851. He called attention to:

> the importance of religious influence, pervading the whole course of study, and sanctifying, so to speak, all the arrangements. This College is open to all denominations, nevertheless, we must claim the right of aiming to imbue literature with the spirit of religion, and of inculcating, from time to time, those principles of our common Christianity, and those moral lessons which are admitted by all who wish to shun the reproach of infidelity.[48]

Yet, the sentiments expressed by Porter and Cramp were becoming more infrequently embraced by higher educators. This pattern was certainly influenced by the development of universities, but it was also coupled by an increasing dissatisfaction on the part of many higher educators with respect to denominational colleges. Due to religious origin, and the common requirement that the president and the trustees must be members of the same particular denomination, educators in denominational colleges started to become recognized as far too narrow or simply representing sectarian interests, rather than the broader interests of society.[49] The rise of a more democratic spirit in higher education meant increased external pressure for institutions to become more pluralistic in nature.

Internal pressures also forced denominational colleges to move away from their strict religious focus. Students started to express themselves in more disorderly ways, resulting in a push by faculty for greater control over discipline and instruction.[50] In attempting to respond to these problems, they developed practices that only weakened their authority and cohesion.

The net result of these internal and external pressures was what educational historian George Marsden called "the secularization of the academy."[51] Of the many colleges that started out as narrowly sectarian establishments, very few remained that way. These institutions found that their distinctiveness and exclusiveness had been compromised. In the United States, "liberal Protestants during the first half of the twentieth century dealt with this problem not by sharpening their identity over against the culture, as did the fundamentalists and Catholic intellectuals, but rather by blurring their identity so that there was little to distinguish them from other respectable Americans."[52]

The secularization of mainline Protestant colleges in Canada followed the pattern of colleges in the United States.

Until the end of the nineteenth century they stood for certain precise religious doctrines which gave them vigour and distinctive viewpoint. . . . The partial abandonment of older doctrinal ideas meant that the character of church colleges changed. . . . to a great extent they became, in effect secularized institutions retaining only a nominal relationship with one or other of religious denominations.[53]

As previously noted, Canadian colleges associated with and sponsored by mainline churches almost all became affiliated with public universities. These affiliations only served to weaken their denominational distinctives as they became more secularized.

This religious decline can be seen in three areas: First, the spiritual formation and curriculum; second, the profiles of faculty and administrators; and third, the nature of graduates.

In the category of religious formation, compulsory prayers and chapel services became less important on college campuses. At one time, they were fundamental to North American higher education, and, of all the characteristics of early colleges, they have in many places been the most enduring. However, they were in many cases more symbolic of collegiate responsibility and religious purpose than a genuine expression of religious conviction. During the second half of the nineteenth century, there was a gradual abandonment of compulsion. Most of the older institutions completely gave up on evening prayers. Compulsory chapels became voluntary.[54]

The most effective agency of religion in college was the revival, that almost unexplainable combination of confession, profession, joy, and tears that brought many young men into the church and into the ministry. Rudolph indicated that "most college presidents and college faculties felt that they or God had failed a collegiate generation if once during four years there did not occur a rousing revival.[55] The revivals occurred for a variety of reasons, such as a day of prayer, an effective sermon, or a tragic event. Whatever the circumstances surrounding the religious experience, the response usually showed itself in confession of sin and the profession of a significant religious experience and conviction. Evangelical religion, however, with its great outpouring of the Spirit and personal profession of faith, would become a thing of the past at most church-related colleges as the nineteenth century came to a close.

Second, the curriculum of church-related colleges underwent changes. The curriculum of the early colleges was designed primarily for the education of prospective ministers of the gospel. Many of the old colleges had also slanted their curriculum toward the education of those interested in becoming leaders of state.[56] Later, the curriculum was altered to serve the interests of those desiring to enter other professions, like medicine, education, engineering, and journalism.

The theological character of the early curriculum illustrated the great influence that clergymen had in political, social, and intellectual areas, as well as in religious affairs. It is not surprising, therefore, that ministers of the gospel would be the most common product of such a curriculum.[57]

The curriculum of the early colleges was also uniform and rigid. In most cases, Latin, Greek, and mathematics were required courses. Some schools also included courses in English and natural philosophy. From the latter evolved departments of physics, chemistry, biology, astronomy, and geology. History gradually edged itself into the curriculum as did the study of romantic languages. These additions led to a curriculum that was more diverse, indicative of the increased secularism of higher education.

Third, and perhaps the most significant sign of a declining religious spirit within colleges, was the faculty. Nine times out of ten, the college president was a minister,[58] and ministers in academic posts were usually ordained by a sponsoring church. "There was no religion of the college president as such; he rather reflected the theological views of the denomination in which he held membership and whose interest he served."[59]

The clergy, however, became less of a factor as higher education moved into the later part of the nineteenth century. This happened as colleges became entirely independent of denominational dogma and wholly committed to the rationalist tradition.[60] While the majority of the early nineteenth century colleges held to a traditional position with a strong influence from the clergy, a minority began recruiting trustees, administrators, and faculty who were from lay ranks. Some clergymen involved in higher education started to view themselves first as educators and second as clergymen. Thus, both laymen, who played a growing role in nineteenth century colleges, and clergymen, who continued to exercise great influence, became more professionalized.[61] This resulted in more influence and control coming from educators within colleges and less from the denominations who sponsored them.

Changes in the character of the faculty also led to changes in the selection of administrators. As faculty started to have earned doctorates, trustees came to feel that college presidents should have the same credentials. Clergy who lacked them had trouble winning the respect of their faculty and often seemed aloof from what was happening in their particular college. This changing conception of higher education also brought changes in the character of trustees themselves, who were increasingly chosen from the laity.[62] These trustees often prided themselves in the academic standing of their colleges, though maintaining a general commitment to religion. They were in many cases more concerned with academic reputation than the moral or doctrinal views of the alumni. In fact, even the denominations were undergoing change—becoming more organized and bureaucratic. This meant that most had special departments for dealing with their colleges. These departments were staffed with scholarly men who were more sympathetic to the claims of secular learning than to the teachings of the church.[63]

Doctrine and religious practice played a far less significant role in the creation of new colleges after 1900. First the teaching faculty and then the administration were recruited from the ranks of the academic profession rather than from the ministry.[64] Denominational affiliation and religious influence became less and less important as church-related colleges accepted the academic profession's view on what, how, and whom a college should teach.

The decline of religious influence in college programming, curriculum, and faculty ultimately manifested itself in a fourth area, the graduates. The number of graduates going into clerical careers started to decline. This decline in graduates going into religious vocations was a natural outcome of the many changes that occurred in church-related colleges in the late nineteenth century as religion became less and less important. The emergence of the university also drew students away from sectarian institutions where there was some religious orientation.

In summary, the period between 1882 and 1920 was not only a time of unparalleled change for North American Protestantism, as cited in chapter two, but a transitional time for North American higher education. In returning to the original hypothesis of Metzger, the transformation of North American institutions of higher learning was so significant that it was in fact an educational revolution. It was the beginning of unusual academic freedom in North America through the influence of the emerging university and the changing church-related college that had dominated higher education from its beginning. The implications of this educational revolution were significant for society in general and for the church in particular. Although the church appeared to be losing ground, fervent evangelical leaders would be raised up in the late nineteenth century. Their labors would come to greater fruition in the early part of the twentieth century.

CHAPTER FOUR

THE RISE OF THE BIBLE SCHOOL:
1882-1920

The early Bible schools cannot be disassociated from the cultural, political, educational, and theological developments of the late nineteenth and twentieth centuries. "It was decidedly a period of change and advance in every area of life, thought, and economic relationship."[1]

Religious historian Frank E. Gaebelein described the impact of these changes on the formation of these early Bible schools:

> Just as conditions in America called for new institutions and patterns in secular education, so the Bible institute movement grew out of the social and religious conditions of the latter part of the nineteenth century and the first part of the twentieth. In a sense it is part of the amazing educational development of this period, a development that saw the tremendous growth of secondary schools and college education, the multiplication of vocational schools, the growth of adult education, and the new opportunities in education for women.... It is not a coincidence that the Bible institute movement grew up during the very period when the philosophy of naturalism became prevalent in American education.[2]

Although most of the early Canadian Bible schools would spring forth in the early twentieth century, the changes that helped to bring about their birth were quite similar to those in the United States.

In the early decades of this century, main-line Protes
tant colleges and seminaries were becoming more closely
articulated with public values, culture, and institutions,
and becoming increasingly liberal in their theology, some
evangelical churches moved to establish new institutions.[3]

Canadian church historian George Rawlyk noted,

"The secularization of Protestant higher education was
accompanied by the extraordinary growth of the Bible
school movement. . . . In a sense, Bible schools in Canada
became the new institutions of higher learning for besieged
fundamentalists and conservative evangelicals."[4]

A major factor associated with a rapidly changing society
was a resurgence of Protestant revivalism in a new form. How
did North American evangelical revivalism in the late
nineteenth and early twentieth centuries relate to the birth and
early development of the Bible college movement? This chapter
addresses that religious phenomenon.

THE BACKDROP FOR REVIVALISM

We have seen that the moral and spiritual decline in the
late nineteenth century was a vicious attack against the
credibility of the Scriptures. In response to these attacks by
Darwinism, higher criticism, and the social gospel movement,
a conservative element in North American Protestantism arose
to defend orthodoxy. The key was always the people involved.
These individuals were raised up by God, were highly trained,
and were deeply and irrevocably dedicated to the Word of God.[5]
They were known as revivalists, many of whom founded early
Bible schools and participated in a new form of revivalism.

Revivalism, like everything else in the last decades of the
nineteenth century, underwent change. Broadly speaking, the
period of discussion falls within what has been termed the
"Third Great Awakening," which extended from 1875 to 1915.[6]
Prior to 1875, revivalism had established itself as a permanent
feature of conservative Protestantism.

There were four distinct "awakenings" in American history. During the first period, George Whitefield was the primary figure as he preached an "evangelical Calvinism." The outstanding person in the second interval was Charles G. Finney, who advocated the "pietistic views of evangelical Protestantism." Even though Finney had developed the patterns of modern revivalism, "with the inadequate facilities and divisive theological issues of his day, he did little more than experiment in the urban application of it."[7]

There were similar spiritual "awakenings" in Canada in the eighteenth and nineteenth centuries. Henry Alline (1748-1784), after experiencing a powerful conversion in 1775, led a revival throughout Nova Scotia. In one sense, Alline extended George Whitefield's revivalism by stressing the power of Christ's death to reconcile men and women to God. In another way, however, Alline departed from Whitefield's Calvinistic theology.[8] In the nineteenth century there were similar revivals that took place within denominational groups, such as the Baptists, Methodists, and Presbyterians, as they recognized the necessity of a definite experience of personal conversion to Christ. In Canada during the late nineteenth century, most Protestants expected to have such an experience, and zealous attempts were made to cultivate it.[9]

Clearly the leading figures for the third period of awakening were D. L. Moody and Billy Sunday. Moody was particularly noted for his unique ability to utilize business techniques to organize and execute revival meetings, particularly in large urban centers across North America.

The backdrop for revivalism in the late nineteenth century was vastly different from the earlier period. Urban growth, a more heterogeneous society, a shift from an agrarian to an industrial economy, big labor and big business, and shifting patterns in the intellectual climate all characterized this new era. As part of this change, class distinctions were being drawn more closely than they were before 1850. There was developing a class called "the people" who distinguished themselves from both "the idle rich" and from "the masses."[10] It was these "masses" that the revivalists often attempted to reach, but with varying degrees of success.

According to church historian John D. Hannah, there were four primary methods used by revivalists of this period in their reaction to what was recognized as a growing liberalism within both Protestant denominations and colleges. These methods included emphasis on oral communication, the Bible conference, polemical literature, and the Bible college.[11]

First, the early revivalists' concern for the problems of their day was manifested through a *resurgence of biblical preaching*. The truths of the Scriptures came through a renewed concern for evangelistic preaching and the establishment of strong preaching centers.

Dwight L. Moody was the most famous revivalist of the era. Between 1873 and 1875, Moody together with Ira Sankey, a Methodist layman, returned from Great Britain to launch successful large-scale campaigns in many cities, such as Chicago, Philadelphia, St. Louis, Boston, and New York City.[12]

Moody and Sankey also staged evangelistic campaigns in two Canadian cities—Toronto in 1887 and Winnipeg in 1897. Such revivalists as the team of N. T. Crossley and John E. Hunter also visited most Canadian cities during the late nineteenth century.[13]

Other individuals sharing the same zeal for evangelism include Reuben A. Torrey. He labored to develop the Chicago Evangelization Society for Home and Foreign Missions, later renamed Moody Bible Institute. Torrey trained at Yale and Leipzig in historical criticism of the Bible. He later held evangelistic services in the United States, Australia, and Great Britain. "His success gave him claim to be considered the successor of Moody himself."[14]

One of the most influential evangelists after 1914 was William Ashley Sunday (1863-1935), commonly known as Billy. A professional baseball player in the 1880s, Sunday was converted to Christ in the Pacific Garden Mission of Chicago in 1888 and subsequently left the sport to serve a YMCA and the

J. Wilbur Chapman evangelistic team. The Presbyterian-ordained evangelist came to prominence after 1914, having successful campaigns in Pittsburgh, Philadelphia, Baltimore, Los Angeles, Washington, D.C., and New York City.[15]

In addition to the itinerant evangelists who emphasized the "essentials" in their preaching, numerous other pastors responded by emphasizing the same biblical truths in their local church pulpits. Many of these pastors became leaders in the early Bible schools and the subsequent fundamentalist movement.

The *Bible conference* was a second major strategy used by the revivalists at the end of the nineteenth century to counteract religious liberalism. In response to the higher criticism of the Scriptures, concerned pastors and teachers began to stress the study of the Bible, particularly employing a literal approach. Out of this concerted effort to defend and propagate the literal truth of the Bible came the Bible conference movement.[16] It began as a private source of spiritual refreshment and fellowship through an informal study of the Scriptures among a small group of scattered pastors. But it became a platform for the defense of the Bible and for the popularization of prophetic doctrine.[17] Three major Bible conferences developed in the last quarter of the nineteenth century and continued through the turn of the present century: The Believers's Meetings for Bible Study (commonly known as the Niagara Bible Conference), the American Bible and Prophetic Conference, and the Northfield Conference. There was a strong correlation between these Bible and prophecy conferences and the early Bible schools (discussed in Chapter six).

The third method commonly employed by the revivalists was *polemical literature*. As religious historian Milton R. Rudnick wrote, the conservative element in the Protestant churches reacted to the inroads of liberal theology producing a vast amount of literature in periodical and book form.

From its inception, liberalism had met with severe criticism from conservative writers. However, in the final third of the nineteenth century, when it became obvious that

liberalism was gaining wide acceptance in the churches,
some strong new literary attacks were launched by these
converts to dispensationalism. These were in the form of
periodicals and booklets in which traditional beliefs were
defended, premillennialism promoted, and liberalism
clearly condemned. This literature was written in a popular, inspirational, and emotional style. It was addressed
not to scholars but to lay people and ordinary clergy.[18]

James H. Brookes was one of the first revivalists to embark
upon a publishing ministry through a periodical entitled *The
Truth*. He began producing *The Truth* while pastoring the Walnut
Street Presbyterian Church in St. Louis in 1875 and continued
as its editor until his death in 1897. In the introduction to the
initial volume, Brookes made it clear that *The Truth* would
combat error by encouraging doubting and despondent
Christians to a "higher practical holiness."[19]

Similarly, a periodical of equal stature and importance was
written by A. J. Gordon of the Clarendon Street Baptist Church
in Boston. In the first edition of *The Watchword* in 1878, its aim
was to "defend the primitive faith, the doctrine of grace,
proclaim the primitive hope, the personal appearing, and
commend primitive charity." After the death of Gordon in 1895,
the magazine was merged with *The Truth* and was renamed
Watchword and Truth.[20]

Although these two are the earliest of the prominent
periodicals of their type, several others deserve mention. In
1879 A. B. Simpson put together the first issue of a new
missionary magazine, *The Gospel in All Lands*. It was intended
to attract a wider audience than other missionary magazines
had. The name of the magazine was changed to *The Word, Work,
and World* and later became the official journal of the Christian
and Missionary Alliance started by Simpson in 1887.[21] In 1894
Arno C. Gaebelein, a German immigrant of Methodist
persuasion, began to edit *Our Hope* with the help of Ernest
Stroeter and W. J. Eerdman. *Our Hope* grew in popularity in
the early 1900s through its association with C. I. Scofield.
Scofield and Gaebelein claimed that the *Watchword and Truth*
was not the true successor of either previous magazine.[22] The

Moody Monthly, which has maintained continuous publication since 1900 under two previous titles, *The Institute Tie* and *The Christian Worker's Magazine,*[23] has maintained a strong evangelical tone for almost one-hundred years. The most prominent Canadian periodical, *The Gospel Witness,* was published by Baptist pastor T. T. Shields.[24] Other noteworthy periodicals included James Inglis' *Waymarks in the Wilderness,* W. B. Riley's *The Christian Fundamentalist, The Bible Champion, The Princeton Review,* and *Bibliotheca Sacra.*[25] These periodicals were significant in adding fuel to the fire of the revivalist theology and ministry and served as a means for promoting many of the early Bible schools. Many of these periodicals were specifically related to the Bible institutes.

In addition to the numerous magazines that set forth an apologetic for the historic doctrines of Christianity, numerous books seem to have awakened interest in Bible study and doctrine. In 1908 William E. Blackstone, a Methodist, wrote a widely influential book, *Jesus Is Coming.* It set forth the doctrine of the premillennial advent of Christ and was eventually printed in forty languages and sold over one-million copies.[26] The *Scofield Reference Bible,* which was the editorial work of Cyrus I. Scofield, also awakened interest in the study of the Scriptures.[27]

The last major instrument used by the revivalists to counteract reputed liberalism in the last part of the nineteenth century was the **Bible institute**.

THE RISE OF BIBLE SCHOOLS

The Bible college movement to which fundamentalism has been said to owe its existence,[28] emerged in the last two decades of the nineteenth century as a protest to the inroads of secularization in higher education and as a base for the education of lay workers and full-time Bible teachers, evangelists, and pastors.

Though increased secularism in higher education had already appeared on one side of the religious ledger in the nineteenth century, a counterforce began to appear on the

opposite side, particularly with the last quarter of the century. Great religious revivals created a new motivation
among evangelicals. As the number of individual Christians increased, as well as new churches, doors began to
open for Christian service in pastorates, in Sunday school
work, in evangelical endeavor, and on home and foreign
mission fields. It soon became apparent that colleges and
seminaries could not fill these vocational positions with
trained leadership, first, because the number of such
schools was limited, and second, the objectives and curricula of these institutions were not comprehensive enough
to meet the variety of needs which appeared on the religious scene. Consequently, an 'auxiliary means of securing recruits' was inaugurated and designated 'Bible institutes.'[29]

Dwight L. Moody believed that there was a need for "gap
men" who could fill the void between the common people and
the highly trained clergy.[30] To meet this need, he proposed to
recruit those who were enlivened with a spirit of evangelism
but who lacked educational training. Moody's commitment to
train lay people was representative of the early Bible schools.
They were founded as practical training schools, not as rigorous
academic centers. Their chief aim was to provide a well-trained,
biblically literate, and spiritually mature corps of lay people to
meet the changing needs in society. Along with training the
laity to serve as urban workers and evangelists, the Bible schools
were committed to preparing young men and women for
foreign missionary service.[31]

The Bible college movement is distinctively North American
in origin and development. There were, however, several
European antecedents. The one that drew most frequent
attention was the East London Institute for Home and Foreign
Missions, established in 1872 by a Baptist clergyman, H. Grattan
Guinness and his wife. Guinness, through visits to the United
States and through the visits of Americans to England, greatly
influenced such Bible school founders as A. B. Simpson and A.
J. Gordon.[32]

Another much admired institution was the Pastors' College founded in 1861 by the famous English Baptist preacher, Charles Haddon Spurgeon. He designed the college for dedicated and devout young men who had been preaching for at least two years but who had inadequate schooling and insufficient money to make up their educational deficiencies. At a time when educational qualifications and financial means were generally required at English Baptist colleges, even the semi-literate and the indigent were welcome at Spurgeon's training school.[33]

Two German pastors, Johannes Gossner (1773-1858) and Louis Harms (1809-1865), also deserve mention because of the type of missionary training they provided. Neither of these men maintained a regular school, but each offered brief missionary training on an informal basis. Bible school founder A. J. Gordon wrote of Gossner, "The experience of Pastor Gossner and his Bethlehem Church in Berlin is wonderful. He sent out and maintained one hundred and forty-one missionaries, two hundred including the wives of those married, who did a work among the heathen second to none."[34]

Although few mention it, the first Bible school in North America was probably "the lay college" formed by T. Dewitt Talmage in 1872. The school, which was part of his great Presbyterian Tabernacle in Brooklyn, New York, was short-lived, and it is not officially recognized as the first Bible school.[35]

The first Bible school in North America to survive was Nyack College, located in New York. Established in 1882 as an outgrowth of the missionary enterprise of Presbyterian minister A. B. Simpson, it was housed in the rear of an antiquated theater in New York City. It was known as The Missionary Training Institute for Home and Foreign Missionaries and Evangelists.[36] Church historian C. B. Eavey described Simpson's motivation for starting Nyack College.

Simpson's missionary zeal and ardor influenced young people of his congregation to offer themselves for missionary service. Most of these lacked a good education; to prepare for college and then to wait seven more years until they had completed seminary was too much. He had studied and had been impressed by the methods of the East London Institute for Home and Foreign Missionaries. Since there was no school like it in America, he decided to start one to give his own young people basic Bible training.[37]

In 1885 Union Missionary Training Institute was started at Niagara Falls, New York, by Mrs. Lucy Drake Osborn. Mrs. Osborn, a veteran missionary, opened her home to young people for the purpose of training them for foreign missionary work. After some years, it was moved to Brooklyn. Its outstanding characteristic was a good combination of medical and evangelistic preparation.[38]

The school that was to become the most famous among the Bible institutes was the Chicago Evangelistic Society, established by Dwight L. Moody in 1886. The early stirrings for the work go back to the days immediately following the great Chicago fire when Miss Emma Dryer, principal and teacher of grammar at Illinois State Normal School, visited the city and remained to do evangelistic work. In 1882 Miss Dryer established "May Institutes" to train lay workers.[39] In 1885 Moody led some short-term institutes in Chicago to complement Dryer's work; out of this involvement and interest came the Training School of the Chicago Evangelization Society. The name of the School was changed in 1900 to Moody Bible Institute to honor its deceased founder.

In 1889, while Moody formally opened his School in Chicago on a year-round basis, A. J. Gordon also launched the Boston Missionary Training School. The immediate impetus for the Institute was the urging of H. Grattan Guinness.

Dr. Guinness offered the Congo Mission to the American Baptist Missionary Union. It was accepted at Detroit at the annual meeting. A. J. Gordon was one of those enthusiastic about it there, and became a close friend of Dr. Guinness. . . . Guinness came over in 1889, and together they prayed and pondered. Guinness suggested a school like his own missionary institute in London, not requiring extended educational preparation for what was then the primitive fields of the Congo.[40]

As a result of Dr. Guinness' challenge, the matter of a school weighed heavily upon Gordon's mind as he discussed the possibilities with others in the city. Much discussion and planning led to the founding of the Boston Missionary Training School in October 1889. After Gordon's death in 1895, it was given the name Gordon Missionary Training School. Today the school exists as Gordon College and Gordon-Conwell Seminary.[41]

Ashley S. Johnson, a well known evangelist, teacher, and author within the Christian Churches/Church of Christ founded the School of Evangelists near Knoxville, Tennessee, in 1893. This training school for men was an outgrowth of a correspondence school that Johnson had started in 1886. The school name was changed to bear his name in 1909, but it did not become an official coeducational institution until 1943. Today, Johnson Bible College stands as the oldest and one of the largest Bible colleges within Christian Church circles.[42]

Several Canadian schools came and went in the first two decades of Bible school development, but the first long-standing institution was the Toronto Bible Training School. It was started in 1894 under the leadership of Baptist pastor Elmore Harris. Harris' church, Walmer Road Baptist, housed the school for the first four years. In 1898 the school relocated to downtown Toronto. In 1968 it merged with London College of Bible and Missions to form Ontario Bible College.[43]

Although the schools founded by such men as Simpson, Moody, Gordon, Johnson, and Harris stood in the vanguard of the Bible college movement by virtue of their early founding dates and immense impact, a modest number of other fine schools developed in scattered sections of the United States before 1900. Several of these early schools were: Western Baptist Bible College (Kansas City, Missouri) (1890) by the Negro Baptist Church of Missouri; Boston Bible School (1897) by the Advent Christian Church and later renamed Berkshire Christian

College; and Training School for Christian Workers (1899) in California, later named Azusa Pacific College.[44]

The Bible college movement had a steady but not phenomenal growth during the first two decades of the twentieth century. Some of the prominent schools founded in 1900 or later were: Rhode Island Bible Institute (Barrington, Rhode Island; 1900); Practical Bible Training School (Johnson City, New York; 1900); The Northwest Bible and Missionary Training School (Minneapolis, Minnesota; 1902); Fort Wayne Bible School (Fort Wayne, Indiana; 1904); Toccoa Falls Institute (Toccoa Falls, Georgia; 1907); The Bible Institute of Los Angeles (La Mirada, California; 1908); and the Bible Institute of Pennsylvania (Philadelphia, Pennsylvania; 1913), and Philadelphia School of the Bible (1914), which would later merge to become Philadelphia Bible Institute. In almost every situation, these and other early Bible schools have evolved into four-year colleges.[45]

Between 1882 and 1920, a total of 40 Bible schools (see Table IV-1) were started in North America. Six of them were founded between 1882 and 1890, eight between 1891 and 1900, ten between 1901 and 1910, and sixteen between 1911 and 1920.[46]

TABLE IV-1

PARTIAL LIST OF BIBLE SCHOOLS
FOUNDED BY 1920

School	Founding Date	Sponsoring Group	Comments
Missionary Training Institute, N.Y.C. & Nyack	1882	C&MA	Became Nyack College
Union Missionary Training Institute, Niagara Falls and Brooklyn	1885	Interdenom.	Merged with National Bible Institute, 1916
Chicago Evangelistic Society	1886	Interdenom.	Became Moody Bible Institute
Northwestern Bible Training School, St. Paul, MN	1889	Interdenom.	Closed in 1899

Boston Missionary Training School	1889	Baptist/ Interdenom.	Became Gordon College
Western Baptist Bible College	1890	Baptist	Trained black ministers
Cleveland Bible	1892	Friends	Became Malone College
Johnson Bible School Knoxville, Tennessee	1893	Churches of Christ	Became Johnson Bible College
Toronto Bible School	1894	Interdenom.	First Canadian school, Became Ontario Bible College
Boston Bible School/New England School of Theology	1897	Advent	Became Berkshire Christian College
Free Church Bible Institute and Seminary	1897	Evang. Free Christian	
Training School for Christian Workers, Los Angeles	1899	Friends	Became Azusa Pacific University
Providence Bible Institute	1900	Interdenom.	Became Barrington College
God's Bible School	1900	Interdenom.	
Practical Bible Training School, Johnson City, NY	1901	Interdenom.	Became Practical Bible College
Northwestern Schools Minneapolis, MN	1902	Interdenom.	Became Northwestern College
Ft. Wayne Bible Institute	1904	Missionary Church	Became Ft. Wayne Bible College
Grayson Normal School/ Christian Normal Institute, Grayson, KY	1906	Churches of Christ	Became Kentucky Christian College
National Bible Institute, New York City, NY	1907	Interdenom.	Became Shelton College
Bible Institute of Los Angeles	1908	Interdenom.	Became Biola University
Heston Bible School Heston, KS	1909	Mennonite	Became Heston College
Chicago Evangelistic Institute	1910	Holiness	Became Vennard College Moved to Iowa
Trinity Bible Institute	1910	Evang. Free	Became Trinity College & Evang. Divinity School
Colorado Springs Bible Training School	1910	Pilgrim Holiness	

Toccoa Falls Schools	1911	C&MA	Became Toccoa Falls College
Metropolitan Bible Institute, North Bergen, NJ	1912	Assemblies of God	
Albany Bible School Albany, NY	1912	Interdenom.	Founded for women
Bible Institute of Pennsylvania, Philadelphia	1913	Interdenom.	Merged to become Philadelphia College of Bible
Philadelphia School of the Bible	1914	Interdenom.	Merged to become Philadelphia College of Bible
Winona Lake School of Theology, IN	1914	Grace Brethren	Became Grace College & Seminary
Minnesota Bible School	1914	Churches of Christ	Became Minnesota Bible College
Denver Bible School	1914	Interdenom.	Became Western Bible College; merged to become Colorado Christian University
Bethel Bible School	1914	Interdenom.	Closed in 1929
St. Paul Bible Institute St. Paul, MN	1916	C&MA	Became Crown College
Hope Bible School, Chicago	1916	Interdenom.	
Midland Bible Institute	1918	C&MA	Closed in 1923
Cascade College Portland, OR	1918	Holiness	
Baptist Bible Institute of New Orleans	1918	Baptist	Became New Orleans Baptist Theological Seminary
Lutheran Bible Institute Minneapolis	1919	Lutheran	
Glad Tidings Bible Institute, San Francisco	1919	Assemblies of God	Became Bethany Bible College, Santa Cruz, CA[47]

ABBREVIATIONS: C&MA-Christian and Missionary Alliance
                        Interdenom.-Interdenominational

EARLY TRAINING CENTERS

In attempting to arrive at certain general characteristics that apply to the early Bible schools, one must exercise caution, because no formal organization of these schools existed until the 1940s. Therefore, there were no regular and official channels through which Bible school educators could exchange ideas, let alone work toward uniform educational practices. Still, it is possible to trace the existence long before 1940 of an informal Bible school movement, which channeled casual but frequent communication among Bible school educators. Such educators met at Bible conferences, evangelistic campaigns, and other events of Protestant revivalism.

In spite of a variety of sponsoring groups, there were common characteristics among these early training schools. First, *the English Bible was at the core of the curriculum.* In addition to the other skills that were taught, a thorough knowledge of the Bible was a central purpose.[48] The Bible was more than a textbook for students. It became their daily companion, their inspiration and primary tool in soul winning.

Second, there were *significant opportunities for both women and men from diverse backgrounds* in the Bible schools in contrast to other types of theological training centers. The distinct constituency of these schools included "women who were not admitted to seminaries or who were not admitted on equal terms with men; and laymen who did not desire ordination, but belonged to denominations requiring four years of college and three years of seminary for any type of full-time service."[49] Many of these students were mature adults who felt called into some type of Christian service later in life.

Because the students were entering the Bible schools with different educational backgrounds, a variety of curricula was provided for those with college, high school, or only grammar school education. Graduation usually meant earning a certificate or diploma. A bachelor's degree in theology, religious education, or missions would follow later.

Third, *the academic program of these training schools was more abbreviated than at traditional colleges and universities.* The student was not to get entangled in what Jane Adams called the "share of preparation," and be delayed in going to the mission field until all the fervor had been burned out.[50]

Fourth, there was *an informal curriculum that worked in tandem with the formal curriculum* within the Bible schools One's personal relationship with the Lord and involvement in Christian service were emphasized just as strongly as the classroom expectations. Prayer meetings, daily chapel services, challenges from missionaries, accounts of student ministry opportunities, and sharing of personal testimonies were all part of the ethos of these training institutions.

Fifth, the *faculty were often pastors or missionaries who had not necessarily been trained as professional educators.* Although they often did not have advanced degrees, they usually brought many years of experience in Christian work to the task. They frequently taught part time, with the exception of the president or perhaps one primary instructor. The salaries were quite limited. Many of the teachers even served on a voluntary basis.

The sixth and final characteristic was the *commitment to train men and women for the Lord's service.* Traditional education did not seem to be producing enough effective Christian workers. Because of a shortage of laborers, training was needed for those who would have ordinarily received no preparation. Revivalist A. T. Pierson offered a plea for foreign missions when he advocated a "grand campaign for Christ" and "the immediate occupation of all unoccupied fields."[51] At home, D. L. Moody lamented over the "hundreds of families in cities . . . never coming in contact with churches or representatives,"[52] and warned of the horrible results if nothing were done. "Either these people are to be evangelized or the leaven of communism and infidelity will assume such enormous proportions that it will break out in a reign of terror such as this country has never known."[53]

A major obstacle to the fulfillment of the vision of aggressive evangelism appeared to be a lack of trained workers. Pierson believed that each trained missionary needed to "assume an average responsibility of one-hundred thousand souls."[54] Although the challenge was extremely ambitious, the need was clearly communicated. "Many city pastors," said Moody in the 1880s, "have asked me to find laymen for them who would be skilled helpers in the Sunday school and mission work; but I could not do it, for there was no school to train them. The call for such men is greater today than ever."[55]

All those who cited the desperate need for "laborers" assumed the existence of a pool of potential recruits who were anxious to serve the Lord at home or abroad but were not able to do so because of their inability to afford a long and expensive education. Pierson stated it this way:

> A pastor whose heart and tongue are on fire urges the claims of a lost world, and there are few who respond, 'Here am I, send me;' but they are generally for the most part from the poor and less-educated classes. . . . The few dormant consciences that do awake under our appeal are generally found in people to whom wealth and learning do not open attractive doors at home. How disheartening, when one offers to go to these regions to be told at the outset that from five to ten years must be spent in preparation.[56]

A. J. Gordon, in his capacity as head of the American Baptist Missionary Union, reflected,

> "I think of those whom we have hesitated over and at first rejected because of a want of qualifications which we considered of first importance. And then to see how God has rebuked us by showing how wonderfully He could use them."[57]

The call went forth for trained lay people. Moody issued his famous pleas for "gap-men" to stand between the laity and the masses and the clergy. C. I. Scofield, founder of Philadelphia School of the Bible, stated, "This is a laymen's age."[58] A. J. Gordon issued the challenge "to call out our reserves—to put into the field a large force of lay workers."[59] A. B. Simpson asked for "irregulars" because "God is building windows for the cathedrals of the skies out of the rejected lives and fragments of consecrated service for which the wisdom of the world has no room."[60]

All the characteristics of the early Bible schools could be summed up in the word "training." The revivalists of the late nineteenth and early twentieth centuries saw a desperate need to equip a corps of men and women for religious service who would probably never have the luxury of pursuing a traditional theological education but truly wanted to serve the Lord at home and abroad.

This new approach to training was, in part, a revolt against the older classical learning, a revolt that was in progress elsewhere in education. Nothing was inherently wrong in learning Latin, Greek, and Hebrew, or in reading classical literature. Many of the Bible school founders were products of a classical education, but recruits for the Lord's service simply lacked the time and resources for this luxury. A. B. Simpson criticized traditional education for "how often it is merely intellectual, scholastic, traditional and many of us have found by sad experience that God has put us to school again to unlearn what man had crammed into our brains."[61] Pierson also spoke against classical education when he stated,

> On the mission field men who have no college diploma, and could furnish no supreme test of scholarship, the 'Latin essay,' if found capable, and willing are licensed and ordained. . . . Facts show that scholastic training is not necessary for effective service. There are scores of heroic men doing valiant battle for the Lord and the faith, who never were in college or seminary.[62]

And Moody warned that "ministers are educated away from" the people they should be attempting to reach.

> A boy is kept at school until he is ready to go to college and then to college, and from college to theological seminary, and the result is he comes out of a theological seminary knowing nothing about human nature, doesn't know how to rub up to these men and adapt himself to them, and then gets up a sermon on metaphysical subjects miles above these people. . . . What we want are men trained for this class of people."[63]

In spite of the preceding statements, it should be noted that the early Bible school founders were not necessarily opposed to longer and better training. They did not reject their own traditional education. Nor did they feel that theological seminaries had run their course. Although they had some obvious concerns, they still saw seminaries as the primary training centers for the professional clergy. They simply wanted to create a new approach for training Christian servants that took less time and was more accessible to lay people rather than insisting on a long course of instruction. The response to this need was the Bible school.

CHAPTER FIVE

EARLY BIBLE SCHOOL LEADERS

Many of the early Bible schools emerged from the activities of dynamic leaders who shared very common backgrounds. Sometimes the founding groups consisted of denominational leaders who, worried about the future leadership of the denomination, sought to provide valuable facilities for training. Often, however, the founders of Bible schools were single individuals who had charismatic personalities and powerful, driving religious objectives. It is important to understand what these individuals were like because their personalities and visions often determined the character of the Bible schools they founded, their precise emphases and theological positions. As teachers and administrators, some founders dominated their institutions for decades while others left an impact for shorter periods of time. However, they had this in common: their influence continued to shape policies and directions long after their deaths. In most situations, they were not professional educators; they resorted to the creation of schools as one way of accomplishing their varied evangelical goals.

The early leaders of Bible schools were also revivalists like those described in the previous chapter. They frequently criticized the state of the churches, particularly those which appeared to be lukewarm. They did not spare the ministers, whom they attacked as being unbiblical in their preaching and unevangelical in their attitudes toward the unchurched. These revivalists condemned the practice of renting pews, the hiring of professional musicians, and the use of church fairs for coaxing money from congregations. Above all, they criticized the church's missionary efforts, both domestic and foreign, as being ineffective.

Rather than limiting themselves to one ministry, the early Bible school leaders were usually quite diverse in their activities. They sought to foster lay excitement for missions, engender interest in Bible study, and cultivate desire for meaningful spiritual growth. They would often conduct Bible classes, organize mission societies, edit periodicals, write books, and pastor churches. Before long, many Bible school leaders came to oversee religious empires that required a high level of energy and strong organizational skill.

In addition to common goals and interests, early Bible school leaders were often linked by personal ties. Almost all of them knew D. L. Moody, or at least had heard him preach. Many of them were popular Bible conference teachers who frequently appeared together on the same program. Some of them taught as guest instructors at other early Bible institutes; A. J. Gordon and C. I. Scofield, for example, were both guest teachers at Moody Bible Institute in Chicago. Many Bible school founders were very close friends. A. B. Simpson and A. J. Gordon maintained a friendship, and Simpson preached at Gordon's funeral service. Likewise, Scofield and Moody were close friends with Scofield preaching at Moody's funeral. Many of the personalities in this study not only knew one another, but were similar in age. These personal ties were very significant because no formal organization of Bible schools and colleges existed until the 1940s. The informal relationship that existed among the early Bible school leaders served as a communication network for sharing ideas and mutual encouragement.

How did the backgrounds of the early leaders reflect themselves in the development of their respective schools? This chapter examines the lives of some of the early Bible school leaders and the impact they made on the colleges they founded.

ALBERT B. SIMPSON

Albert B. Simpson (1843-1919) was the founder of what is commonly recognized as the first Bible school in North America.

His life was full of religious upheavals and unique experiences. As a youth, he suffered an extended crisis of faith. Later, after a series of successful Presbyterian pastorates, he abruptly left his conventional church and launched into a ministry on his own. Starting with a single independent congregation in New York City, he went on to establish an international organization. The network of institutions that came to be called the Christian and Missionary Alliance included a system of churches, a newspaper, a publishing house, annual conventions, and several Bible schools in the United States, Canada, and abroad.

Simpson was born in Bayview, Prince Edward Island (Canada) on December 15, 1843. He was the fourth of nine children to James and Jane Simpson.[1] His father was originally a Prince Edward Island shipbuilder, miller, merchant, and exporter, as well a Presbyterian elder. After the 1847 failure of his father's business due to difficult economic times, the family bought a farm in western Ontario.[2] There Albert B. Simpson spent his youth, never very strong physically but very alert mentally.

His parents were pious Presbyterians who believed both in the "efficacy of the rod" and strict religious instruction.[3] Even before he was fourteen years of age, Simpson was determined to be a minister. He was tutored in Latin, Greek, and higher mathematics by a retired minister as well as by his own pastor. When his health permitted, he attended classes in the Chatham High School. It was during his early adolescence that he experienced conversion, solidifying his call to the ministry.[4]

At age seventeen Simpson appeared before the Presbytery of London, Ontario, to demonstrate his fitness to study for the ministry. Passing his examination, he was recommended as a student at Knox College, now situated on the campus of the University of Toronto. He entered the school in the fall of 1861 to pursue literary studies and theology.[5]

At that time, the college required a ministerial student to complete either the full arts course at the University of Toronto, or three years of academic work at Knox; not until then would he be eligible to take three years of theological training.

However, because Simpson's academic background had been so thorough, he was admitted to the third or senior year of the literary course. Upon completion of the literary course, he took the regular three years in the theological department. He graduated in April, 1865.[6]

Simpson was ordained into the ministry on September 12, 1865, when he assumed the pastorate of the Knox Presbyterian Church, Hamilton, Ontario.[7] The following day he was married to Margaret Henry, the daughter of his college landlord from whom he rented a room. They were to give birth to four sons and two daughters.[8]

During his eight-year ministry at Knox Church, 750 members were added to the rolls. He then accepted a call to the Chestnut Presbyterian Church, the largest Presbyterian church in Louisville, Kentucky. He began this work in January 1874, and concluded it in November 1879.[9]

It was during his Louisville pastorate that he became intensely interested in the work of foreign missions. In the Knox Church, he had stressed this work, but now, as never before, the need of "the regions beyond" challenged his attention. So greatly interested did he become in missionary work that he himself applied for missionary service. However, poor health and hesitation on the part of his wife made it an impossibility. Therefore, he determined that he would labor for the people of the world "just the same as if I were permitted to go among them."[10]

This missionary desire prompted his acceptance of the call from the Thirteenth Street Presbyterian Church in New York City. He believed that New York City offered the most advantageous location for launching such a missionary outreach. He served as pastor of the Thirteenth Street Church for only two years, 1879 to 1881. His early departure was prompted by the lack of congregational support for his evangelistic ventures in the community. As Simpson recalled this situation, "What they wanted was a conventional parish for respectable Christians. What their young pastor wanted was a multitude of publicans and sinners."[11]

Leaving a comfortable church and salary, Simpson resigned from the Thirteenth Street Church and the Presbyterian ministry. With his withdrawal from his Presbyterian pastorate, he started a new and independent work in New York City. This new congregation, the Gospel Tabernacle, used a variety of rented facilities for the first eight years of its existence until a permanent building was constructed in 1889 at Eighth Avenue and Forty-Fourth Street. By the end of 1893, the membership of the Tabernacle had grown to over one thousand.[12] This growth came about through a very strong evangelistic emphasis. The services were simple and brief, in the style of Dwight L. Moody. A. B. Simpson continued to serve as the pastor of the Gospel Tabernacle while simultaneously providing leadership for other religious endeavors.

After establishing the independent congregation, he started the Missionary Training College for Home and Foreign Missionaries and Evangelists. With a growing number of zealous followers for missions, the need for training them became more pressing. The school opened in 1882 to "a few enthusiastic followers."[13] This institution would serve as a prototype for many other Bible schools that would follow.

Two years later, in 1884, Simpson introduced what he called a "convention" in Old Orchard, Maine, "to gather Christians of common faith and spirit for fellowship; to study the Word of God; and to promote a deeper spiritual life among Christians."[14] This was the first of many national and regional Bible conferences.

In 1887 Simpson organized his followers into two "alliances." The first focused on work at home and the second on activity abroad. The "Christian Alliance" took as its purpose "the wide diffusion of the Gospel in its founders, the promotion of a deeper and higher Christian life, and work of evangelization, especially among the neglected classes by highway missions and other practical methods." The second group, the "Evangelical Missionary Alliance," was committed to sending "qualified lay people as well as regularly educated ministers" to all parts of the world with the Gospel message.[15] In 1897 the two alliances, which involved virtually the same personnel, merged to form the Christian and Missionary Alliance.

Simpson founded a newspaper in 1888. About the same time, he initiated a "Colportage Library" to publish, sell, and distribute inexpensive Christian literature.

As these accomplishments suggest, Simpson's efforts multiplied. The Christian and Missionary Alliance quickly became an international organization, as he and his associates launched conventions, local Bible classes, churches, Sunday schools, and missions in many regions of North America. A Bible training institute, modeled after Simpson's first school in New York City, was established in Toccoa Falls, Georgia; St. Paul, Minnesota; Regina, Saskatchewan; Seattle, Washington; and Boston, Massachusetts.

In the face of myriad administrative duties, Simpson did not shift any energy from his spiritual concerns. In fact, his spiritual commitment and enthusiasm permeated the institutions and agencies of the Alliance by means of his writing and his personal example.

Simpson was the guiding hand in all these enterprises. He pastored the mother church in New York City, edited the Alliance paper, and travelled to conventions until his death. In his lifetime, he wrote 155 hymns, authored over eighty books, and taught at the Missionary Training Institute.[16] He died on October 29, 1919, at the age of seventy-five. He was buried on the campus of the Missionary Training Institute at Nyack, New York.[17]

DWIGHT L. MOODY

Dwight L. Moody (1837-1899) is the most famous of all the revivalists of the late nineteenth century. He was an entrepreneur and promoter par excellence, endowed with the ability to recognize and seize an opportunity. This was true in his endeavors as a young businessman, a pastor, YMCA leader, evangelist, conference speaker, and educator. Many of his contemporaries possessed similar talents but exercised them in a quieter and less exuberant manner.[18]

Moody was born in the small New England town of Northfield, Massachusetts, on February 5, 1837.[19] He was the son of a brick and stone mason who died when Moody was just a boy. His mother insisted on rearing and keeping the family together even though she was left with practically nothing.

At the age of seventeen, and armed with only a very meager education from Northfield's one-room schoolhouse, he made his way to Boston to work in his uncle's shoe store. It was in there that Moody's Sunday school teacher, Edward Kimball, specifically came to talk to him about spiritual matters. Finding Moody in the back of the store wrapping shoes, Kimball asked the young man if he was ready to commit himself to Christ. Kimball "simply told him of Christ's love for him and the love Christ wanted in return."[20] To these disarming gestures, Moody's response was positive. His life was not radically changed, but there was gradual spiritual development.

Moody soon became restless in Boston and decided to head for the rapidly growing city of Chicago. Motivated by a driving sense of ambition and aided by an outgoing personality, he accomplished early financial success. He obtained a better job and started to invest his money. This same drive would bring him to the task of evangelism in later years. With his genius for hard work, he might well have been a leading business tycoon of the budding industrial age had he not chosen another course.

Business, however, was not his only area of concern in Chicago. He engaged in church work, joined the newly formed YMCA, spoke so often at prayer meetings that he was asked to refrain from taking part, and finally rounded up youngsters to fill four pews that he rented for that purpose at Plymouth Congregational Church.[21] But all that was not enough. He wanted to do more. He desired to teach in a mission Sunday school, but since no classes were available, he could teach a class only if he rounded up the pupils. He started his own class in the city's North Market, a poor immigrant section, and rented a former saloon. In recruiting students for the school, he sometimes recruited prospective students from the streets until ten or eleven at night. For the parents of his pupils, he organized prayer meetings and evening classes "in common English branches."[22] Assisted financially by business leaders, such as Cyrus McCormick and George Armour, he soon had over one thousand pupils and so decided to construct his own building at a cost of $10,000.[23]

In 1860 Moody made one of the most difficult decisions of his life—to leave business in order to devote himself fully to religious work. During this time he met and courted Emma C. Revell, daughter of an immigrant English shipbuilder. They were married in 1862. It was Emma Moody who constantly inspired him and helped to smooth out the roughness from his outspoken and sometimes impulsive demeanor.

The twelve years following his decision to enter full-time Christian work were filled with numerous activities and accomplishments. He became a leading figure in the National Sunday School Movement; was president of the Chicago YMCA; worked with the United States Christian Commission during the Civil War to assist soldiers in a variety of ways; conducted street-corner evangelistic services; approached at least one person each day with the question, "Are you a Christian?" and founded the Illinois Street Church, a work which grew out of his ministry to slum children and their parents.[24]

The Chicago fire of 1871 was a major blow to Moody's work. It destroyed his home, Church, Sunday School, and the YMCA. While in the process of securing funds to rebuild them, he accepted a six-month preaching engagement in England. It turned out to be a pivotal decision in his life. He arrived in Liverpool in 1873 as an unknown and returned to the United States in 1875 as a world figure.[25]

When he returned two years later, he preached in many of the major cities in North America, including Boston, Baltimore, Philadelphia, Chicago, Toronto, and New York City.[26] Sandwiched between these meetings were a host of other activities related in some way to evangelistic work. The establishment of the Northfield Schools and the Bible Institute in Chicago were two of these. But Moody was first and foremost an evangelist. All else was subordinated to that end.[27] He believed that God had called him to preach, and he was engaged in that task in Kansas City when he was overtaken by the illness that caused his death on December 22, 1899.

Although D. L. Moody made his greatest impact through mass evangelistic campaigns on both sides of the Atlantic, his accomplishments in founding schools is our focus here. The Northfield School for Girls and the Mount Hermon School for Boys (both are located in Northfield, Massachusetts) were started in 1879 and 1881 to provide high school education in a Christian atmosphere at low expense. Moody never completed high school himself, but was a firm believer in education. He once stated, "A man who knows his Bible can never be said to be illiterate; and a man who is ignorant of the Bible can never be said to have a broad culture."[28]

The third school that Moody founded was the Bible Institute in Chicago in 1886, later renamed Moody Bible Institute. While he provided the vision for the school, he was not the one who cared for the details. The earliest administrator was Miss Emma Dryer, a former principal of the Illinois State Normal School who heavily engaged in works of mercy after the 1871 Chicago fire. With Moody's encouragement, she carried on an active "Bible Work" in the 1870s and early 1880s of training men and women as Bible teachers and city missionaries.[29]

In 1886 Moody determined to expand the "Bible Work" to train lay workers by securing the necessary funding. After raising a total of $250,000, in 1887 the Chicago Evangelization Society was organized to conduct a series of brief training institutes. In 1889 these successful efforts were extended to a year-round program called the "Bible Institute for Home and Foreign Missions" under the academic leadership of Reuben A. Torrey.

Moody's aggressive sales approach set the tone for this new institution even though he was never involved in its daily operations. Some of his contemporaries were more actively engaged in the administration of their respective schools, but none was more renowned as a Bible school founder, and therefore his choice of the institution as the training ground for Christian workers give it visibility and a legitimacy it would otherwise have lacked.

ADONIRAM J. GORDON

Although A. J. Gordon (1836-1895) may not have received the international acclaim of Simpson or Moody, he followed the familiar pattern of the late nineteenth century revivalists.

He was born on April 19, 1836, in New Hampton, New Hampshire, to John Calvin Gordon and Sallie Robinson Gordon. Impressed with the need for modern missions and those willing to answer the call of God to foreign lands, they named their eldest son after pioneer American missionary, Adoniram Judson.[30]

A. J. Gordon was reared in a religious home and experienced conversion when he was fifteen years of age. A short time later, he felt the call of God into the gospel ministry, and thus entered the New London Academy, a Baptist preparatory school in New London, New Hampshire, in the fall of 1853.[31] He graduated with honors and spent the next four years at Brown University, Providence, Rhode Island. After graduation from Brown, he enrolled at the Newton Theological Institution in New Centre, Massachusetts, finishing his work there in 1863. All of Gordon's formal training was in Baptist schools and was directed toward preparing for the ministry.[32]

Gordon's first pastorate was at the Jamica Plain Baptist Church, a suburb of Boston, where he was ordained into the ministry and officially installed as pastor in 1863. That same year he married Miss Marie Hale. Eight children were born into their home.[33]

After ministering for six and one-half years, in 1869 Gordon reluctantly resigned to accepte the persistent call of the Clarendon Street Baptist Church in Boston. He served twenty-five years there until his untimely death on February 2, 1895. His ministries of writing, organizing missionary activities, frequent speaking engagements, and starting his own Bible school took place during his long tenure at the Clarendon Street Baptist Church.

Gordon accomplished much during his twenty-five years at Clarendon, even by his own standards. By the time of his death in 1895, his church supported twelve foreign missionaries and twelve local evangelists (compared to only one of each before Gordon's arrival). Church membership had increased from 358 in 1869 to 1,083 in 1895.[34] In addition, the ministries supported by the church had become multifaceted: an "Industrial Temperance Home" for the unemployed, a young people's group, women's missionary organizations, and missions directed toward black and Chinese Bostonians.[35]

Many of Gordon's convictions about the role of the church grew out of his formative religious experiences. A revival by D. L. Moody in Boston in 1877 had reinforced his conviction of the importance of evangelism. He became a close associate of Moody and, beginning in 1880, a participant and speaker at Moody's Northfield (Massachusetts) conferences.

In addition to Gordon's lengthy tenure as a pastor, he was also a prolific writer. He authored several books and edited a monthly journal, the *Watchword*, from its inception in 1878 until his death in 1895. He also served on the editorial boards of *The Christian Herald and Signs of Our Times* and *The Missionary Review of the World*.[36] Articles and sermons by Gordon were published in many of the well-known journals of his day.

Gordon's Bible-centered preaching, particularly his emphasis upon the deeper life and prophetic themes, brought him into great demand as a speaker at many of the popular Bible conferences. He was also called upon to conduct special meetings on college and seminary campuses. Even though he was active as a member of the executive committee of the American Baptist Missionary Union, Gordon's philosophy of missions was closer to that of the faith mission movement, emphasizing simple dependence upon God for mission workers and their support.[37] Biographer George C. Houghton summarized Gordon's philosophy of missions as follows: The missionary task is one of reaching people with the gospel; it is the Holy Spirit's ministry to draw people to salvation in Christ; and the missionary ought to sense his own calling to the work by the Spirit as well as have a continued dependence upon the Spirit for life and service.[38]

Gordon recognized the need for a school that would give practical and biblical training to men and women who felt called of God into missionary service. As a result, he opened the Missionary Training School in Boston in 1889. Despite opposition from some denominational leaders who viewed the principles of the newly Institution as encouraging "the short cut method," he went ahead with the school.

Gordon died in 1895, only six years after the school's founding. As a result, his influence was limited in comparison to A. B. Simpson, who guided the Missionary Training Institute for almost four decades. Yet, Gordon gave the school the vision for training men and women for missionary service and conferred upon it an honorabe position among conservative evangelicals.[39]

CYRUS I. SCOFIELD

Cyrus I. Scofield (1843-1921) deserves attention because he was not "just another preacher" to come out of the late nineteenth century who started a Bible school. Other revivalists did what he did, but seldom in the same combination. Few Congregational ministers, other than Scofield, served as a United States district attorney. Few served two terms in the state legislature of a rowdy frontier state. Few Confederate Army privates had three books published by the Oxford University Press or were elected to membership in the French Société Académique d' Histoire Internationale. These, and other key events in his life, make him deserving of brief attention.[40]

Scofield was born near Clinton, Michigan, on August 19, 1843. His mother died shortly after his birth, leaving him as the youngest of seven children. While Cyrus was a young boy, his father moved the family near Lebanon, Tennessee. It was here that he received his early education, but it was not formal in nature.[41]

At the age of seventeen, young Scofield enlisted in the Confederate Army to serve for twelve months. He served successfully and participated in eighteen battles and minor engagements. Although his tenure in the army did not include the entire Civil War, he was awarded the Cross of Honor for bravery in the Battle of Antietam.[42]

After the Civil War, Scofield lived with his oldest sister in St. Louis. Through the influence of his brother-in-law, he entered the practice of law and began to prepare for the bar examination. It was also in St. Louis that he married and started his family.

In 1869, Cyrus moved his family to Atchison, Kansas, to handle the lawsuit for his wife's family. While in Kansas, he finished his law studies and successfully passed the bar examination. After being admitted to the Kansas Bar, he became involved in politics. Twice he was elected as a representative to the Kansas State Legislature. On June 9, 1873, he was sworn in as a United States district attorney for the fourth district of Kansas, appointed by President Grant. Being only twenty-nine years of age, Scofield was the youngest U. S. district attorney in the nation.[43]

Scofield's success was short-lived. By 1879 he started to drink, destroying both his legal practice and his personal life. Because of his severe drinking, his wife and two daughters left him and never returned.[44]

Although this was perhaps the lowest point in his life, it also led to his conversion through a friend who explained the gospel to him. His conversion empowered him to abandon alcohol.[45]

It was just after his conversion that D. L. Moody came to St. Louis to conduct a five-month evangelistic campaign. Scofield met Moody and became one of his active volunteers.[46] This marked the beginning of a friendship and association that lasted until Moody's death in 1899.

In 1880 Scofield joined the Congregational church and began preaching to railroad men in East St. Louis. In this same year, he was made acting secretary of the YMCA in St. Louis and was licensed to preach. He organized and pastored the Hyde Park Congregational Church of North St. Louis.[47]

Scofield would spend much of his career pastoring Congregational churches in North St. Louis, Dallas, and Northfield, Massachusetts. The First Congregational Church in Dallas, however, was where he served with greatest distinction on several different occasions. The church changed its name to Scofield Memorial Church after his death.

Following Scofield's resignation from the First Congregational Church in Dallas, his ministry became more diversified, particularly with his speaking at Bible conferences and contributing to Christian periodicals. His greatest writing contribution, however, was editor-in-chief of the *Scofield Reference Bible,* which was published by Oxford University Press in 1911.[48]

Scofield was also a strong promoter of foreign missions. This grew out of his association with Hudson Taylor at the Niagara Bible Conference. Scofield became so burdened about the spiritual needs of Central America that he called three of his church members to his home in Dallas on November 14, 1890. Together they formed the Central American Mission with Scofield becoming the secretary.[49]

In 1914 Scofield undertook another project. He and other key church leaders founded Philadelphia School of Bible. His primary associate in this undertaking was William L. Pettingill. Beginning October 1, 1914, the school offered evening classes in rented quarters. As the first president, Scofield addressed the opening session and lectured in Bible classes when his health permitted.[50]

Beginning in January, 1915, he began his contributions to the widely distributed *Sunday School Times.*[51] The Comprehensive Bible Correspondence Course had grown to ten-thousand students. Starting in 1915, it was published by Moody Press, the publishing division of Moody Bible Institute.[52]

In January, 1919, Scofield was notified of his election to the 38-member Société Académique d' Histoire Internationale in recognition of his work on the reference Bible.[53] At the time of the election, he was planning a new revision of the reference Bible, but never had the opportunity to carry through because of his failing health.   In July, 1921, he lapsed into semiconsciousness and died quietly on July 24. He was buried in Flushing, New York. William L. Pettingill conducted the funeral.[54]

C. I. Scofield, like the other leading revivalists, was a man who involved himself in a variety of religious endeavors. He was a pastor, Bible conference speaker, founder of a foreign missionary society and a Bible school, and author. The last role is the one for which he is most remembered, particularly as editor of the *Scofield Reference Bible*. This is clearly the most significant legacy which he bequeathed to Protestant Christianity.

REUBEN A. TORREY

Reuben A. Torrey (1856-1928) was called an apostle for the hour in which he lived. His life bears striking resemblance to the Apostle Paul. Both were well educated and converted from scepticism. Both labored for some time in rather insignificant ministries and eventually were thrust into global evangelistic efforts. Both were preachers and teachers, and their writings made an indelible imprint on the generations which followed.[55] R. A. Torrey was also a key figure in the early growth of two key Bible schools, Moody Bible Institute and the Bible Institute of Los Angeles, not as a founding president but as a dean.

Reuben was born in 1856 in Hoboken, New Jersey, the third of five children. His father was a banker who later directed a prosperous manufacturing company. The family was actively involved in the Congregational church. Enjoying the advantages of a strong private education, Torrey entered Yale in 1871 at the age of 15 to pursue a law career.[56]

At the end of his second year at Yale, Torrey made a public profession of faith and joined the church. In 1875, instead of going to law school, he began his studies at Yale Divinity School. While in seminary, he was licensed to preach by the Congregational church. He completed his seminary training in 1878.[57] He also did further graduate training in Leipzig, Germany, in historical criticism of the Bible.[58]

Torrey served in relative obscurity as pastor of Congregational churches in Garrettsville, Ohio, and Minneapolis, Minnesota. However, his career as a pastor, teacher, and evangelist took a major step forward in 1889 when D. L. Moody invited him to serve the Bible Institute in Chicago as superintendent. His responsibilities included organizing and directing the new school. Because Moody lacked a formal education, he extended a call to one who could provide strong academic leadership.[59] He worked as superintendent or dean at Moody Bible Institute until 1908.

It was also during these years in Chicago that Torrey distinguished himself as an author of a number of theological books, as a Bible conference speaker, as pastor of the Moody Memorial Church, and most of all, as a world renowned evangelist. He held evangelistic services in the United States, Australia, New Zealand, and Great Britain. Religious historian Ernest Sandeen wrote, "His success gave him claim to be considered the successor of Moody himself."[60]

Upon leaving Moody Bible Institute in 1908, he continued his itinerate ministry of evangelism and Bible teaching. In 1914 he also established a Bible conference center in Montrose, Pennsylvania, which attracted popular Bible teachers and thousands of people to the small town in the mountains of northeastern Pennsylvania.

In 1911 Torrey accepted the invitation to become dean of the newly established Bible Institute of Los Angeles. He served there with distinction until 1924 while simultaneously pastoring the Church of the Open Door.[61] He spent the balance of his life in itinerate ministry until his death on October 25, 1928, at the age of 72. Torrey was a strong voice for the cause of fundamentalism in the twenties, though he was in the twilight of his career.

ELMORE HARRIS

Elmore Harris (1854-1912), like many of the other leaders of Bible schools in the late nineteenth century, was a successful pastor, Bible conference speaker, ardent supporter of the faith mission movement, writer, and personal friend of many of the well known revivalists of his day. The one key difference, however, was that Elmore Harris was a Canadian who spent his entire life in the Toronto area.

Harris was born near Brantford, Ontario, in 1854 into a prosperous farm machinery family. His father, Alanson Harris, was the founder of the A. Harris, Son and Company. This business later merged with Hart Massey's firm in Toronto to become Massey-Harris, a company that soon became the largest and most successful farm implement company in the British Empire.[62]

Harris became a follower of Jesus Christ at the age of sixteen at the Beamaville Baptist Church where his parents were prominent members. It was in this church that he preached his first sermon and felt the call of God into the gospel ministry. Determined to be a pastor, he enrolled at the University of Toronto in Classics and Hebrew and graduated with a B.A. in 1876.[63] It was also during his student days that he became active in evangelistic work with the YMCA.

In 1875, while still a university student, Harris accepted the pastorate of St. Thomas Baptist Church where he was ordained into the gospel ministry. After six years in St. Thomas, Ontario, he left to pastor the Yorkville Baptist Church in Toronto. In both of these churches, his pastoral ministry was remarkably successful. When the Yorkville Church on Bloor Street reached a high degree of prosperity in 1889, he withdrew in order to establish a new congregation at Walmer Road in Toronto. This church was his own creation and his most successful pastorate. For six years he devoted a high degree of energy to its growth and development, and out of his wealth helped to build what was at that time the largest Baptist church in Canada.[64] Threatened by failing health in 1895, he resigned and became Pastor Emeritus of the church.

During the last year of his pastoral ministry at Walmer Road Baptist Church, Harris began what he regarded as the chief work of his life. In conjunction with a group of pastors and lay leaders from various denominational backgrounds, he established the Toronto Bible Training School. The school was first held in the Walmer Road Baptist Church until a building was erected on College Street, largely through the benevolence of Harris. In association with William Stewart, the first principal, Harris devoted most of his time and energy during the remaining years of his life to the school. Until his death in December 1911, he served in the presidency and taught on a regular basis.[65]

In addition to his successful ministry as a pastor and then Bible school president, he became a popular speaker for Bible conferences and deeper-life meetings and a well-known visiting instructor at other Bible schools throughout the United States. Although he was loyal to his own denomination and its work, he was very interdenominational in matters that evangelical churches had in common. His interdenominational approach to Christianity was also reflected in his serving as a contributing editor for the 1911 edition of the *Scofield Reference Bible*.[66]

ASHLEY S. JOHNSON

Ashley S. Johnson (1857-1925) did not fit the same profile as most other early Bible school leaders of the late nineteenth century. His ministry was limited to one particular geographic area, the upper southern states, and to one specific denomination, the Disciples of Christ/Christian Church. The impact of his ministry, however, was quite significant within this particular sphere. His concern for evangelism, missions, and education was consistent with developments that were taking place within North American Protestantism during this time period of evangelical revivalism.

Ashley was born on June 22, 1857, in Knox County, Tennessee, the eldest of seven sons born to Jeremiah and Barbara Johnson. Because of family circumstances, his formal educational opportunities were limited. After having his early education supervised by his father, he enrolled in two successive neighborhood "subscription schools." At the age of seventeen, he passed the county examination for a teacher's certificate. After a year's study at the University of Tennessee, he took a job at a law office in Knoxville with the hope of becoming a lawyer while continuing to teach on a limited basis.[67]

Johnson's religious background was also quite limited. His family joined a Disciples of Christ congregation during his adolescent years, but he remained indifferent to his family's religious awakenings until he was converted at the age of twenty after attending a Baptist revival meeting. He was baptized by immersion on October 14, 1977,[68] and immediately focused his attention on preparing for preaching and evangelism. He began an intense program of studying the Bible and reading the works of Alexander Campbell, founder of the Disciples of Christ.

Johnson soon embarked upon what would be a very successful writing career. He began to publish a theological journal, the *Christian Watchman*, in 1879, and wrote his most popular book, *The Great Controversy*, in 1882. Johnson's works included a Bible encyclopedia, a "self-interpreting" New Testament, Bible commentaries, hermeneutical and doctrinal studies, devotional literature, an autobiography, and collections of public sermons. Much of the financial capital for the Bible college he would later found came from the sale of these books.[69]

Although Johnson did serve for short periods of time as pastor of the First Christian Church of Knoxville and the First Christian Church of Chattanooga and as the State Evangelist for South Carolina, the majority of his career was spent in theological education. He founded and developed the School of the Evangelists, later called Johnson Bible College.

Johnson Bible College, which was officially started in 1893, originated as the Correspondence Bible College in 1886. The purpose of the school was to train young men to preach the gospel and to provide instruction for those who could not afford a traditional education. The Correspondence Bible College claimed a total enrollment of nearly three-thousand students from 1886-1912.[70]

Johnson began the School of the Evangelists with three sincere convictions: preachers must be trained to evangelize the world; a Bible-centered education was absolutely necessary to this training; and special opportunity must be given to poor young men who desired to preach but could not afford an education. As the institution developed, it continued to embody those same convictions.[71] There were two distinguishing characteristics that set Johnson's institution apart from most of the other early schools. Admission was limited to male students and emphasis and attention was focused on training men to be pastors and evangelists whereas other early Bible schools were coeducational and placed a very strong emphasis on lay training.

Johnson served faithfully as the president of Johnson Bible College until his death on January 15, 1925. During his 32 years of leadership, there was a steady growth in students, graduates, facilities, and financial base. There were 3879 students and 200 graduates during his presidency (1893-1925). These students came from over thirty states (although the largest percentage came from the Upper South and Midwest) and at least eight foreign countries.[72]

COMMON CHARACTERISTICS

After examining the lives of these early Bible school leaders, certain observable common characteristics can be summarized and highlighted. These are reflected in their contributions and religious activities.

In common with other conservative Protestant leaders of their era, these Bible school leaders experienced a dramatic conversion which produced significant modifications of their conduct. Some abandoned secular careers in order to carry on full-time evangelical activities. For example, D. L. Moody was a shoe salesman before his conversion. Attorney C. I. Scofield's conversion resulted in an instantaneous cure for alcoholism. Reuben A. Torrey and Ashley S. Johnson both abandoned their original plans to go into law in order to pursue Christian ministry. The fact that each had a life-changing conversion experience certainly helps to explain their strong commitment to evangelism. Their preaching and writing ministries centered around a strong revivalistic message, and the schools they founded were committed to training students for evangelism at home and abroad.

These men were also fervent students of the Bible. Each one spent large amounts of time reading and meditating upon the Scriptures. This practice grew out of a firm belief that the Bible was the infallible, inspired Word of God and was the basis for life and godliness. In fact, these men were extremely critical of those who did not hold to the same literal interpretation of the Bible, particularly those embracing higher criticism. Because these revivalists had such a love and appreciation for the Bible, they dedicated their lives to communicating its message. This is why their Bible schools centered around a strong Bible curriculum. They believed that the Bible should be at the center of the educational program.

Most of these individuals also engaged in broad ecumenical activities to carry out their evangelical endeavors. While these Bible school leaders retrained denominational affiliations (A. B. Simpson was the exception), they tended to minimize the importance of denominational loyalties. They recognized the value of nondenominational efforts, such as city-wide revivals, Bible conferences, and the YMCA, in combating apostasy and religious indifference. A significant percentage of the early Bible school leaders had worked as YMCA directors or secretaries at a time when it had a strong evangelical emphasis. Just as many of these leaders were ecumenical, their schools also attracted faculty and students from many different denominations.

Another common characteristic was their commitment to train lay men and women to assume more significant responsibilities within local churches. These men were also anxious to promote evangelism and Bible teaching as there was a lack of trained workers. Because of the desperate need for "laborers" who would complement the clergy, they committed themselves to the mobilization of lay workers to carry out their evangelical tasks. Their instrument to accomplish this was the Bible school.

Finally, most of these men founded or directed their respective Bible schools late in their careers. Only A. B. Simpson and Ashley S. Johnson were under forty when they founded their Bible schools. Although they were successful pastors, Bible conference speakers, writers, and evangelists, they realized that a primary way to accomplish their varied evangelical goals was through the establishment of Bible schools. These training schools could perpetuate their theology and their methodology. In fact, they could serve as more permanent legacies for the church. In support of this argument, D. L. Moody stated, "My school will not tell much until the (nineteenth) century passes, but when I am gone, I shall leave some grand men and women behind."[73] Less than a year before his death, C. I. Scofield said, "I hope and pray that it will please God to give me many years of service in connection with the school. But if He does not, I know that my dream of a Bible school in the east has come to pass."[74]

The apparent informality and spontaneity with which these training schools appeared might suggest that the schools sprang up as a result of the fundamentalist-modernist controversy of the 1920s and 1930s. To a great extent, the issues and priorities of the fundamentalist movement did shape the policies and practices of the schools. However, the early Bible schools took on the characteristics of the late nineteenth century and the early twentieth century revivalists who founded and directed them. These were missions-minded individuals who were responding to the needs of their society and times by establishing schools to equip skilled lay people who could serve in areas of evangelism and Christian education. They were to become models for future generations.

CHAPTER SIX

COMMON THEOLOGICAL THEMES

As we saw in the previous chapter, the founders of the early Bible schools maintained certain theological convictions and values that had a corresponding impact on the institutions they represented. The leaders all shared a very high regard for the Bible and applied systems of study and interpretation particularly to the subject of prophecy. All believed in the need for personal conversion and ongoing dedication of oneself to Christ. They placed very strong emphasis on personal evangelism, both at home and abroad. Most were premillennialists who looked forward with anticipation to the imminent return of the Lord Jesus Christ.

They also held similar viewpoints on issues related to education, morality, and culture. Most looked to common heroes, such as Dwight L. Moody, Charles Spurgeon, J. Hudson Taylor, and George Mueller, as examples for truth and practice. These theological convictions and shared values helped to influence the birth of the early Bible schools. Their schools in turn helped to preserve and perpetuate common themes.

Those who sought out and supported Bible schools had experienced common spiritual experiences or events—conversion, sanctification, success in personal evangelism, and sometimes divine healing and/or speaking in tongues in the case of Pentecostals. Though these experiences were quite common in the lives of those involved in the early Bible school movement, religious historians have paid little attention to them, perhaps because those who were writing from within took them for granted and those who were from without could not or would not comprehend or sympathize.[1] The result is that doctrine has been overemphasized within the movement while the personal application or experience has been diminished. Furthermore, the revivalists of the nineteenth century and the fundamentalists of the early twentieth century tended to stress doctrine because of the struggles in which they engaged with opponents whom they felt gave far too much attention to subjective experience. However, the personal experiences of these leaders and their students cannot be overlooked in understanding their theology and their institutions. John Roach Straton, an ardent fundamentalist leader of the early twentieth century, in spite of his uncompromising commitment to theological orthodoxy, conceded that "sceptics and infidels can answer argument with argument, they can pit philosophy against philosophy, but there is one thing they cannot answer and that is a personal experience of the redeeming grace and power of Jesus Christ as the Son of God."[2]

What were common theological themes and experiences that characterized the early Bible schools and colleges? How did these theological views influence the formation and early development of these institutions? This chapter will answer these questions by examining many of the shared theological convictions and experiences of these early leaders.

CONVERSION EXPERIENCE

From the time of Luther to the beginning of the twentieth century, the primary event in the life of most Protestant Christians was their conversion experience. The experience occurred at different ages and under varied circumstances, but a major spiritual turning point was necessary for Christians to believe that they had been saved. It was often initiated by feelings of worthlessness and "a conviction of sin." Finally, often through the agency of Scripture, a close friend or relative, or a compelling evangelist, pastor, or Bible teacher, the need to be rescued from the consequences of sin would surface. This need would lead the individual to an act of faith in the saving power of Christ's death and resurrection. This was recognized as a glorious experience that was described in the Scriptures as spiritual rebirth, a high point in the Christian life.[3]

During the late nineteenth century, however, conversion gradually came to be seen as a less important part of the Christian life. Fewer and fewer North American Protestants viewed this radical experience as part of their understanding of Christianity. A leading spokesperson for this particular argument was Horace Bushnell, a Congregational pastor from Hartford, Connecticut, and author of *Christian Nurture* (1847). Bushnell rejected the traditional theology of the "conversion experience" and maintained that "the child can grow up as a Christian and never know himself to be otherwise."[4] He argued that conversion was not a one-time experience but the result of culture and education as Christians were growing and being nurtured in their faith.[5] His ideas may have been ahead of his time, but by the end of the century his views helped to shape liberal revisions of Protestant orthodoxy and conservative emphasis on the primacy of the Christian experience as opposed to the conversion experience.

One of the first evidences for change in attitude toward conversion change was in higher education. Prior to the Civil War, church-related colleges and theological seminaries attempted to foster spiritual development. With the declining impact of religion in these institutions and the emergence of public universities, however, student conversions ceased to be a major concern of college professors and administrators. Instead, the responsibility for evangelism rested with outside agencies, such as the Young Men's Christian Association and its sister organization, the YWCA, both of which operated on college campuses. The secularization of college and university campuses continued to increase. The books and articles accusing colleges and universities of abandoning their religious moorings began to increase in the late nineteenth century, and reached a crescendo in the 1920s.[6]

The Bible school movement emerged in the later nineteenth century as a protest against secularization in higher education and as an educational center for lay workers and full-time Bible teachers, evangelists, and pastors. It was in these early Bible schools that conversion was regarded as central to one's Christian experience. It also provided an environment where the convictions of young converts could be fostered, confirmed, and deepened by the presence of like-minded peers and instructors. While most college and university professors viewed students as scholars and critical thinkers, Bible school teachers served as role models of the consecrated life.

COMMITMENT TO BIBLICAL AUTHORITY

Equal in importance to conversion was an intense and reverent approach to the Scriptures that characterized all the early Bible school leaders and their students. This unwavering commitment to the authority of Scripture was not unique to the Bible school. North American Protestants of many descriptions shared it, at least until the emergence of higher criticism in the late nineteenth century. As we saw in Chapter two, higher criticism openly attacked the validity of the Scriptures and the very foundation of evangelical Christianity.

The higher critics' challenge to traditional ideas about the Bible could not easily be overlooked. Many of these critics served in Protestant churches and church-related colleges and seminaries. The revivalists and the later fundamentalists that followed responded to their critics with strong teaching on biblical inerrancy, biblical literalism, and verbal inspiration. Benjamin B. Warfield (1851-1921) of Princeton Theological Seminary was perhaps the most forceful defender of the Bible's "inerrancy" at the end of the nineteenth century. By inerrancy, Warfield meant that all of the statements in the Bible were truthful if interpreted according to the sense in which the biblical authors had intended them. In 1881 Warfield and his colleague A. A. Hodge wrote that "the Scriptures not only contain, but ARE THE WORD OF GOD, and hence . . . all their elements and all their affirmations are absolutely errorless, and binding in faith and obedience of all men."[7]

The teachers in the early Bible schools demonstrated no less of a commitment to the authority of the Scriptures. The Bible was the foundation of instruction in in all their departments. For example, the catalog of Central Bible Institute stated that the Bible was "the primary textbook of the curriculum."[8] Similarly, the 1920 catalog of the Bible Institute of Los Angles pointed out that the Bible was to be "the chief textbook of the Bible Institute." Furthermore, the publication made it quite clear that this statement applied to all courses in the curriculum including the department of "Psychology and Sociology." The catalog declared, "The best textbook on psychology is the Bible. The Bible sets forth man as he really is, and not as speculative philosophers imagine him to be."[9] These statements were characteristic of many other Bible schools in regard to their Bible-centered approach to education.

PREMILLENNIAL ESCHATOLOGY

At the end of the nineteenth century, North American evangelicals least expected a resurgence of premillennialism, the belief that Jesus Christ would return before establishing his peaceful kingdom on the earth for one thousand years.[10] Premillennialism had long been associated with periods of intense religious activity. The early Christians lived in expectation of Jesus Christ's swift bodily return. Since the time of St. Augustine, the church in general had not been premillennialist, but every age had given rise to groups that preached the imminent second coming. These groups self-consciously patterned themselves after the Christians of the apostolic age. In the United States, the premillennialist tradition flourished in the early nineteenth century, but the belief fell into dispute after a leading millenarian, William Miller, a Baptist pastor from Vermont falsely predicted the Lord's return in 1843 (and then in 1844).[11] Miller's failed predictions were particularly devastating because of his large following and wide publicity.

By 1875 a new kind of premillennialism called "dispensationalism" began gaining wide acceptance among the same conservative Protestants who had considered the earlier Adventists fools and heretics. The new premillennialists fought to establish two related truths: that they had essentially nothing in common with the discredited Millerites and that they were just as legitimate and orthodox as the rest of the Protestant mainstream.[12] They developed a very elaborate system to codify the study and interpretation of the Bible. Dispensationalism could reasonably be called a systematized form of premillennialism, although not all premillennialists were dispensationalists. Briefly put, it divided the contents of the Bible into several time periods, each with its own characteristic theme. The name "dispensationalism" came from one of its chief tenets, the belief that all history is divided into ages or dispensations. It was also a method of interpreting biblical prophecy.

Before coming to North America in the late nineteenth century, the new premillennialism had flourished in Great Britain, thanks in large part to the influence of the Plymouth Brethren. The most gifted teacher within the Brethren was John Nelson Darby (1800-1882), who popularized this new premillennialism through his many volumes of writing. Along with other Brethren leaders, Darby came to the United States and Canada after the Civil War and with him came new concepts.[13]

Among North American dispensationalists, William E. Blackstone and Cyrus I. Scofield, both followers of Darby, became prominent advocates of this belief system. Blackstone's influence came through his well-known book, *Jesus Is Coming*, written in 1878. Scofield's greatest influence stemmed from his heavily annotated *Scofield Reference Bible* (1909) and his previous work, *Rightly Dividing the Word of Truth*. Scofield defined dispensationalism as "a period of time during which man is tested in respect to some specific revelation of the will of God."[14] Furthermore, "these periods are marked off in Scripture by some change in God's method of dealing with mankind with respect to two questions: of sin and man's responsibility. Each of the dispensations may be regarded as a new test of the natural man, and each ends in judgment— marking his utter failure in every dispensation."[15]

A number of reasons explain why dispensationalism carried an inherent appeal. First, at the most elementary level, the system furnished the faithful with a way of reading the Bible that was reverent and methodical. Second, students of the Bible were struck by how large a portion of Scripture was devoted to prophecy. Adherents of dispensationalism appreciated the attention given to prophecy and the literal approach to the interpretation of Scripture. Dispensationalism, they thought, gave proper recognition of prophetic books and passages such statements were interpreted literally. Third, despite its apparent complexity, dispensationalism offered a simple view of the Bible. To dispensationalists, the Bible was one voice and the creation of a single mind. Fourth, it conveyed a bleak picture of the world and of human ability. To people convinced that morality, civilization, and true religion were in decline, this was a legitimate viewpoint. Conservative Protestants felt that their views were appropriate for their era as liberal religious leaders increasingly received important denominational posts, secular scholars trained in historical and scientific methods monopolized universities, and the world was seemingly becoming less oriented toward a religious value system.

Moreover, dispensationalism aided the understanding of history. This worldview divided the history of mankind into different time periods or dispensations from creation to final judgment when God will ultimately establish a new heaven and a new earth. People of the late nineteenth and early twentieth centuries were historically conscious; they were particularly concerned about "evolution," "growth," and "development." Any system that attempted to offer a religious and philosophical explanation had to take history into account. Dispensationalism gave God the leading role. He was the "mover" and "doer," not humanity. Therefore, dispensationalism offered a welcomed alternative to the emerging visions of history that assumed that human beings were the primary agents and progress the dominant direction. It posed a cyclical history culminating in a blessed end. Other current histories envisioned a straight, upward line, whose termination was a troubling question mark.

The appeal of this new premillennialism could be summed up in the certainty and clarity it offered to Protestants who otherwise would have felt anxious about the present and the future. But it went a step further in that it created an attitude of hope and anticipation. It was the bridge between the old traditions of conservative Christianity and the rapidly changing secular society.

During the last quarter of the nineteenth century, the premillennial movement took on a new form in North America through a series of newly founded Bible and prophecy conferences. These conferences furnished an opportunity for the prorogation of the new form of premillennialism. It also provided occasions for the formation of new friendships and the development of new leadership. This new phenomenon was the key instrument that really brought premillennialism into its own after 1875.[16]

In addition to the Bible and prophecy conferences, which helped to promote premillennialism in the late nineteenth and early twentieth centuries, another factor that changed the character of the millenarian movement was the founding of Bible institutes. The popularity of the Bible schools among premillennialists was consistent with their theological outlook. "That blessed hope," as the second coming of Christ was often called, transformed the way they lived their lives. It created a sense of urgency for missionary activities as well as the need to be properly trained. Believers who were convinced that only a little time remained before the Lord's coming understood their duty as preparing His way by proclaiming the gospel around the world.

Because of this sense of urgency, premillennialists felt the necessity of training as many believers as possible to do some type of missionary service. Their base for training was the Bible school, but their premillennial views altered their thinking about the way education should take place. Since time was short before the Lord's return, schooling should be brief and intense. A 1921 graduate of Moody Bible Institute captured the sense of urgency when he recalled, "Everyone was going into the ministry. The coming of the Lord would be very soon. We had to get some training."[17]

The growth of the Bible schools, particularly in the early twentieth century, also helped to promote the doctrine of premillennialism. As one might expect, the Bible school classroom and chapel service were used to teach this belief. Just as delegates from the Bible and prophecy conferences returned to their churches and taught the theology they received, the Bible school students took their millenarian viewpoint with them to their fields of service. Therefore, as Bible schools increased and produced a growing number of graduates, so the popularity of premillennialism increased. The Bible schools became a means whereby their premillennial leaders could reproduce their own.

EMPHASIS ON HOLINESS

Another spiritual emphasis alongside premillennialism was the Victorious Living or Keswick Higher Life Movement.[18] Its emphasis on holiness took on a variety of forms. Within Methodism, there was growing discontentment over the lack of teaching on John Wesley's doctrine of Christian perfection. In 1867 the National Campmeeting Association for the Promotion of Christian Holiness was formed in Vineland, New Jersey, by John S. Inskip and several associates. This new organization attempted to foster holiness expectations among Christians, primarily from within the Methodist constituency.[19]

The concern for the doctrines and practices of holiness ultimately led to a break-away movement within Methodism in the late nineteenth century. Methodists who continued to promote the possibility of entire sanctification and who looked for a distinct second work of grace after conversion sponsored a wide variety of camp meetings, mission initiatives, and independent churches. The Church of God, Anderson, Indiana, was started in 1881 after breaking from the main denomination under the leadership of Daniel Sidney Warner. Similarly, former Methodist minister Phineas F. Breese organized an independent congregation in Los Angeles in 1895 known as the Church of the Nazarene. It later became a national organization or denomination promoting distinctively holiness teachings.[20]

Concepts such as "laying it all on the altar," a "deeper work of grace," a "higher life," the "baptism of the Holy Spirit," and "victorious living" were not unique to the Nazarenes or the Methodists. Among the Baptist and Presbyterian groups, the holiness emphasis did not usually involve belief in a conclusive post-conversion experience, but there was still a very strong emphasis on living a deeper spiritual life. The Keswick Movement, which originated chiefly among Anglicans and Calvinists in England, came to the United States in the late nineteenth century where it helped to renew the holiness movement. The "Victorious Life Movement," was formed in 1913, and a site in New Jersey, "Keswick Grove," became its permanent home in 1923.[21]

There were many similarities between the Wesleyan and Keswick traditions of holiness. The most obvious difference between the two approaches was terminology. For example, the Wesleyan holiness tended to emphasize "sinless perfection," the total eradication of human sin made possible by the experience of holiness. On the other hand, the Keswick adherents remained Calvinistic in orientation, stressing that humanity could never be completely set free from sin in this life. But they went far beyond what traditional Calvinists would have allowed in arguing that those who managed constantly to experience the "indwelling Christ" in their lives could achieve "victory" over at least their conscious sins.[22]

Although sanctification, or the achievement of holiness, was often described as an instantaneous experience, it required continuous and careful cultivation through prayer, personal Bible study, and encouragement from other Christians who shared a common experience. Such an experience made a significant difference in the way believers conducted themselves. A. T. Pierson, a revivalist of the late nineteenth century, declared that Keswick followers avoided as sinful those things which were "done primarily to please one's self," which gave "undue prominence to self."[23] Although part of Pierson's reference may have been to outward behavior, such as tobacco, alcohol, dancing, and the theater, it no doubt related to personal character qualities, such as controlling one's temper or gaining victory over impatience.

Holiness also involved "trusting the Lord" enough to "step out upon his promises." In a very literal sense, "promises" referred to prophetic declarations about the imminent return of the Lord and eternal rewards awaiting the saints. When believers referred to "promises," however, they also meant that God would provide for their daily needs.[24]

Two of the most respected individuals for "trusting the Lord" were George Mueller (1805-1898) and J. Hudson Taylor (1832-1905). Mueller, who established a large orphanage in Bristol, England, never made his needs known to the public but simply prayed for what he needed when he needed it. J. Hudson Taylor, founder of the China Inland Mission, promoted the message that missionaries could find their own support in the field by relying upon the Lord. Using this particular approach, Taylor was able to send out hundreds of missionaries to the interior of China at a much lower cost than denominational mission boards could. The China Inland Mission paradigm was later adopted by many other "faith" missions that were started in the late nineteenth and early twentieth centuries.[25]

The doctrine of holiness, or sanctification, was communicated with enthusiasm among North American evangelicals through books, periodicals, conferences and conventions, camp meetings, holiness denominations, but also through the early Bible schools. One of the major reasons why Iva Durham Vennard founded the Evangelistic Training Institute in Chicago in 1910 was to ensure that future Christian workers would receive instruction in holiness from teachers who had themselves been sanctified.[26] The cultivation of holiness was also a major objective in the founding of the Training School for Christian Workers in Los Angeles by the Quakers in 1899. An early schedule for the school mentioned that "many prayer meetings including one on Monday evenings especially devoted to seek the second blessing."[27] These are just two examples of how the holiness emphasis took form in the early Bible schools in North America. Although this doctrine took on other expressions in the early schools, it was a pervasive influence.

PENTECOSTALISM

In 1906 an abandoned Methodist church at 312 Azusa Street in the industrial section of Los Angeles became the birthplace of modern Pentecostalism. William J. Seymour (1870-1922), a black holiness preacher, founded the Apostolic Faith Gospel Mission on Azusa Street, where a new emphasis on the work of the Holy Spirit rapidly became a local sensation and grew into an international religious phenomenon. Before arriving in Los Angeles, however, Seymour had been greatly influenced by the teaching of Charles Parham (1873-1929), a Methodist of holiness upbringing who directed a revival at Bethel Bible College in Topeka, Kansas, in 1901.[28] Parham taught that the baptism of "the Holy Spirit and fire" should be expected among those who were Christians and had sought the deeper life of holiness. He also promoted the "speaking with other tongues" as a special sign of the baptism of the Holy Spirit and placed a strong emphasis on such gifts of the Spirit as divine healing.[29] It was out of this context that William J. Seymour, one of Parham's students, went on to preach this experience in the Azusa Street Mission in Los Angeles.

The revival that began on Azusa Street in 1906 quickly drew international attention. It was characterized by fervent prayer, speaking in tongues, enthusiastic singing, and healing of the sick. Another distinguishing quality was the full participation of women in public activities. Azusa Street caught peoples' attention because of the way blacks and whites joined together in worship while setting aside racial and cultural differences. This new model for worship attracted thousands of visitors from around the world. When these visitors returned home, they promoted this new form of Pentecostalism in their home churches.[30]

Pentecostalism initially had a strong nondenominational flavor. Because it faced growing opposition from both the mainline evangelical denominations and some of the newer holiness churches, Pentecostal leaders soon adopted denominational ways. For example, A. J. Tomlison founded the Church of God (Cleveland, Tennessee) in 1906, and Charles H. Mason formed the Church of God in Christ a year later. Eventually the latter became the largest black Pentecostal church in the world.[31] From a series of alliances and the networking of preachers and faith-healers, the Assemblies of God, established in 1914, emerged as the largest Pentecostal denomination.[32]

Pentecostalism also tended to be one of the issues that most divided conservative evangelicals. Fundamentalist leaders, particularly those who embraced dispensationalism and valued order, were quite sceptical of what they perceived to be unruly outpourings of the Holy Spirit. This carried over to the Bible schools. At non-Pentecostal schools where speaking in tongues was discouraged, this and other more extreme displays of spirituality among the students was a problem with which many administrators had to deal.[33]

In spite of opposition from within more traditional evangelical groups, Pentecostalism was eventually responsible for the founding of a number of Bible schools. The Pentecostal schools resembled Bible schools of other fundamentalist traditions in most respects, but they often tended to struggle under scarcer economic resources and lower academic standards. Pentecostal schools also suffered from a high attrition rate. As of 1959, for instance, only nine of forty Bible schools started by the Assemblies of God had survived.[34]

In summary, the Bible schools that were started in North America in the late nineteenth and early twentieth centuries shared many common theological viewpoints. These commonalities served as a uniting force in drawing them together. Although the leaders of these schools came from different denominational backgrounds, they experienced a definite spiritual kinship because of these shared convictions and values.

First, the conversion experience was regarded as central to the Christian life. In spite of the influence of theological liberalism, which tended to diminish the importance of the experience, conversion was recognized as a necessary and glorious experience that was foundational to Christianity. Conversion was a prerequisite for Bible school faculty and staff, and it was an expectation for students.

Second, and just as important as conversion, there was a clear commitment to biblical authority. With the emergence of higher criticism in many of the Protestant colleges and seminaries of the era, the Bible schools served as a reaction to the open attacks on the authority of the Scriptures through their strong, Bible-centered education.

Third, premillennialism, the doctrinal belief that Jesus Christ would return to the earth before establishing His one thousand year reign on the earth, began gaining a strong following in North America at the end of the nineteenth century. Premillennialism, particularly the dispensational approach to biblical interpretation, provided Christians with a systematic method for Bible study, and it created an attitude of hope and anticipation. Bible school leaders taught this form of eschatology with a sense of urgency. They saw the need to train as many believers as possible to do the Lord's work.

Fourth, biblical teaching on holiness took on a variety of forms in the early Bible schools. Whether this theological viewpoint was promoted as a post-conversion experience or an ongoing process of sanctification, there was a very strong emphasis on living a deeper spiritual life. Holiness required continuous cultivation through prayer, Bible study, and support from other Christians who shared the same experience, all of which were characteristics of the Bible schools.

Fifth, Pentecostalism was not necessarily emphasized in all of the early Bible schools, particularly those that had a strong dispensational emphasis. Yet, Pentecostalism was a major force in the founding of a number of the early schools. These particular institutions were quite instrumental in promoting Pentecostal theology while serving as training centers for Pentecostal missionaries and church leaders.

The common theological themes that characterized the early Bible schools were by no means limited to the five cited in this chapter, though they certainly were some of the most prominent. These theological convictions and shared values helped to influence the birth and development of the Bible schools, and the schools in turn helped to perpetuate these teachings.

CHAPTER SEVEN

THE FAITH MISSION MOVEMENT

Another major factor in the rise of the early Bible schools was the great forward movement of world missions and evangelism. During the second half of the nineteenth century missionary societies grew and multiplied, resulting in an increasing number of missionaries being sent to countries around the world. They were commissioned by traditional mission boards and by new independent groups that had sprung up in Canada, the United States, and England. From the famous Haystack Prayer Meeting in the first decade of the nineteenth century to the great Student Volunteer Movement with its rallying cry, "The evangelization of the world in this generation," the century was marked by significant growth of foreign missions.[1]

Following the lead of William Carey, often called the father of "modern missions," from the late eighteenth to early twentieth centuries, some 400 missionary societies were formed. The nineteenth century in particular demonstrated great missionary expansion and development.[2]

At first, mission societies were not denominational in the strict sense. They were independent organizations. Like William Carey's Baptist Missionary Society, they may have arisen within a single denomination. The denominations as such, however, did not sponsor them nor did they direct their affairs.

In the early nineteenth century, a major change took place, especially in Britain and North America. More and more of the mission societies came under the control of the various Protestant denominations. Denominations, as such, began to initiate missions. Even the interdenominational London Missionary Society found itself becoming the organ of British Congregationalism. In the United States, the American Board of Commissioners for Foreign Missions went through the same process. It came to represent only American Congregationalists while Presbyterians and others set up their own boards. By the close of the century, practically every Protestant denomination had its own missionary society. Because the greatest multiplication of Protestant denominations occurred in the United States, more mission societies arose here than in any other country.[3]

While missionary activity in North America was directed primarily toward native Americans or Canadians on the expanding frontier, the visit of English missionary Robert Morrison, who sailed for China in 1807 by way of the United States, furthered interest in foreign missions. Subsequent to Morrison's visit, missionaries of the London Missionary Society frequently made their way to the east via North America. Their visits did much to excite interest in the spiritual needs of people in other lands.

This rise in enthusiasm for world evangelization at the beginning of the nineteenth century gave rise to many kindred organizations. Religious historian William W. Sweet wrote:

> The increased demand for missionaries led to the establishment of schools where they could be adequately trained. To aid in this important work, education societies began to be formed, and a national organization known as the American Education Society was organized in 1815. This society had for its purpose the aiding of all young men, of suitable talents, who appear to be called to preach Christ, and who belong to any of the evangelical denominations.[4]

However, in the late nineteenth century, theological liberalism, which was so prominent in Germany, had begun to draw a following in North America and to affect missionary activity. "In essence, it stripped Christianity of its supernatural elements," wrote historian Robert T. Linder, "especially its miracles and the deity of Christ. It taught instead what it considered to be the essential virtues of the fatherhood of God, the brotherhood of man, and the necessity of living in love."[5] The Bible, historically the authority for faith and practice in the Protestant churches, was no longer considered trustworthy because of apparent errors and contradictions. Critical studies seemed to undermine its authority. According to missionary historian Ruth Tucker, this had a significant effect on Protestant foreign missions:

> Virtually one-hundred percent of Protestant missionaries during most of the (nineteenth) century were evangelicals who held to a literal interpretation of Scripture and defended the cardinal doctrines of the faith. But, by the end of the century, carrying the title of missionary was no guarantee that an individual was orthodox in his Christian beliefs.[6]

The impact of higher criticism was starting to be felt in foreign missions. Those colleges and seminaries that started rejecting traditional Evangelicalism in favor of higher criticism no longer produced as many graduates who were interested in home and foreign missions. Those holding higher critical views of the Scripture believed that man was not lost and thus did not need to be saved from sin; because everyone was a child of God, there was no need for evangelistic attempts to convert others to the Christian faith. As a result of this higher criticism, existing Protestant denominational boards sent out fewer missionaries.

As a reaction to this new theological trend, a period of Protestant revivalism occurred in North America in the late nineteenth and the early twentieth centuries that included a significant increase in missionary activity. As part of this reaction, a new breed of missionaries emerged, not necessarily so different from their forbears, but intensely determined to keep their faith pure and to trust God alone for their needs. They were largely graduates of Bible schools as opposed to denominational colleges and seminaries, and they founded and filled the ranks of new independent faith mission societies. The China Inland Mission, the Africa Inland Mission, the Christian and Missionary Alliance, and the Central American Mission are examples of these faith mission societies. Unlike many of their predecessors, this new breed of missionaries had no qualms about evangelizing "nominal" Christians and areas of the world traditionally regarded as evangelized. This was particularly true where Roman Catholicism was strong. In fact, they did not distinguish such efforts from missions in non-Christian countries, believing all must hear the gospel message of Jesus Christ and experience conversion. Some missionaries went abroad with the express purpose of "converting" Roman Catholics.[7]

Concurrent with the growth of independent faith mission groups came a change in the nationality of the missionaries themselves. As the nineteenth century drew to a close, the home base shifted from England to North America, more specifically to the United States. Missiologist Harold R. Cook estimated that fifty percent of all Protestant missionaries came from the United States by 1900.[8] Although many missionaries continued to come from Great Britain, New Zealand, Australia, and the Scandinavian countries, the United States took the lead.

By the early twentieth century, the United States had become the missionary "sender" of the world. This missionary expansion and commitment to world evangelization resulted in a larger number of foreign missionaries than ever before. While some of these missionaries continued to come from established Protestant denominations, most came from independent faith mission societies.

In what ways did the rapid growth of the faith mission movement make an impact on the birth and growth of the Bible college movement in North America? This chapter examines this new movement in foreign missions and answers the question.

THE FAITH MISSION MOVEMENT

The faith mission movement began in 1865 with the founding of the China Inland Mission by J. Hudson Taylor, who directly and indirectly influenced the founding of over forty new independent mission groups.[9] Born in Yorkshire, England, of Methodist parents, Taylor (1832-1905) felt called to the mission field as a youth. In 1853, at the age of twenty-one, he went to China under the China Evangelization Society. He served in China for seven years, and then was forced to return to England because of failing health. While in China, however, he learned the language, became familiar with the country's interior, and adopted Chinese dress to identify more closely with the people. He also resigned from his mission board, deciding to rely on God alone for his financial and medical needs.[10]

When he returned to England in 1860, he was uncertain if he would ever be able to return to China. Despite severe health problems, his concern for the unevangelized millions in China continued to grow. In 1865 he undertook the founding of a new independent mission dedicated to reaching the people of the Chinese interior. He believed China would never be evangelized if it had to wait for highly educated, ordained missionaries; instead, he looked for dedicated men and women from among England's massive laboring class. By appealing to this segment, he avoided competition with other denominational mission societies. Unlike his denominational counterparts, he saw the need to establish his missionary headquarters in China where it could be more responsive to the needs of the missionaries. He succeeded in raising financial support and volunteers even though his new endeavor was an independent one without denominational backing.[11]

He started by calling twenty-four volunteers, two for each of China's twelve provinces. In 1875 Taylor enlisted eighteen, in 1881 seventy more, and in 1886 one-hundred more. By 1895 the China Inland Mission had grown to 641 full-time missionaries and 462 Chinese helpers who served in 260 stations and outstations, making it the largest missionary agency of its time.[12]

The Regions Beyond Missionary Union was founded in 1878 by Dr. Grattan Guinness, one of the foremost prophetic scholars of his day. Convinced that he was living in the "end times" and burdened by those who had not been reached with the gospel of Jesus Christ, he started one of the first missionary training institutes in England.[13]

During the first year of the school's existence, an urgent plea came from missionary leader David Livingstone, who was serving in Central Africa. A number of young aspiring missionaries responded by going to Central Africa. They were organized into the Livingstone Inland Mission, later called Regions Beyond Missionary Union. The second major mission field to be entered by Regions Beyond Missionary Union was India. At the turn of the century, a group of students from Guinness's missionary training school landed in North Binar, a mission field that experienced significant growth.[14]

In the late nineteenth and early twentieth centuries, a significant number of faith mission groups were started, more or less patterned after the China Inland Mission and the Regions Beyond Missionary Union. This early group of mission societies included the Christian and Missionary Alliance (1887), the South Africa General Mission (1889), the Central American Mission (1890), the Evangelical Alliance Mission (1890), the Sudan Interior Mission (1893), the Gospel Missionary Union (1894), the Africa Inland Mission (1895), the Japan Evangelistic Band (1903), the Bolivian Indian Mission (1907), the Evangelistic Union of South America (1912), and the South American Indian Mission (1914). These independent faith missions became a significant feature of world evangelization. These "glorious achievements," according to missiologist J. Herbert Kane, were "stranger than fiction and more marvellous than miracles."[15]

The term "faith mission" is commonly associated with those missions whose financial policy guarantees no set income for its missionaries. Some missions carried the policy to the point of refusing to solicit funds or even making known the needs of their missionaries, thus professing to rely entirely upon God for financial needs. Living by faith, however, went far beyond the matter of finances. These missions were born out of faith, often at great risk, and experienced a high mortality rate among the early faith missionary pioneers.[16]

The faith missions did not regard themselves as being in competition with the efforts of mainline Protestant denominations. The latter, however, tended to regard the faith missions as something of a "Cinderella" and referred to them as "sects." Faith missions commonly adopted a statement of faith that each member was expected to sign. In this way, they could be more certain that their members would maintain a conservative theological stance.[17]

The faith mission movement grew so rapidly in the late nineteenth and early twentieth centuries that by 1920 it was considered to the strongest missionary force in North America, surpassing the efforts of many Protestant denominational groups.[18] Certainly the spirit of revivalism that blazed within the hearts of these missionaries was a key consideration, but there were other factors that contributed to this missionary growth. Modern inventions served to accelerate missionary activity. Railroads and steamships carried the missionaries and made their journeys easier and more rapid. Possession of machines, knowledge, and scientific methods gave them prestige among the heathen cultures. Because of increased travel and communication, Christians became acquainted with conditions in other countries and were impelled to missionary activity. The relative absence of war in the late nineteenth century created more favorable circumstances for missionary endeavors. The individualism of the period found at least partial expression in the courage and tenacity of the missionaries. Increased wealth provided means for spreading the gospel. Printing presses produced quantities of literature in various tongues, while many languages of the earth were reduced to writing and translations of the Bible were produced. Missionary historian Kane described the impact of the faith mission movement during this time period:

> Never before in a period of equal length had Christianity or any other religion penetrated for the first time as large an area. The emissaries of the cross were to be found in all parts of the habitable globe, from the frozen wastes

of Greenland to Africa. . . . There were, to be sure, a few areas of the world where there were no resident missionaries; but that was because of government restrictions, not because the church lacked either the will or the power to press forward with the task of world evangelization. Included in the Christian church, for the very first time, were representatives of every tribe and tongue and people and nation. . . . Although denominational missionary activity cannot be overlooked, the primary force behind the proliferation of the gospel was the faith mission movement.[19]

THE IMPACT OF FOREIGN MISSIONS

The vitality generated by the revivalism of the late nineteenth and early twentieth centuries was expressed through missionary expansion. Large numbers of young men and women, impelled by people of other lands who were not familiar with the gospel, offered to serve Christ in foreign missions. Many of these volunteers were willing to devote their lives to missionary work, but they needed suitable training and practical experience.[20]

Missionary societies were often totally unprepared to provide this training and experience. Although some of the Protestant denominational groups had been inclined to send to the foreign fields only highly educated men with a seminary education, there were those from within the faith mission movement who believed that the field did not only need the highly educated workers. They believed that workers of all classes were needed abroad as well as at home. This is where Bible institutes and training schools were able to play a very crucial role in the expansion of foreign missions. They were the link between the need for foreign missionaries and an abundant supply of men and women ready to be utilized.

Some missionary historians associate the growth of the faith mission movement with the Bible institute/college movement.[21] Truly, the early Bible schools provided training for a very high proportion of the missionaries who served under various independent groups. However, as missionary historian Harold

R. Cook claimed, "the Bible institute/college movement itself was more a result than a cause."[22] The Bible schools were started because there was a recognizable need to train workers for the mission field. Most of the early Bible school founders had a commitment to foreign missions, which had some impact on the establishment of their respective missions.

Although many of the early Bible schools were started by individuals, such as A. B. Simpson and A. J. Gordon, who were most noted for their relationship with foreign missions, there were other early Bible schools started specifically to prepare and provide workers for the foreign mission field. These included the following:

1. Union Missionary Training Institute (Niagara Falls, New York, 1885);
2. Toronto Bible Training School (Toronto, Ontario, 1894);
3. Training School for Christian Workers (Los Angeles, California, 1895);
4. Northwest Bible and Missionary Training School (Minneapolis, Minnesota, 1902);
5. Fort Wayne Bible School (Fort Wayne, Indiana, 1904);
6. Toccoa Falls Institute (Toccoa Falls, Georgia, 1907);
7. The Bible Institute of Los Angeles (California, 1908);
8. Philadelphia School of the Bible (1914); and
9. St. Paul Bible Institute (St. Paul, Minnesota, 1916).[23]

In summary, the forward advance of foreign missions during the closing decades of the nineteenth century and the early decades of the twentieth century motivated many young men and women to pursue foreign service for Christ and His church. In response to this missionary fervor, a number of revivalists started schools to train recruits to be foreign missionaries. A new day in Protestant missions demanded new methods and a new approach to training. For many who could not or chose not to attend college and seminary, the Bible school was the educational alternative. Clifford E. Larsen, Bible institute researcher, summarized the way the missionary impulse affected the rise of Bible schools:

The faith mission movement inevitably involved the establishment of specific schools where workers could be trained who would go out with the necessary qualifications and be willing to live under the indefinite arrangement provided. It was felt that the existing colleges and seminaries were inadequate in that requirements financially and academically were such as to prevent many from getting the needed training. Then also it was felt that such schools did not have a practical enough program. . . . In other words, the Bible institute/college movement began as a sort of vocational trade school for a specific type of lay missionary, who would serve either abroad or at home.[24]

THE IMPACT OF THE EARLY BIBLE SCHOOLS ON FAITH MISSIONS

The faith mission movement was certainly a factor leading to the establishment of many of the early Bible schools. Conversely, the Bible schools provided the majority of candidates for faith mission organizations. David Rambo, former President of Canadian Bible College and Nyack College (started by A. B. Simpson), stated that "the missionary movement over the last one-hundred years owes an inestimable debt to the Bible institute, now the Bible college movement.[25] S. A. Witmer, a leading figure in the development of the Accrediting Association of Bible Colleges, stated in 1962, "It is conservatively estimated that half or more of foreign missionaries from North America receive their training or part of it in a Bible school."[26] Missiologist Kane estimated that the actual figure may be over 75 percent.[27]

Although the estimates just cited involved the first one hundred years of the Bible college movement, its impact on foreign missions was significant even during its formative years. From the very beginning, faith missions were associated with conservative Evangelicalism, and the majority of the missionary recruits were either without higher education or graduates of Bible institutes and colleges.[28]

The impact of the early Bible schools on the faith mission movement was both deliberate and circumstantial. In the case of the Missionary Training Institute, it was deliberate. The school was started by A. B. Simpson for one purpose—to train missionaries in a short-term undergraduate program because existing seminaries simply were not supplying enough missionaries to respond to the needs of new missionary societies. He believed conventional training was simply too lengthy to provide an adequate supply of missionaries. Although the first class from Simpson's school in 1882 only had twelve students, by 1884, the first vanguard of institute pioneers sailed for the Congo to begin work in a totally unevangelized region. In each succeeding year, other bands of devoted young people went forth from the school into what were considered spiritually neglected regions of the world. The 1922-1923 issue of the *Missionary Training Institute Catalog* reported that "about four hundred are laboring under the Christian and Missionary Alliance in seventeen different mission fields and many others are found in the ranks of other societies everywhere."[29]

In addition to the graduates of the Missionary Training Institute who went into missionary service with the Christian and Missionary Alliance, there were alumni who were instrumental in starting other faith missions. Rowland Bingham, Walter Gowans, and Thomas Kent, all of whom completed their studies in 1893, were the first missionaries with the Sudan Interior Mission, which was originally based in Canada.[30] The Africa Inland Mission owed a similar debt to the Missionary Training Institute because its founder, Peter Cameron Scott, was a graduate of the school.[31]

Although the training of foreign missionaries was not part of the original plan for Moody's Bible Institute in Chicago, it developed an excellent record of missionary recruitment. Between 1889 (when the school opened full-time) and 1923, 1143 Moody students became foreign missionaries. Of that number, 818 were still serving on the field in 1923 under 55 denominational and independent mission boards. The largest number were in China (227), but others were in Africa (194), India (87), Japan (55), Korea (31), the Pacific Islands (25), Europe (20), and Southeast Asia (5). Those students who did not travel overseas had a deep concern for those who did. In 1922 the student body at Moody Bible Institute donated $6,950 for foreign missions.[32]

A. J. Gordon started the Boston Missionary Training School for the primary purpose of training lay workers for the foreign mission field. These lay workers were not expected to have all of the background and knowledge of college and seminary graduates; rather, they were to be "men and women, who knew enough of their Bibles to lead souls to Christ, and to instruct converts in the simple principles of the gospel."[33]

Did Gordon's school accomplish its goal of sending workers into the foreign fields? In June of 1895, just six years after its founding, the following report was given about the school's alumni:

> And as we look over the lists of those who have been in the school in the past (six) years, we can discern about one hundred who may well be reckoned as such living epistles. Of these, twenty-five have gone to the foreign shores, and . . . . The large majority are faithfully herald-ing the good news in the far-off places on earth—in Af-rica, India, China, Korea, Japan, and the West Indies.[34]

The early Bible schools succeeded in equipping a large number of missionaries by fostering an enthusiasm for foreign missions on their respective campuses. The students of these early schools could not help but be exposed to the needs and activities of foreign missions. Consider the situation of many students: a number of fellow students, possibly a best friend or roommate, had pledged their futures to the foreign mission fields, and some had even gone so far as to select a particular area of the world for service.

Graduates of these schools, who were foreign missionaries, contributed letters and articles about their experiences. Photographs and maps of missionaries in distant lands hung on the walls of classrooms and dormitory rooms. The library and bookstore offered heroic accounts of missionary endeavors, written to engage a popular audience. It was not unusual for graduates to die in the course of missionary service; they might be killed or they might succumb to tropical disease or uncongenial climate. When news of such deaths reached a school, it stimulated other students to pledge themselves to take the place of "martyred" missionaries.

In place of the lighthearted fare common to student yearbooks, the student publications at Bible schools often described the urgency of missionary needs. Biblical quotes often exhorted other students to offer themselves as foreign missionaries:

> Truly "the field is the world, and the harvest is plente-ous, but the reapers are few." "Pray ye therefore the Lord of the harvest that He may send forth more laborers." Hear the voice of Jesus say, "who will go and work for me?" And behold they also call us from the uttermost ends of the earth. Who, who, will answer gladly saying, "Here am I, O Lord, send me."[35]

Most Bible schools had at least one foreign missionary organization. The student body was commonly divided into "prayer bands," each of which concentrated upon a particular part of the mission field, such as Africa, or China, or South America. The prayer bands usually met weekly to study a particular mission field, keep track of progress, pray for the success of missionaries, and raise money for a designated field.

Bible school graduates who had pledged themselves to become foreign missionaries frequently belonged to the campus branch of the Student Volunteer Movement. This national organization was the product of three men: Princeton University graduate Robert T. Wilder provided the missionary vision; evangelist D. L. Moody gave it spiritual power; Cornell University student John R. Mott was the organizing genius.[36] It grew out of a summer conference in 1886 at Moody's Northfield Conference Center at Mount Hermon, Massachusetts when one-hundred college and seminary students signed a pledge, "I purpose, God willing, to become a foreign missionary." The watchword of the movement, coined by Wilder was "The evangelization of the world in this generation."[37] Although the Student Volunteer Movement ceased to exist by the early 1930s, it was a significant missionary force during the late nineteenth and the early twentieth centuries.

The leaders of the Student Volunteer Movement generally favored college or seminary-educated missionaries, while the work at most Bible schools was below the college level. John R. Mott of the Student Volunteer Movement cautioned, "The ultimate success of the missionary enterprise does not depend primarily upon vast numbers of missionaries so much as upon thoroughly furnished missionaries."[38] The organization, however, did not prohibit branches on Bible school campuses.

Very early in the history of Moody Bible Institute, the foreign missionary band was organized as a branch of the Student Volunteer Movement. This was not surprising because Moody himself was a key figure in helping to found the national movement. After the Missionary and Prayer Union was formed at Moody in 1900, the Student Volunteer (Foreign Missionary) Band became an arm of this larger organization. But until 1927, it still continued to function as part of the Student Volunteer Movement. In those early days, the Missionary Study and Prayer Union was almost synonymous with the regular curriculum. The outline for the Missionary Union meetings formed the basis for the first informal missionary course. [39]

The Gordon Missionary Training School also had its branch of the Student Volunteer Movement. Students who pledged themselves to become foreign missionaries usually belonged to this group. The Student Volunteer Band at Gordon in 1914 held meetings every Tuesday night. The first Tuesday of the month was a business meeting; the meeting on the second Tuesday was convened for the purpose of "asking God's blessing upon our missionaries and our efforts here." The third Tuesday was a "study night," when students usually chose textbooks on foreign missions as their point of departure. On the fourth Tuesday, the students presented "some special feature of interest for students." The speaker at these meetings was frequently a returned missionary or "some of our own students representing some mission field."[40]

Visiting foreign missionaries stirred up enthusiasm for their cause. One missionary to Africa spoke at the (Nyack) Missionary Training Institute in 1912 for the student missionary group. One account of a missionary challenge follows:

> Amusingly, and yet surprisingly, Dickinson told how sanctification of the eyes, ears, nose, stomach, was necessary and that nothing in the way of preparatory training in the death of one's senses was amiss for a missionary to Africa. Prayer-habit, long patience, and faith in the cleansing power of Jesus' blood were emphasized.[41]

Mrs. Graham, a missionary to Sudan, who spoke on two occasions, described how she was led there

> despite her initial conviction that Africa, the Sudan, was not the place for a fleshly person like her. And it cost her a very death itself to say 'yes' to the forcible call. But the result had proved that the Lord made no mistake in calling her and that she made no mistake in following.[42]

In summary, the energy produced by the revivalism of the late nineteenth and early twentieth centuries expressed itself in a period of missionary expansion, particularly through the developments of the faith mission movement. Concurrent with, and in some respects as a result of, the faith mission movement was the development of the Bible institute/college movement. Because many of the new missionary societies were unprepared to provide adequate training for foreign missions, the early Bible schools were able to respond by serving as a link between the need for workers on the foreign fields and the supply of zealous young men and women who were volunteering themselves for Christian service. Moreover, because many of the seminaries and Protestant denominational colleges were producing too few graduates for the mission fields of the world, the Bible schools were able to provide what was viewed as a practical type of education in a shorter amount of time. One after another, Bible schools were started to provide training for lay workers to fill the gaps at home and abroad.

Although it is impossible to determine exactly how many Bible school/college graduates were serving overseas during the early years of the movement, Bible school educators were claiming that their graduates made up the overwhelming majority of the missionary force that was sent out from North America. Even though some of the claims may have been overstated, Bible school graduates were well represented on the various mission fields, particularly where the faith mission movement had an impact.

CHAPTER EIGHT

PROTESTANT FUNDAMENTALISM: 1918-1930

The early Bible schools were closely related to the Protestant fundamentalist groups of the early twentieth century and their spiritual forebears. Fundamentalism and its roots, however, have not always received sufficient exploration. Therefore, a description of the Bible schools runs the risk of lacking richness and depth unless a portrayal of the fundamentalist movement so closely associated with them is considered. It is necessary to understand the fundamentalists, their theology, their objectives, and even their hopes and fears before there can be a thorough comprehension of why they set up the institutions they did.

A DEFINITION OF FUNDAMENTALISM

Over the past sixty-five years, a handful of historians and sociologists have attempted to define fundamentalism. Many of these definitions have been grossly inadequate for several reasons. The attempts have been too few and too specific. Because of the lack of sustained historical interest, the sources have remained scattered or have even disappeared. Most writers who have taken notice have been partisans committed to one side or the other of the "fundamentalist-modernist" conflict and, as partisans, have tended to see only limited aspects of their subject.

The first major attempt to define fundamentalism came from Richard Niebuhr, who wrote the section on "fundamentalism" for the *Encyclopedia of the Social Sciences* in

1931.[1] Niebuhr's definition had two main aspects: First, he described the phenomenon in terms of its struggles for influence, particularly its attempts to outlaw the teaching of evolution. He viewed the Scopes Trials of 1925, which focused on the issue of the teaching of evolution in Tennessee schools, as the paradigmatic conflict. Second, Niebuhr portrayed fundamentalism as a rural protest against urbanization and industrialization. In his estimation, fundamentalists appeared as ill-educated farmers who were threatened by the changes of a modern world.

The next major attempts to arrive at a definition of fundamentalism came from Stewart G. Cole, *The History of Fundamentalism* (1931) and Norman F. Furniss, *The Fundamentalist Controversy, 1918-1931* (1954).[2] Both understood fundamentalists to be conservatives in the struggle for control of Protestant denominations and, from the perspective of their particular bias, they traced the battles for leadership of foreign mission boards and theological seminaries. Their theological definitions of fundamentalism were built around a listing of the so-called "five points," which in their view summarized the movement's position: the inerrancy of Scripture, the virgin birth, the substitutionary atonement, the bodily resurrection, and the second coming of Jesus Christ.[3] These five points were based on a literal interpretation of the Bible.

The most important definition within the last twenty-five years has come from Ernest R. Sandeen, in his book *The Roots of Fundamentalism: British and American Millenarianism, 1800-1930*, and also in his shorter work, *The Origin of Fundamentalism*.[4] Sandeen offered a primarily theological definition of fundamentalism. He saw it as a grouping of conservative Christians, mostly from Calvinist backgrounds, Baptists and Presbyterians, whose theological "roots" consisted of two parts: a premillennialism which he traced to British and American millenarianism of the early nineteenth century, and a doctrine of biblical inerrancy that he ascribed to the tradition of Princeton Seminary theology. Not only was Sandeen one of the first historians to take the theology of fundamentalism seriously, but he was also the first to explore carefully the network of relationships that existed among early fundamentalists, pointing out the high degree of structure in the movement's Bible schools, Bible conferences, missionary societies, and publishing ministries. Each of these activities was part of the changing pattern of revivalism that came to the forefront in the late nineteenth century as a counter-reaction to liberal trends within Protestantism.

Although Sandeen's definition improved on previous attempts, his work has received criticism. LeRoy Moore, for example, has questioned whether a theological understanding such as Sandeen's is sufficient to account for the political events of the twenties. Many people who associated themselves with what Moore referred to as the "fundamentalist party" did not fit Sandeen's definition. William Jennings Bryan, the most famous American figure associated with fundamentalism and a prominent participant in the Scopes Trial, was a lifelong Presbyterian who never embraced the doctrine of premillennialism. This may cast some doubt upon the comprehensiveness of Sandeen's definition.[5]

George M. Marsden has objected to Sandeen's definition of millenarianism as the one "root" of fundamentalism. He has suggested other roots—enduring elements of nineteenth century Evangelicalism that emphasize the place of personal holiness, the shock from the rapid decline of what had been a solidly Protestant culture, and a continuing current of anti-intellectualism.[6] In response to Marsden, Sandeen has claimed that the additional roots mentioned by Marsden were merely "characteristics" of millenarians shared with other descendants of nineteenth century Protestantism. He also argued that the colorful decade of the twenties, which has received so much attention from students of fundamentalism, was not as crucial in its history as has been supposed. He further remarked that acrimony, defensiveness, and aggressiveness displayed by fundamentalists during this decade were likewise characteristic of some non-fundamentalists of the twenties.[7]

Although not all religious historians would go so far as to say that premillennialism is the only root of Protestantism, most would agree that it was at least a prominent source to be considered. In his *Living in the Shadow of the Second Coming: American Premillennialism, 1875-1982,* Timothy P. Weber specifically cited a number of leading American Bible teachers of the late nineteenth and the early twentieth centuries who preached the doctrine of premillennialism. Some of these spokespeople included: D. L. Moody, R. A. Torrey, A. T. Pierson, James H. Brookes, A. B. Simpson, A. J. Gordon, and C. I. Scofield,[8] all of whom were involved in the early Bible college movement to one degree or another. In support of this contention, Weber also stated, "The new premillennialists not only had their share of respectable leaders, they produced their own through a number of Bible institutes, which they helped establish at the end of the nineteenth century.[9]

The argument can be made that there were other themes besides premillennialism that helped to shape the fundamentalist movement, but few were more dominant. It was also this brand of fundamentalism that had a strong influence on Bible schools and colleges in the early twentieth century as they started to come of age. It was equally true, however, that the Bible schools in turn influenced fundamentalism and allowed it to survive.

How did Protestant fundamentalism of the early twentieth century influence the emergence of the Bible college movement? What part did the Bible college movement play in the growth of fundamentalism? This chapter answers these questions by examining the fundamentalist-modernist controversy.

THE FUNDAMENTALIST-MODERNIST CONTROVERSY

The Protestant Church in the United States and Canada experienced major conflict after World War I. Although the church was devoted to the service of God and the continuation of the patterns of Christianity, the various denominational groups were often divided among themselves over theology and purpose. Discontentment over these theological differences ultimately came to a head with the development of a movement known as fundamentalism. The term "fundamentalism" first became popularized when a widely circulated set of twelve booklets called *The Fundamentals: A Testimony to the Truth* was published between 1910 and 1915. This published series contained nearly one hundred articles that were written by a group of British, American, and Canadian writers who were the leading evangelicals of that time period. Copies were sent to lay and clerical leaders in an effort to swing Protestantism away from liberalism. These articles defended the "fundamentals" or basics of the faith that had been called into question by newer forms of thought sometimes referred to as "modernism."[10] Included in this series of "fundamentals" were assertions that (1) the Bible is the inspired Word of God; (2) Jesus Christ, God in human flesh, was born of a virgin, lived a sinless life, died on the cross for the salvation of men and women, rose from the dead, ascended into heaven, and will return at the end of this age to set up in great glory his earthly kingdom; (3) sin is real and not the product of human imagination; (4) God's grace and not human effort is the source of salvation; and (5) the church is God's institution designed to build up Christians and to spread the gospel.[11]

Authors of these articles included some of the leading theologians of the early twentieth century: Scottish theologian James Orr, Princeton theologian B. B. Warfield, Anglican bishop H. C. G. Moule, American dispensationalist C. I. Scofield, evangelist and Bible school leader R. A. Torrey, and Southern Baptist scholar E. Y. Mullins.[12] Although there were differences among these individuals on how to interpret the Bible, they were able to set them aside in order to publish *The Fundamentals*.

A more clearly defined movement arose shortly after the publication of *The Fundamentals*, particularly among Northern Baptists and Presbyterians. This fundamentalism was defined by historian George Marsden as "militantly anti-modernist Protestant Evangelicalism" that contained many of the revivalist themes, such as the inerrancy of Scripture, premillennialism, Victorian morality, and a common-sense philosophy of life.[13] The sense of crisis within western civilization created by World War I also helped to add fuel to the movement. The term "fundamentalist" was coined by Baptist editor Curtis Lee Laws in 1920 as a designation for those who were ready "to do battle royal for the Fundamentals."[14]

The fundamentalist movement built up steam in 1919 when the World's Christian Fundamentals Association was founded in Philadelphia with 6500 people attending. William Bell Riley, pastor of the First Baptist Church of Minneapolis and president of Northwestern Bible Training School, captured the tenor of the conference when he addressed the opening crowd:

> The issue of the hour is Christ! It is a question far more fundamental than formulated creeds . . . a question far more fundamental than the scientific accuracy of the Old Testament. . . . It is this question: Is Christ the Son of God or not?[15]

Led by Riley, John Roach Straton, and Jaspar C. Massey, all Baptist pastors, the Association "launched a revivalistic campaign to recapture for orthodoxy the pre-eminent place in American life." Their plan was to disseminate fundamentalism through the distribution of polemical literature, public debate between modernists and fundamentalists, and Bible conferences throughout North America.[16] Fundamentalist fellowships were formed in several northern denominations in an effort to win supporters to a conservative stance and to resist liberal theology.

Conflict between the conservatives and liberals continued to intensify in Northern Baptist and Presbyterian churches. Harry Emerson Fosdick (1878-1969), a well-known Baptist preacher and faculty member at Union Theological Seminary in New York City, added fuel to the fire with a controversial sermon that he delivered on May 22, 1922. While serving as a guest speaker at New York City's First Presbyterian Church, he spoke on the theme "Shall the Fundamentalists Win?"[17] Attacking what he perceived as the fundamentalists' apparent intention to drive those of liberal persuasion out of the churches, Fosdick pleaded for a spirit of tolerance so that Christians of various theological persuasions might address common human needs. This attempt to hold middle ground was criticized sharply by both extremes, but those who did sympathize were chiefly on the liberal side.[18]

In the wake of controversy, Fosdick left the Presbyterian Church but went on to gain even greater recognition as a national radio preacher and as pastor of the liberally-minded Riverside Church in New York City. Among the Northern Baptist and Presbyterian groups, the battles ensued over denominational control of educational and mission programs. Those who were more liberal in their theological convictions were quite inclusive, willing to embrace a wide range of opinions in their denominations. The inclusivists, commonly referred to as moderates, preferred peaceful coexistence rather than theological conflict. The moderates triumphed over the stricter conservatives, but they also rendered theology considerably less important.[19]

The more militant conservatives were not willing to coexist with moderates. They felt such a relationship would compromise their own theological convictions and further promote modernism. In 1932 the General Association of Regular Baptist Churches was established as a separate denomination, a fundamentalist contingent that left the Northern Baptist Convention.[20] In 1936 Presbyterian dissidents under J. Gresham Machan formed an alternative church. The following year these Presbyterian militants, who would not compromise with modernism, divided into two separate groups, the Orthodox Presbyterian Church and the Bible Presbyterian Church. The former represented efforts to preserve a confessional Calvinism, the latter a desire to mix modern Calvinism with premillennialism, the prohibition of alcohol, and other more American emphases.[21]

There was a clear geographic pattern among American fundamentalists. Robert Wenger, after examining a number of sources from the teens and twenties, concluded that fundamentalist population centers were in the Middle Atlantic and East North Central States, with an additional contingent on the Pacific Coast.[22] The southern churches were less sharply divided by the controversy. They regarded themselves as citadels of orthodoxy, and liberal theology had few prominent representatives. With conservative theological leadership in control in most places, the challenges raised by modern scientific thought and higher criticism were less troublesome for southern churches, either white or black. The focus of the fundamentalist-modernist controversy in the south was more in the legislatures and the courts. Laws to prevent the teaching of evolution were passed in Mississippi, Florida, Tennessee, and Arkansas.[23]

The Tennessee anti-evolution law of 1925 brought about the famous Scopes Trial. When John Scopes, a young high school teacher, was brought to trial for teaching evolution, both sides brought in nationally known figures. Clarence Darrow, a prominent criminal attorney, represented the defense; William Jennings Bryan, former presidential candidate and Secretary of State under Woodrow Wilson, became the fundamentalists' spokesman on behalf of anti-evolution laws. Scopes was found guilty, but the attention accorded to fundamentalism in the general press hurt its cause.[24] Although fundamentalists formally won, it was at the expense of having their positions severely and publicly criticized. This proved to be very damaging to the movement.

Following the Scopes trial, American fundamentalism became stereotyped as southern, rural, and anti-intellectual. In reality it was more typically led by northern, urban, educated men who developed a network of institutions that would be a substitute for the colleges, seminaries, and mission societies that had been lost to modernism.

Fundamentalism also had an impact on Canadian church life, particularly in the Baptist churches and in the emergence of independent religious movements in the western provinces. T. T. Shields (1873-1955), a prominent pastor of the Jarvis Street Baptist Church in Toronto for 45 years, was Canada's most ardent fundamentalist.[25] He associated with many of America's most prominent conservative leaders and conducted a strong attack on the leadership of the Baptist Convention of Ontario and Quebec and McMaster University. When he was censured by his convention in 1926 for his tactics, he founded his own college (Toronto Baptist Seminary) and mission board, and two years later drew many churches away from their conventions into the Union of Regular Baptist Churches.[26] During his lifetime, Shields isolated himself from all but a few Baptists and fundamentalists of other denominations. His militancy seemed to prevent him from forming lasting alliances that would give him enduring influence upon Canadian religion.[27]

William Aberhart (1878-1943) was a prominent political and religious leader who has received a great deal of scrutiny from political scientists and church historians. He founded a political party (Social Credit Party) during the depression and led it to dominance in the legislature of Alberta. Because of his political influence and religious activities, he has been given a place of prominence in Canadian church history.[28] A Baptist laymen from Calgary who embraced a strong dispensational approach to the Scriptures, Aberhart developed a large following as a Bible teacher. In 1925 he began to broadcast his Bible lectures throughout the province of Alberta with a very strong emphasis on the Lord's return, repentance, and conversion. He founded the Prophetic Bible Institute in 1927 and built his own independent fundamentalist movement.[29] Much like T. T. Shields, Aberhart became quite militant as he denounced other Protestant denominations. This critical spirit actually worked against him. Although he became prominent in politics, he lost much of his influence within the Canadian religious community.[30]

The theological debates in the United States and Canada in the 1920s and 1930s had larger and more lasting consequences than might at first appear possible. First, the results were an occasion for weakening the position of these denominations in national religious life. Second, debates within these denominational groups also had something to do with the increasing propensity of fundamentalists to form independent churches. After the fundamentalist-modernist controversy, the number of such churches grew rapidly across North America.[31]

Outside the churches, the fundamentalist-modernists debates eroded the general influence of Protestantism in North American life. Historian Martin Marty has perceptively summarized the situation with these words:

What had come of the conflict of the twenties was a deeply, permanently divided Protestantism. . . . Original-stock Protestantism—from which both sides derived—no longer presented a single front. . . . They were splitting up what was left of a Protestant establishment, leaving it ever less prepared to hold its place of dominance in American culture in the decades to come.[32]

Although this may be perceived as a blessing to Christianity that such influence has waned, at the time it was a blessing very much in disguise.

Inside the churches, fundamentalist-modernist strife had a more obvious negative effect. The debate left confusion that still exists. After the 1920s, theological discussion between Protestants in the marketplace of North American religion has regularly had a self-defeating character. As church historian Mark Noll asserted,

"Those who protest the errors of modernism and attack the intellectual environment in which inclusivism was at home have been pushed toward sectarian and anti-intellectual affirmations of faith for fear of being labelled modernists."[33]

On the other hand, "inclusivists, moderates, and liberals who scorn sectarianism and the populist environment in which Protestant anti-intellectualism flourishes have been pushed toward expansive and barely Christian definitions of faith for fear of being labelled fundamentalists"[34] Of all the results of the fundamentalist-modernist conflict, this may be the most tragic.

THE INFLUENCE OF FUNDAMENTALISM ON THE BIBLE COLLEGE MOVEMENT

In losing the battle for control of Protestant denominational agencies and institutions, fundamentalists claimed that the denominational colleges and seminaries had sold out to liberal Protestant teaching. The denominational struggles, which became quite public at the heat of the fundamentalist-modernist battle in the 1920s, had started more quietly several decades before. Virginia Brereton insisted that the fundamentalists had all but lost the battle for control of the educational institutions by the 1920s.[35]

From the late nineteenth century until the 1920s when the theological controversy within Protestantism came to a head, denominational colleges and seminaries had been moving away from a conservative approach to theology and were more accepting of critical approaches to the Scriptures. In the 1890s, conservatives had ignited several heresy trials to examine the orthodoxy of professors. Charles A. Briggs of Union Theological Seminary in New York City and Henry P. Smith of Lane Theological Seminary (as previously cited in Chapter two) were among those put on trial. It was not until after World War I, however, that the conservatives in many denominations, particularly Presbyterians and Baptists, appeared to react more strongly. The strong reaction from the conservative element generally had two foci: restoring orthodoxy to foreign mission organizations, and purifying denominational colleges and seminaries of modernist influences. Almost without exception, the fundamentalists lost these battles for control. By the early 1920s, they realized that almost every seminary had been given over to liberals and moderates, and most church-related colleges had abandoned their denominational affiliations or had at least patterned their curricula after secular institutions.[36]

In response to their losses in the denominational struggles, and because of their unwavering commitment to biblical orthodoxy, many of the conservatives split from their old church bodies.   Other conservatives had already left their denominations in preceding decades because of theological dissatisfaction and religious upheaval. For example, the Pentecostals had "come out" from a number of groups, and holiness groups had departed from the Methodists and Presbyterians when they encountered opposition.

Although there were differences among these various groups, they were united by their dissatisfaction with the intellectual and theological currents within denominational colleges and seminaries and agreed on the need to develop solid evangelical institutions to train men and women for religious service. Simply put, they saw a need to establish theological training schools because of what had been lost to modernism.

First, in the teens and twenties, the fundamentalists created new theological seminaries: Northern Baptist Theological Seminary (founded in Chicago, 1913); Dallas Theological Seminary (Interdenominational, 1924); Eastern Baptist Theological Seminary (Philadelphia, 1925); and Westminster Theological Seminary (Philadelphia, 1929).[37] Many additional seminaries were started in subsequent decades as the need for graduate-level training centers for evangelical leaders increased. Second, fundamentalists also started a handful of liberal arts colleges or maintained control of some longer-standing schools, such as Wheaton College and Taylor University.

The creation of new colleges and seminaries was often difficult because of limited financial resources among many of the newly formed fundamentalist groups. Furthermore, what funding these groups did possess was often channelled toward evangelistic and missionary activity. It was difficult for these groups to develop colleges and seminaries that were equal in prestige and resources to the ones they had seen swept away by the "tides of apostasy."[38] It would be many years before the newer evangelical institutions would rival or even surpass the denominational schools in enrollment and resources.

The primary educational alternative for many of the fundamentalists, however, was the Bible school. With limited resources, the Bible school of necessity became the most pervasive form of higher education. Furthermore, there were already a significant number of Bible schools in place that had been started in the later part of the nineteenth century or the early part of the twentieth century. So the precedent was already set.

It must be remembered, however, that most of the instruction was well below college level; high school graduation was seldom a requirement for entrance. Many of the early faculty were part-time employees or volunteers who generally lacked advanced (or even college) degrees. The early Bible schools did not even pretend to compete with the colleges and seminaries in terms of academic credibility.

These early Bible schools have been compared to the "log colleges" that were established by eighteenth century revivalists. Brereton, however, used the analogy of the junior or community colleges of our time, which have been established in many states and provinces as less expensive, less ambitious, and less selective than four year colleges or universities. The community colleges have typically had a stronger vocational focus than a liberal arts focus.[39] It could be argued that the early Bible schools and liberal arts colleges shared many of the same characteristics as they trained Christian workers in methods of Bible teaching, evangelism, and missionary work.

With few exceptions, the fundamentalists did not try to use the Bible school as a substitute for college or seminary. They certainly recognized that the Bible schools were less rigorous academically and did not offer a bachelor's or master's degree. This type of academic advancement would come later as the programs were expanded, accreditation was received, and they were able to offer education that was just as competitive as their more liberal counterparts. As a general rule, the schools established in the earlier part of this century just did not have the financial resources to offer traditional undergraduate- and graduate-level education. The Bible schools did, however, serve as a satisfactory educational vehicle for those groups who had limited resources and a desire to provide training for dedicated Christians who wanted to serve the Lord.

The Bible college movement actually experienced expansion and stability during the 1920s and 1930s. Many of the fledgling schools started in the later nineteenth century started to come of age and showed signs of maturity. Furthermore, the fundamentalist-modernist controversy generated a particular energy among the fundamentalists that led to the establishment of additional Bible schools. Because of their firm commitment to biblical orthodoxy, these established schools perpetuated conservative theological teaching and trained a new generation of church leaders.

Of the many religious groups that were formed as a result of the fundamentalist-modernist controversy, the Baptists were the most active in starting Bible schools. The following is a partial list of their denominations:

Northern (American) Baptist Convention:
- Baptist Union (1923);
- General Association of Regular Baptist Churches (1933); and
- Conservative Baptist Association of America (1947).

Southern Baptist Convention:
- American Baptist Association (1925);
- World Baptist Fellowship (1931);
- Baptist Bible Fellowship (1950);
- Baptist Missionary Association (1950); and
- Southwide Baptist Fellowship (1956).[40]

Most of these groups established at least one Bible institute or college of its own, although some came into being several decades after the fundamentalist-modernist controversy. The General Association of Regular Baptist Churches helped establish five institutions:

1. Omaha Baptist Bible Institute (Omaha, Nebraska, 1921);
2. Baptist Bible Seminary (Johnson City, New York, 1932);
3. Baptist Bible Institute (Grand Rapids, Michigan, 1941);
4. Baptist Bible Institute of Cleveland, Ohio (1943); and
5. Denver Baptist Bible College (Denver, Colorado, 1952).

The Baptist Missionary Association helped support Southeastern Baptist College in Laurel, Mississippi (1948). The World Baptist Fellowship was the work of fundamentalist leader J. Frank Norris, who also established the Fundamental Bible Institute in Arlington, Texas (1939). Baptist pastor Lee Robertson founded the Southwide Baptist Fellowship along with Tennessee Temple Schools (Chattanooga, Tennessee, 1946); and the Baptist Bible Institute (Springfield, Missouri) was started by the churches of the Baptist Bible Fellowship (1950).[41] As a result, these and other Bible institutes helped the cause of fundamentalism across the United States.

A number of characteristics demonstrated the maturity that was starting to take place within the early Bible schools. First, many of the longer-standing institutions were able to *move to more desirable locations and purchase or build more permanent buildings*. The original schools were often housed in temporary and makeshift locations. In 1897 the Missionary Training Institute moved from its quarters in the Gospel Tabernacle in New York City to Nyack, New York, where a campus was developed. After using rented quarters, the Bible Institute of Los Angeles completed construction of two dormitories and an auditorium in 1915. Gordon Bible College moved to a new campus on Boston's Fenway in 1917. By 1920 Moody Bible Institute had already developed a large downtown Chicago campus.

Second, the *course of study in many of the schools expanded to three or even four years*. The earlier curricula were either one or two years, and students often did not complete the full program because of a desire to engage quickly in some type of religious service. With the development of curricular programming, more students desired to finish and earn either a diploma or certificate. As the length of study increased, so did the number of course offerings, but the focus continued to be practical and vocational. Besides the core of biblical studies, students were able to take specialized programs, such as missions, music, Christian education, or even pastoral care.

Third, the Bible schools *started to employ a number of permanent and full-time faculty*, though part-time instructors were still quite common. There were also more faculty being hired who made education their primary responsibility as opposed to pastoral or itinerate ministry. Career educators started to make long-term contributions to the Bible college movement.

Fourth, the Bible schools started to employ *new delivery systems which attracted larger numbers and varieties of students*. For example, they might offer night or summer courses, if these options were not already available. In addition, they sometimes offered correspondence courses, and published

Bible study guides, Sunday school curricula, and missions information. They often produced books from their own presses, sponsored Bible and missions conferences, put on radio programs, and sent out touring music groups. In some cases, such as Moody Bible Institute and the Bible Institute of Los Angeles, extension centers were established.

Last, it was also during this time frame that most of the Bible schools adopted *official statements of faith which faculty and trustees were required to sign*. Although theology had always been important to the Bible schools, the doctrinal battles of the teens and twenties caused conservatives to be even more precise in stating their theological positions. Not all the disputes, however, were with liberal Protestants. Some Bible school statements of faith were designed to guard against the influence of those who might have been regarded as fundamentalist extremists.

The decades of the twenties and thirties were very difficult for North American Protestantism, in general, and fundamentalism, in particular. First, the losses were great on both sides as the battle was waged in the twenties between conservatives and liberals. In spite of the preservation of biblical orthodoxy through the strong stand taken by the fundamentalists, denominations and even local church bodies were badly fractured through the controversy. Second, the fundamentalist-modernist controversy of the twenties and especially the Great Depression of the thirties had an impact on just about every business, school, church, and government in North America.

In spite of these challenges, the Bible college movement continued to grow. There were seventeen Bible schools started in the United States in the decade of the twenties and another thirty-nine during the thirties. Because Bible schools could be operated relatively inexpensively, this may have worked to their advantage during times of economic hardship. There was also a large number of Canadian Bible schools started during this twenty-year period, but because many distinguishing qualities set them apart from American schools, the subject will be addressed in Chapter nine.

THE IMPACT OF THE BIBLE COLLEGE MOVEMENT ON FUNDAMENTALISM

Heretofore, much of the discussion has centered upon the ways in which fundamentalism helped to shape the Bible college movement in the two decades following World War I. It is equally true, however, that the Bible schools in turn influenced fundamentalism, and, as Sandeen averred, allowed the movement to survive. He specifically stated that "fundamentalism owed its survival to the Bible institutes, and the institutes were the product of millenarian leadership."[42] The Bible schools and colleges served as a base of operations for fundamentalists, who, in addition to being Bible instructors, concurrently worked as pastors, evangelists, missionaries, editors, and conference speakers and organizers. Some of these key leaders who engaged in other fundamentalist activities included: Reuben A. Torrey of the Bible Institute of Los Angeles, James M. Gray of Moody Bible Institute, William Pettingill of Philadelphia School of the Bible, and William B. Riley of Northwestern Bible Training School. Many of these fundamentalists had left their denominations because of religious disagreements or had embarked on evangelistic activities that their denominations would not or could not turn back. Consequently, the Bible schools provided stability. They offered a community of sympathetic colleagues and dedicated students.

In addition to supplying a base of operations for fundamentalist leaders, Bible schools gave them freedom to participate in outside ministries. They could teach there part time and still manage to carry on evangelistic or Bible teaching activities. The respect with which fundamentalism treated missionaries and evangelists justified and even encouraged those who preferred not to devote all their time to teaching and working in a single institution. These circumstances might not have applied at the more traditional college, where professors would have been discouraged from dividing their hours between the school and other pursuits.

To state the matter more positively, the Bible schools provided freedom and scope for evangelistic enterprises. Because their leaders had few preconceived notions of what a Bible school should or should not attempt in the way of religious education, restless and energetic evangelists did not seem to confine themselves to classroom walls by associating themselves only with Bible schools. It is also doubtful that Bible school educators limited their attention exclusively to regular matriculating students, if indeed they recognized such a neat category. They organized evening classes, correspondence study, Bible conferences, Bible camps, periodicals, city missions, foreign mission societies, evangelistic campaigns, and the distribution of Christian literature. The list was often limited only by the size of the available personnel and financial resources. Given the flexibility of Bible schools, the fundamentalists felt free to use all the entrepreneurial ingenuity, energy, and zeal they possessed.[43]

In the time period immediately following World War I, when fundamentalism was a major recognized influence on North American church life, the Bible schools served as a base of operations for the movement. Historian George W. Dollar, himself an ardent fundamentalist, acknowledged the role played by the Bible schools relative to fundamentalism:

> Fundamental Bible schools have played a very large part in the growth of fundamentalism. The movement owes an immeasurable debt to the Bible school movement, for their leaders and teachers have been willing to work and serve at great sacrifice, living out their lives in devoted service.[44]

It was from these schools that fundamentalism gained the strength to deal with the theological controversies of the 1920s and became a legitimate religious force in the decades that followed.

CHAPTER NINE

THE MOVEMENT IN CANADA

Although Canada and the United States are both well developed North American countries that share a common border, they are vastly different. Canada, unlike Mexico, is similar enough to the United States to provide a helpful comparison, and yet different enough to suggest options unrelated to the American experience. This is particularly true when it comes to higher education. There are many similarities between the two countries with regard to institutions that have been established: Bible colleges, independent or "free standing" liberal arts colleges, theological seminaries, and private and public universities. But there are also many educational differences, particularly when it comes to the historical development of church-related colleges and seminaries.

Whereas a large number of evangelical seminaries and liberal arts colleges in the U. S. were started in the early part of the twentieth century, such paradigms of Christian higher education were virtually absent in Canada until the 1960s. As a result, the majority of Canadian students who enrolled in evangelical postsecondary education selected the Bible school or college. In 1985 the Evangelical Fellowship of Canada reported that 60,000 students had graduated from these schools.[1] Knowing that many other students attended such schools but never graduated, Bruce Guenther estimated that at least 200,000 people spent at least one academic term at a Canadian Bible school or college.[2] This figure does not include the thousands of other individuals who were influenced through the auxiliary ministries of these schools, such as weekend conferences, polemical literature, and radio broadcasts. The Bible college movement has had a profound impact on the growth of the evangelical church in Canada in the twentieth century.

Despite the scope of this educational movement and its influence on Canadian Evangelicalism, the Bible schools and colleges have not received the attention they deserved. Ben Harder noted in 1980 that these schools were "largely ignored or else played down as the relatively minor activity of some rather small, fundamentalist sectarian groups."[3] Although a few of the larger schools have garnered some attention within recent years, there has never been a comprehensive study on this educational movement in Canada. Because this gap exists in Canadian religious historiography, this chapter will answer the following questions: How was the growth of Bible schools and colleges in Canada different from the United States? What were the major factors that influenced the growth of the Bible college movement in Canada?

THE GROWTH OF CANADIAN BIBLE SCHOOLS AND COLLEGES

The Bible college movement in Canada grew out of a strong revivalist tradition that had a significant impact on religious life in the late nineteenth and early twentieth centuries, particularly in the western provinces. This revivalist tradition of the western frontier, however, was quite different from that in Eastern Canada and the United States where the institutional church was more firmly established. Because Western Canada was still being settled by different ethnic groups well into the twentieth century, this created very different religious and educational needs. This was reflected in the types of churches and schools that were started.

There are actually two different paradigms that help to explain the growth of the Canadian Bible college movement. First, there were a smaller number of institutions started because of secular trends in the church-related colleges. As mainline Protestant colleges and seminaries were identifying more closely with public values, culture, and institutions, and becoming more liberal in their theology, certain evangelical leaders established new institutions. Historian George Rawlyk contended that "Bible schools in Canada became new institutions of higher learning for the besieged fundamentalists and conservative evangelicals."[4] He demonstrated a strong correlation between the secularization of Protestant higher education in Canada and the growth of the Bible college movement. This was quite consistent with the U. S. pattern. A majority of the Canadian schools that fit into this category were interdenominational, influenced to a greater or lesser degree by Protestant fundamentalism.

A second model, however, is far more common in the western provinces. Many denominational schools were started to serve a very defined constituency and to provide a very specific type of religious instruction. Guenther suggested that viewing the Bible college movement purely as a fundamentalist reaction to liberal Protestantism is far too limiting. In his examination of Mennonite schools in Western Canada, he proved that they were also established to perpetuate "their religious and ethnic values to successive generations."[5] They were nurturing a linguistic and cultural tradition as well as a theological one.

Interdenominational Bible Schools

The first Canadian school, Toronto Bible Training School (now called Ontario Bible College and Theological Seminary), was founded in 1894.[6] The school was started under the leadership of Elmore Harris, pastor of the Walmer Road Baptist Church. Harris was a successful pastor, Bible conference speaker, writer, foreign missions advocate, and well known revivalist of his day. Just as Harris fit the profile of many of the revivalists of the late nineteenth and early twentieth centuries, the school he founded was very similar to others that were founded in this time period.

Convening a meeting on May 14, 1894, Harris challenged a group of church leaders with his vision to establish a Bible school. He wanted to train lay people as Sunday school teachers, pastors' assistants, and missionaries. "It is intended for those who believe they have been called of God to Christian service, and who, for age or other reasons, cannot pursue a full collegiate or theological course of study."[7]

The group was primarily made up of Baptists and Presbyterians, but there were Methodists, Anglicans, and other church bodies represented.[8] Historian John Stackhouse stated that "from the start the school would be avowedly interdenominational and stress those things the evangelical churches had in common."[9] The institution arose out of a period of Protestant revivalism in Ontario in the late nineteenth century and is very characteristic of a number of American schools started at this time. It was interdenominational, Bible-centered, missions-oriented, spiritually vital, and extremely practical in its training. Because of its transdenominational flavor, Toronto Bible Training School was able to build strong alliances with a wide range of evangelical groups.

Although Toronto Bible Training School was one of the earlier Bible schools to be founded in North America, almost twenty years would pass before other Bible training schools would be started in Canada. The Herbert Bible School began in Saskatchewan in 1913 under the leadership of the Mennonite Brethren. The Lutheran Collegiate Bible Institute was also started in Saskatchewan in 1916 by the Evangelical Lutheran Church. Vancouver Bible Training School was founded in 1917 by the Baptists in British Columbia.[10]

Although Eastern Canada was much more developed culturally and religiously than the western frontier by the early twentieth century, this is not the part of the country that birthed the majority of Canadian Bible schools. To understand more fully the Bible college movement in Canada, it is necessary to examine the origin of the Bible schools in Western Canada and their distinguishing characteristics.

First, 75 percent of the Bible schools started in Canada were, and still are, located west of the Ontario-Manitoba border. Second, by 1952 about 90 different Bible schools were started in Canada's four western provinces. Of these schools started in Western Canada, almost 20 percent came into being during the first two decades of the twentieth century; more than 50 percent were started during the depression of the 1930s; the remaining 26 percent made their debut between 1940 and 1952.[11] A small number of Canadian Bible schools and colleges was started after 1952, but the growth of these institutions has been quite limited.

Just as Toronto Bible Training School was founded in 1894 for the purpose of serving students from various denominational backgrounds, a number of interdenominational schools were started in Western Canada in the 1920s and 1930s. These schools shared a commitment to provide a strong Bible-centered curriculum and practical training for church-related ministries and often reflected the influences of Protestant fundamentalism.

Prairie Bible Institute was the most famous of the interdenominational schools. In 1921 several Presbyterian farming families in Three Hills, Alberta, led by Fergus Kirk, sought to provide theological education for their children through the formation of a Bible school. By the fall of 1922, L. E. Maxwell (1895-1984), a recent graduate of Midland Bible Institute (Kansas), was called to give direction to the new school that started in an abandoned farmhouse. The first student body consisted of ten, but grew to nine hundred students in 1948-49, making Prairie the largest Bible school in Canada and one of the largest in the world at that particular time.[12] Prairie was perhaps most known for its impact upon world missions through its training of several thousand missionaries, but the interdenominational school also had an enormous impact on numerous evangelical denominations. Many PBI graduates who did not go into foreign missions saw the vast, often isolated regions of western Canada as an important home mission field where they planted large numbers of churches.[13]

In spite of the size and impact of Prairie Bible Institute, the school was much slower than many of its Bible college counterparts in advancing itself academically. Stackhouse described Prairie as the "Bible institute" type of school with homegrown teachers, independence from accrediting associations, a curriculum that did not include liberal arts instruction, and a very rigid set of community life standards. On the other hand, Stackhouse classified Toronto Bible College as the "Bible college" type of school with an emphasis on university and divinity training for its teachers, accreditation and degree offerings, and greater willingness to offer liberal arts courses.[14]

Another interdenominational institution was started in the city of Winnipeg in 1925. The Winnipeg Bible Training School (now called Providence College and Theological Seminary) began under the leadership of Rev. H. L. Turner, a Christian and Missionary Alliance missionary who wanted to train women and men for Christian work in the fast-growing prairie west. He was assisted by Muriel Taylor, a missionary with the Canadian Sunday School Mission. She provided strong leadership for the fledgling school. Largely because of frequent changes in leadership and inadequate facilities, the growth of the Winnipeg school would come much later than some of the other Western Canadian interdenominational schools. It occupied thirteen different premises, most of them rented, in its first forty-five years of operation.[15]

One of the early graduates of the Winnipeg school, Henry Hildebrand, responded to a call in 1935 from the members of a small nondenominational gospel assembly in southern Saskatchewan. They wanted him to be their pastor and to start a Bible school. The school was the Briercrest Bible Institute (now called Briercrest Bible College and Biblical Seminary), and was in many ways modeled after the Winnipeg Bible school. A number of the early students and teachers received at least some of their education from the Winnipeg school.[16] Briercrest would eventually grow to become the largest Bible college in Canada with thousands of graduates serving churches or mission organizations across Canada and around the world.

The development of interdenominational types of Bible schools was not limited to the institutions mentioned in the preceding paragraphs. Other interdenominational schools started during the decades of the 1930s and 1940s included Kingston Bible College (independent Baptist) in Kingston, Nova Scotia (1930); Millar Memorial Bible Institute in Pambrun,

Saskatchewan (1933); Nipawin Bible Institute in Nipawin, Saskatchewan (1935); Peace River Bible Institute in Sexsmith, Alberta (1935); and New Brunswick Bible Institute in Victoria, New Brunswick (1944). These schools, with their own distinctives, managed to build solid financial and prayer support bases in their respective geographic regions. Many of these schools also built strong alliances because they had no official ties with a particular denomination. This often worked to their advantage as their denominationally mixed constituencies became strong and cooperative.

Denominational Bible Schools

The second paradigm that must be considered in examining the establishment of Canadian Bible schools, particularly in the western provinces, involves the denominational institutions that were started between 1913 and 1952 and often coincided with the settlement in western Canada by different ethnic immigrant groups. According to Guenther,

> It is active involvement by some of these ethnic communities that accounts for the disproportionate number of Bible schools in Western Canada, and it is this cultural and religious pluralism that calls for a more multifaceted interpretation of the Canadian Bible school movement than allowed for in previous studies—studies which have allowed religious factors to overshadow ethnic and social aspects, and studies which usually characterized the entire movement in light of the non-denominational schools that have now become the larger, more prominent schools.[17]

There were a variety of ethnic groups that started Bible schools in the first part of this century. The most active group was unquestionably the Mennonites. They were the first to introduce Bible schools to the Canadian prairies, and they also started the largest number of them. Guenther purported that of the 90 Bible schools that existed in Western Canada prior to 1952, the largest proportion were started and operated by Mennonites. A few others identified themselves as interdenominational, but they were essentially Mennonite schools.[18]

The three Mennonite groups most active in establishing Bible schools in Canada in the early part of the century were the Mennonite Brethren, the Mennonite Brethren in Christ, and the General Conference Mennonite Church. These three groups became quite involved in organizing institutions and networks to respond to the needs of the Canadian culture while holding to their ethnic distinctives. These groups were often quite entrepreneurial, starting churches and businesses in rural communities as well as in growing prairie towns.

The Mennonite Brethren were by far the most active group in starting Bible schools. The first Mennonite Brethren institution was Herbert Bible School. It was also the second Bible school in Western Canada.[19] Started by John F. Harms in 1913 in Herbert, Saskatchewan, the stated purpose of the school was twofold: "to establish and strengthen youth in the fundamental principles and doctrines of the Scriptures" and "to provide sound biblical training for definite Christian service in such work as Sunday school instruction, daily vacation Bible school, young peoples and choir work, as well as extended mission work at home and abroad."[20] The language of instruction was German.

The Mennonite Brethren established a second Bible school in Winkler, Manitoba, in 1925. Through the influence of Abraham H. Unruh, a former teacher at Tschongraw Mennonite Brethren Bible School in Russia who had immigrated to Canada, Pniel (meaning "the face of God") Bible School (later called Winkler Bible Institute) came into being. In 1944 Unruh left Winkler to head the Mennonite Brethren Bible Institute in Winnipeg (later called Concord College).[21]

Beginning in the late twenties and carrying through the thirties, the Mennonite Brethren started at least sixteen additional schools in Western Canada. Most of these schools eventually closed or merged with other institutions.[22] One such school deserves mention. In 1927 the Mennonite Brethren started Bethany Bible Institute in Hepburn, Saskatchewan; it was modeled after the school in Herbert. Although at least five other schools were established in Saskatchewan during the same time frame, all, including Herbert Bible School, were incorporated as part of Bethany in 1957.[23]

A number of Mennonite Brethren schools were also started in Alberta and British Columbia, though most lasted for only a few years. The most noteworthy of these schools was Bethel Bible School, started in Abbotsford, British Columbia, in 1936. In the mid-forties, several other Mennonite Brethren institutions amalgamated with the Abbotsford school. The most unique merger took place in 1970 when this school joined with a Mennonite General Conference school, Bethel Bible Institute, to become Columbia Bible Institute (later called Columbia Bible College).[24]

The Mennonite Brethren were also instrumental in establishing the Steinbach Bible School (Manitoba) in 1936. The school (now called Steinbach Bible College) is operated by three different Mennonite conferences, all of which have a very strong evangelical orientation.[25]

The second Mennonite denomination to start a Bible school in Western Canada was the Mennonite Brethren in Christ. Strongly influenced by Methodist revivalism, this group of predominately Swiss Mennonites was very evangelistic and reached beyond its ethnic borders. This group started the Mountain View Training School in Didsbury, Alberta, in 1921.[26] The institution was among the first Mennonite schools to use English as the language of instruction. In 1992 this school merged with Hillcrest Christian College to become Rocky Mountain College in Calgary.

The third Mennonite denomination involved in the Bible college movement was the General Conference of Mennonites. In contrast to the Mennonite Brethren in Christ, who deliberately reached beyond the Mennonite boundaries, the General Conference worked at consolidating Mennonite congregations that were in danger of drifting away because of geographic isolation, cultural differences, congregational practices, or doctrinal variance.[27] The first General Conference School, Elim

Bible School, was started in Gretna, Manitoba in 1929 as an extension of the Mennonite Collegiate Institute. The school moved to Altona, Manitoba, in 1939,[28] where it operated until its closure in 1985.

Despite a slower start than the Mennonite Brethren, there was a proliferation of General Conference Bible schools in the 1930s. More than a dozen schools were founded by the denomination between 1929 and 1939.[29] Unfortunately, almost every one of these schools closed or was forced to be amalgamated with other institutions. One of the longest standing schools, Swift Current Bible Institute, which started in 1936, just closed its doors in 1996. The General Conference later established the Canadian Mennonite Bible College in Winnipeg in 1946; it has remained strong in comparison to most of the other schools within the denomination.

After looking at the various Mennonite groups that have made a significant contribution to the Bible college movement in Canada, brief attention must also be given to some of the other denominational groups that started Bible schools in the first part of this century. The largest Canadian evangelical denomination, the Pentecostal Assemblies of Canada,[30] started four Bible schools in the 1930s and 1940s which have remained relatively strong: Central Pentecostal Bible Institute in Saskatchewan in 1935 (now called Central Pentecostal Bible College), Eastern Pentecostal Bible Institute in Ontario in 1939 (now called Eastern Pentecostal Bible College), British Columbia Bible Institute in 1941 (now called Western Pentecostal Bible College), and Northwest Bible Institute in Alberta in 1946 (now called Northwest Bible College). Another one of Canada's larger denominations, the Christian and Missionary Alliance, founded its own school in Regina, Saskatchewan, in 1941. The Western Canadian Bible Institute (now called Canadian Bible College and Theological Seminary) was started in Regina, Saskatchewan, under the leadership of George Blackett, a former president of the Winnipeg Bible Institute.[31] This institution has remained a strong national center for theological training for the Christian and Missionary Alliance.

The Christian and Missionary Alliance established its school to serve the denomination nationally. A number of other Protestant groups followed this pattern in the first half of the twentieth century. These schools aimed to provide solid biblical instruction, to train clergy and laity for their particular churches, and to perpetuate many of their denominational, and in some cases, ethnic distinctives. Some of these denominational schools included the following:

1. Alberta School of Evangelism (Canadian Nazarene College) in Calgary, Alberta, by the Church of the Nazarene in 1921;
2. Alberta Bible College in Lethbridge, Alberta, by the Christian Church/Church of Christ in 1932;
3. Canadian Lutheran Bible Institute in Camrose, Alberta, by the Lutheran Church in 1932;
4. Alberta Bible Institute (Gardner College) in Edmonton, Alberta, by the Church of God Anderson in 1933;
5. Hillcrest Christian College (later merged with Mountain View Bible College to become Rocky Mountain College) in Medicine Hat, Alberta, by the Evangelical Church in 1939;
6. Emmanual Bible School (Emmanual Bible College) in Stouffville, Ontario, by the Evangelical Missionary Church in 1940;
7. Moose Jaw Bible Institute (Aldersgate College) in Moose Jaw, Saskatchewan, by the Free Methodists in 1940; Christian Training Institute (North American Baptist College) in Edmonton, Alberta, by the North American Baptist in 1940;
8. Covenant Bible Institute (Covenant Bible College) in Prince Albert, Saskatchewan, by the Evangelical Covenant Church of Canada in 1941;
9. Full Gospel Bible Institute in Eston, Saskatchewan, by the Apostolic Church in 1944;
10. Radville Christian College (Western Christian College) in Radville, Saskatchewan, by the Church of Christ in 1945;
11. Northwest Baptist Bible College (Northwest Baptist Theological College) in Vancouver, British Columbia, by the Fellowship Baptists in 1945;
12. Holiness Bible Institute (Bethany Bible College) in Woodstock, New Brunswick, by the Reformed Baptists in 1945, who later merged with the Wesleyan Church;

13. United Baptist Bible Training School (Atlantic Baptist University) in Moncton, New Brunswick, by the United Baptist Convention in 1949; and

14. Central Baptist Seminary and Bible College (later merged with London Baptist Seminary to become Heritage Baptist College and Seminary) in Ontario by the Fellowship Baptists in 1949.

CONTRIBUTING GROWTH FACTORS

How did these schools, often considered academically unsophisticated and operating on limited resources, become so influential in Canadian religious life? Why were these institutions able to attract financial support and significant numbers of students? Roland Miller, who wrote a chapter on Bible schools in *Religious Studies in Manitoba and Saskatchewan*, explained that any attempt to understand the many contributing factors must be done in terms of their own distinct mission,

> .... they are schools committed to the effective teaching of specific syllabus and the development of lifestyles exemplifying their understanding of life and truth.... The Bible school system in Saskatchewan represents an impressive edifice dedicated to the learning and practice of religion, defined as the Christian faith.[32]

Bible schools used similar language in defining their mission. Phrases such as the provision of "training. . . . in a thorough and practical knowledge of the Bible,"[33] "character development and spiritual maturity,"[34] and the sending forth of "workers with an extreme love of souls"[35] are found throughout their records.

The twin purposes of the Bible schools—teaching the Bible as truth, rather than as an academic subject and training for practical Christian living and ministry—are key to understanding their growth. The Bible schools were reliable alternatives that were firmly committed to the truth of the Scriptures during a time when many evangelicals had lost confidence in the theological departments of universities that once had a strong religious orientation.[36] In these evangelical schools, the Bible became the center of the curriculum and the focus of the students' lives. The students learned to think, feel, react, and speak biblically as a primary goal.

The Bible schools' practical, ministry-oriented approach was also highly regarded. Students were given the opportunities to participate in a variety of church and community-oriented ministries. For example, students distributed evangelistic tracts, visited hospitals and old age homes (as they were called), conducted street meetings, preached sermons, taught Sunday school classes, and led Bible studies. The practical work outside the classroom was designed to develop Christian leaders who could speak the language and respond to the everyday needs of people. Most of the institutions regarded these student ministries as fundamental to the Bible school experience.

The focus on laity training served as the attraction for the largest number of students. Because of limited educational backgrounds, most of the students would not be admitted to theological seminaries; yet, they comprised the majority of the student body in Bible schools. Although most evangelical groups, apart from some Holiness and Pentecostal churches, did not approve of women in formal pastoral roles, the practical approach to ministry did not prevent women from playing active roles in home and foreign missions. For thousands of women, it was Bible school training which provided them with a degree of knowledge and skills that was otherwise not available.[37]

Although the primary focus of the early Canadian Bible schools was biblical and practical instruction for lay people, there was also an opportunity for full-time pastors, evangelists, and home and foreign missionaries to receive training. For example, in 1928 Winkler Bible Institute provided both "general" and "special" training. The "general" purpose of the school was to provide training for the laity "who desire to enter into a deeper spiritual life and who seek to understand the Word of God, for private as well as general use." The "special" purpose was to provide training for those ". . . who desire a preparation for public life, that is, as ministers, evangelists, missionaries. . . ."[38]

The modest budgets with which the Bible schools operated made them affordable to a large number of students. While liberal arts colleges and seminaries often demanded more expensive facilities, and regularly paid faculty and staff, Bible schools operated more cheaply. Although there were several Bible schools started in major cities, such as Toronto, Winnipeg, and Vancouver, the majority were located in small town and rural locations where costs were lower. It was not at all uncommon for schools to raise much of their needed food on their own farms as students worked in the fields, or to have much of what was needed donated from nearby rural supporters. Almost all the schools began operations in humble facilities that were rented or donated.[39]

A major factor in holding the Bible college costs down was the willingness of faculty and staff to work for very low salaries, often at levels comparable to or even lower than foreign missionaries. The majority of the Bible school teaching staff were not highly educated, sometimes having no more than a Bible school diploma. More than academic degrees, experience and success in evangelism and Bible teaching were viewed as necessary qualifications. Many of the young Bible school teachers began working as home missionaries, evangelists, or pastors and, while still in their twenties, responded to requests to begin local Bible schools with no expectations of job security or high salary. In addition to teaching duties, their responsibilities usually included a combination of administration, preaching, fund raising, student recruitment, dorm parenting, and maintenance. Because of their low salaries, they often supplemented their salaries through itinerant preaching during the spring and summer when classes were not in session. In some situations, local pastors or missionaries on furlough served as part-time instructors, for which they received little or no remuneration.[40]

Flexibility was also another contributing factor in the success of the Canadian Bible schools. With a strong focus on practical lay training, these schools felt fewer restraints than accredited colleges that had more conventional academic requirements and traditions. Freedom from such constraints gave schools the flexibility needed to adapt to the conditions of their local communities and the needs of their constituents. The Bible schools in Canada demonstrated an excellent example of the unusually adaptable nature of Evangelicalism.[41]

One of the clearest examples of this flexibility was in the area of admissions requirements. Bible schools were open, at least until the 1960s, to students without high school graduation. The reality is that if high school graduation had been a requirement for admission to Canadian Bible schools, the vast majority of the young people would not have been eligible. That would have been an unacceptable limitation given the mission of these early schools. During the 1920s and 1930s, only about 15 percent of Canadian students graduated from high school; not until several years after the second World War did more than 25 percent of Canadian students graduate. That number just reached 50 percent by 1960.[42] This increase in numbers of students graduating from high school was consistent with the changes taking place in Canadian Bible schools and colleges. In 1960 S. A. Witmer, Executive Director of the Accrediting Association of Bible Colleges, stated that Canadian Bible schools and colleges reported that just over half of their students were high school graduates [43]

Accessibility also helps to explain why many students were able to take advantage of a Bible school education. First, the schools were geographically accessible communities—such as Caronport or Pambrun, Saskatchewan; Three Hills or Sexsmith, Alberta; or Winkler or Steinbach, Manitoba. Rather than expecting students to travel great distances to attend Bible schools, institutions were often started in small communities at the request of local residents in order to accommodate their young people. Second, the academic calendar was also designed to fit with student work schedules. The academic year was often shorter than at traditional colleges, beginning after harvest and ending before spring seeding.[44] Urban schools often attempted to accommodate working students by offering classes only in the morning or evening, thus allowing them to hold daytime or evening jobs.

A final factor that may have contributed to the growth of the Canadian Bible schools and colleges was the informal alliances that were formed between the different institutions. Strong, mutually supportive relationships were formed between the schools and their supporters. For example, the founding presidents and longtime leaders of Prairie Bible Institute and Briercrest Bible Institute (L. E. Maxwell and Henry H. Hildebrand), worked very closely together. Unhindered by traditional denominational barriers and taking advantage of an evangelical cooperation that viewed most denominational differences as secondary, they built strong, denominationally mixed constituencies. Some of the schools also developed radio broadcasts that assisted in attracting students and financial support. Many schools hosted large missions rallies or Bible conferences that drew hundreds of people each year to their campuses.[45]

The Bible schools were viewed as resource centers for churches and mission organizations as they provided preaching, musical talent, childrens' and teens' camps, and missions conferences. In many cases, the interdenominational schools actually offered more resources than many denominational schools. This resulted in constituencies that were denominationally and ethnically diverse, sometimes showing more loyalty to Bible schools than to their own denominations. Church historian Joel Carpenter's observes that Bible schools often functioned as "regional coordinating centers"[46] for conservative Protestants. Bible schools managed to develop strong constituencies that were a contributing factor to their success.

The impact of the Bible college movement on Canadian Evangelicalism may be much greater than many people realize. With the absence of evangelical seminaries and liberal arts colleges before 1960, the Bible institutes and colleges were the only post-secondary education option for thousands of men and women who wanted strong religious instruction in an evangelical context. Although many Bible schools had obvious shortcomings or were short-lived, there is little doubt about the contribution they made. The Bible schools trained men and women for pastoral, educational, and cross-cultural ministries; they provided strong lay leadership within their churches and communities. Furthermore, despite the development of evangelical seminaries and liberal arts colleges in Canada over the last three decades, Bible institutes and colleges still remain the choice of thousands of Canadian students who enroll in postsecondary education each year.

CHAPTER TEN

THE GROWTH YEARS:
1930-1960

One of the most decisive factors in determining the future direction of the Bible college movement was the quality of second-generation and even third-generation leadership. A number of the early Bible schools in the United States and Canada were started by strong, highly committed, and charismatic leaders. Many of them served their schools for decades. Their educational values, theology, and leadership styles left long-lasting impressions on the institutions they started and the students they taught. Yet, the time came for each of them to pass the torch to a new generation of leaders. The new group of leaders was called upon to lead the Bible college movement into a new era in North American theological education.

The institutions that survived or grew in subsequent decades did so because the early leaders had the foresight to prepare new leadership to perpetuate the original vision. Thus, their institutions were able to advance to new levels of effectiveness amid the changing needs and expectations of the church and society. Some institutions, however, died with their original founders or survived for only a short time because the new leaders were unable to maintain or advance the founders' vision. Some schools changed directions with new mission statements and educational philosophies. The educational paradigms they adopted were outside the traditional Bible college framework.

How did Bible college leaders respond to the changes that took place in the church and higher education between 1930 and 1960? What was the state of the Bible collage movement by 1960? This chapter examines the role of this new generation of leaders in directing the educational movement toward future growth.

GROWTH YEARS

Although some early Bible schools had difficulty making the transition to second generation leadership. The Bible college movement in general, especially in the United States, experienced moderate but steady growth between 1900 and 1930 and greater development in the next thirty years.

In 1962, S. A. Witmer, Executive Director of the Accrediting Association of Bible Colleges, looked at the founding dates of 234 institutions in North America (see Table X-1). He reported that nine existing schools had their beginning from 1901-1910, fifteen from 1911 to 1920, and 26 from 1921 to 1930. Of those schools started between 1882 and the turn of the century, 61 of those Bible institutes and Bible colleges founded during the first 48 years of the movement were still in existence in 1962.[1] The number of Bible schools established but later discontinued is not known.

The table, originally compiled by Witmer, indicates that the major development of Bible institutes and colleges took place between 1931 and 1960 when 73 percent of the existing institutions were started.[2] The peak decade was 1941-1950 (World War II decade) when 35 percent of all existing Bible schools were founded.[3]

There is an unexpected contrast in the growth patterns of the Bible college movement in Canada and the United States. As mentioned in Chapter nine, the greatest increase in Canadian schools took place between 1931 and 1950. According to Witmer, 69 percent of the Canadian institutions were founded between 1931 and 1950, while only eight percent were started in the decade after that.[4] The majority of the Canadian institutions were established in the western provinces and by specific

TABLE X-1

BIBLE INSTITUTES AND COLLEGES
FOUNDED BEFORE 1962
(by decade)

Decade	United States		Canada		Total	
	#	%	#	%	#	%
1881-1890	3	1.3	0	0	3	1.3
1891-1900	7	3.0	1	0.4	8	3.4
1901-1910	9	3.8	0	0	9	3.8
1911-1920	13	5.6	2	0.9	15	6.5
1921-1930	17	7.3	9	3.8	26	11.1
1931-1940	26	11.0	19	8.2	45	19.2
1941-1950	66	28.2	16	6.8	82	35.0
1951-1960	40	17.1	4	1.7	44	18.8
1961	2	0.9	0	0	2	0.9
Total	183	78.2	51	21.8	234	100.0

denominations. Many of these schools, however, were discontinued or merged with other institutions.

Conversely, the greatest increase in American institutions took place between 1941 and 1960, one decade later than in Canada. The founding of American schools hit a high point during the 1940s when 66 schools were started. Another 40 came into being during the decade of the 1950s.[5]

ACADEMIC ADVANCEMENT

During this period, Bible schools began to upgrade themselves academically. This was precipitated by a general rise in the level and quality of education across North America. In the post-World War II era, the number of men and women pursuing postsecondary education increased significantly. The 1957 President's Committee on Education Beyond the High School reported that "without realizing it we have become a 'society of students.'" More than forty million Americans (25 percent of the U. S. population) were enrolled in some type of postsecondary education.[6] The increase in postsecondary education involvement was slower in Canada. Statistics for Canada reported that only 8.1 percent of the population was enrolled in postsecondary education in 1961, but the figure grew to 43.1 by 1991.[7] The Bible college movement was also part of this trend, particularly as churches and parachurch organizations developed higher educational expectations for their leaders.

When the early Bible schools were first started, few high school graduates enrolled. By 1960 the reverse was true. Seven members of the Accrediting association of Bible Colleges reported not a single non-high school graduate in their 1959-1960 enrollments. Although the Association permitted institutions to admit up to five percent non-high school students as special students, the number had decreased steadily from 4.1 percent to 1.2 percent between 1951 and 1960.[8] Furthermore, students with previous college or university experience started to enroll at Bible colleges in larger numbers.

The increase in academic level was also evident among the faculty. More and more faculty earned advanced degrees in contrast to the formative years of the Bible college movement when many instructors held only a Bible school diploma. Further reinforcement for this pattern came from the U. S. Department of Education in 1947 when they advised AABC that faculty would be expected to hold a master's degree or its equivalent from a collegiate level institution.[9] A comprehensive 1946 study of full-time faculty members at 47 Bible institutes and colleges indicated that 80 percent possessed an undergraduate degree, 25 percent a master's degree, and 11 percent an earned doctorate. By 1979, however, faculty members of AABC institutions had completed an average of nearly eight years of post-high school study.[10]

The library holdings also started to increase as the curriculum was amplified to include more courses in the liberal arts and professional areas beyond the core of biblical and theological studies. Many schools, for the first time, started to charge tuition, and the larger schools achieved a higher degree of financial stability. This enabled them to expand their facilities and place more of an emphasis on academic excellence.

The rate of academic changes was different for each school. Some schools moved rapidly toward academic respectability while others proceeded more slowly. The changes were inevitable in view of the developments in North American higher education. These trends in academic advancement reflected a willingness for Bible institutes and colleges to be identified with more formal educational patterns. It could be said that the Bible college movement was simply upgrading to keep pace with higher education.

EXPANDED CURRICULUM

In the formative years of the Bible college movement, the curriculum was quite limited in most schools. The emphasis was on the provision of a basic Bible knowledge and the development of solid spiritual formation in the lives of the students. The curriculum might even be called "paltry" apart from biblical and practical Christian ministry subject matter. In most cases, the Bible courses were not graded, and students were given two years maximum of instruction. Quite appropriately, the older institutions were often called "Bible training schools."

In the 1920s and 1930s, a trend toward an amplified curriculum started. The two-year curriculum was expanded to three years. At the same time, professional programs were developed in such specialized areas as pastoral ministry, missions, Christian education, and church music. In some cases, very specialized programs that were added, such as missionary aviation, missionary nursing, journalism, communications, and linguistics. With an expanded curriculum to three years, the schools evolved into "Bible institutes."[11]

As more and more of the students enrolled in Bible institutes with a high school diploma, there were requests for an even more amplified curriculum. There was a need for broader general studies in addition to course offerings in biblical and professional studies. This resulted in many of the Bible institutes adding a general studies (liberal arts) component to the curriculum. They made these changes both to ease the process of transfer for students going on to a liberal arts degree and to satisfy students more completely with their own curricular offerings.[12]

As part of this academic evolution, students became more course credit and degree conscious. Previously students often completed two or three years at a Bible institute and then needed to matriculate another two or three years at a liberal arts college or university to earn a bachelor's degree. This prompted a number of institutions to develop an integrated program of biblical, general, and professional studies leading to a baccalaureate degree. With this type of curriculum amplification, many of the Bible institutes changed their names to "Bible colleges."[13]

Witmer's 1962 survey indicated that 52 percent of the Bible training schools were classified as Bible colleges; the remainder were viewed as Bible institutes. The percentage was considerably higher among members of the Accrediting Association of Bible Colleges. Forty of the 49 members (or 82%) were classified as degree-granting institutions and used the name "Bible college."[14]

THE ACCREDITING ASSOCIATION OF BIBLE COLLEGES

One of the most significant developments in the maturation of the Bible college movement was the founding of the Accrediting Association of Bible Colleges in 1947. This new association brought standardization, accountability, and higher levels of academic excellence to many Bible institutes and Bible colleges in both the United States and Canada.

Although the Accrediting Association was not officially started until 1947, there had been previous consideration given to such an organization. In 1918 James M. Gray, president of Moody Bible Institute, called a group of Bible school leaders to attend the Moody Founder's Day Conference of that year to discuss the possibility of forming an accrediting body. The leaders who were present appointed an investigative committee to review the feasibility of organizing an association of Bible schools and of standardizing training courses.[15]

When the committee conducted its research, it concluded that significant differences existed among the institutions relative to curriculum, educational methodology, and even theology. With these differences identified, it was found "impossible to draw up any method of unifying the whole Bible school system, or of establishing a system of interchangeable credits."[16] Gray never called for the report and the effort was abandoned; But the idea did not die. Rather, the need increased for Bible institutes and colleges to have some type of standardization and accountability beyond what took place through the informal networking between the various schools.

When the National Association of Evangelicals met in Minneapolis in 1946, Howard W. Ferrin, president of Providence Bible Institute, identified the critical need for an accrediting association as he issued the following statement:

> The distinctive elements of Bible institute education are indispensable and must therefore be preserved. No existing agency assists Bible institutes to upgrade their programs by the process of accreditation. Accreditation by the regional associations is possible only by converting to liberal arts colleges, which obliterates their distinctives. The only solution, therefore, is to establish an accrediting agency according to sound collegiate standards which will be predicated on principles of Bible college education.[17]

The momentum continued to build for an accrediting association when Samuel Sutherland of the Bible Institute of Los Angeles wrote a letter to key Bible institute and Bible college leaders in December 1946. He declared, "Now is the time to do something about it. It is our conviction that the time is ripe for organizing an association of like-minded institutions in order to stabilize the whole field of Christian training in which we are specializing."[18] He went on to suggest that a conference be held in Winona Lake, Indiana, from January 28-31, 1947. He

attached to his letter a list of suggested agenda topics. Some of
the topics were doctrinal position, minimum curriculum, faculty
resources, library holdings, academic calendar, and quality of
instruction.[19]

Twelve administrators from eight institutions gathered in
Winona Lake at the Westminster Hotel for the planning meeting.
Before the meeting had concluded, an official doctrinal
statement, which embraced the principal tenants of evangelical
Christianity, was adopted. The meeting also addressed such
issues as fees, future meetings, financial structure, appointment
of a constitutional committee and an executive committee, and
the date (October 28, 1947) for the first annual meeting.[20] The
results of this historic planning meeting were contained in the
document: "Academic Standards for Bible Institutes and Bible
Colleges." This document served as a precursor for what would
become the association's *Manual of Criteria*.[21]

The association's first annual meeting, referred to as the
"Constitutional Meeting," was held at the same location in
Winona Lake on October 28, 1947. Delegates considered it their
primary task to develop a founding instrument that would serve
as the organizational document for the new agency. The
meeting was primarily consumed with organizational matters.
It was at this gathering that the Accrediting Association of Bible
Institutes and Bible Colleges was officially formed with Samuel
Sutherland elected as the first president.[22]

The association quickly sought the counsel of experts in
the field of college and university education, particularly John
Russell, the director of higher education for the U. S. Department
of Education.[23] The result was that the association became
recognized by the United States Office of Education in 1948 as
the only accrediting agency in the field of undergraduate
theological education.[24] Thus the Office of Education began to
recognize the undergraduate institutions approved by AABIBC
just as it recognized the seminaries approved by the Association
of Theological Schools.

The association adopted two categories of membership:
accredited and associate. Accredited membership included

institutions that satisfactorily met association standards. Associate memberships identified with the association in a nonaccredited relationship. Schools in both categories of membership were required to show evidence of academic and financial integrity, valid educational service, and conformity to the spirit and objectives of the association.[25]

In 1948, at the second annual meeting, 18 institutions officially received accredited membership.[26] By 1960 the membership had grown to 36 accredited and 13 associate schools. Those figures represented twenty percent of the Bible institutes and Bible colleges in the United States and Canada. It included 44 percent of the total day school enrollment.[27]

There were some Bible schools, however, that did not seek accreditation with the association. For example, L. E. Maxwell, longtime president of Prairie Bible Institute, stated:

> We are personally not interested about becoming uniform, or in becoming accredited. God has given us a special method of Bible study second to none, and we are content to do what God wants us to do without having to adjust to that which others feel led to do. . . . We are concerned that many of the present trends take these Bible institutions into modernism. . . .[28]

A key to the association's success during its formative years was the strong leadership that the member institutions brought to the organization. The first presidents were:
1. Samuel Sutherland of the Bible Institute of Los Angeles (1947-1949);
2. Thomas Mosley of the Missionary Training Institute (1949-1951);
3. S. A. Witmer of Fort Wayne Bible College (1951-1953);
4. William Culbertson of Moody Bible Institute (1953-1955);
5. William Mierop of Philadelphia Bible Institute (1955-1957); and
6. Cornelius Haggard of Azusa College (1957-1960).

Terrance Crum of Providence Bible Institute served as secretary-treasurer of the Association for its first 22 years.[29]

During the 1957 annual meeting the first full time officer was elected. S. A. Witmer became the executive director and was able to serve the organization with distinction until his untimely death in 1962. While active with conferences, workshops, campus visits and association administration, he also made two key literary contributions to the Bible college movement: *Education with Dimension: The Bible College Story* (1962) and *Preparing Bible College Students for Ministries in Christian Education* (1962).[30]

THE STATE OF THE MOVEMENT BY 1960

How many Bible institutes and Bible colleges were there by 1960? Where were most of these institutions located? What type of sponsorship or affiliation did they have? How many students were actually enrolled? The answers to many of these questions were received through a comprehensive study that was conducted in 1959-1960 by the Accrediting Association of Bible Colleges on the daytime Bible institutes and Bible colleges in the United States and Canada. The research did not include evening Bible institutes that were operated primarily in local churches for the training of lay people.[31]

In 1960 there were 248 known Bible institutes and Bible colleges in the United States and Canada. Of this number, 54 were located in Canada and 194 in the United States. They were found in nine provinces, 41 states, and the District of Columbia.[32]

Although Bible institutes and colleges were located all across North America, there was not a distinct pattern of distribution. The American institutions were more commonly found in the densely populated areas. The greater percentage of institutions were located in the North Central states (20 percent), the Pacific Coast states (15 percent), and the states of the Upper South (13 percent). Smaller concentrations were found in New England, the Deep South, and the Rocky Mountain area.[33]

The earlier American schools were commonly started in large cities because of larger populations and for very practical concerns. Practical training was needed to equip the students to reach the masses, particularly within these urban centers. This was provided through churches, missions, Sunday schools, and other agencies that were more commonly based in cities. Most of the larger metropolitan areas in the United States had one or more Bible colleges even though a trend had started for institutions to move from congested downtown locations to larger campuses in suburban and rural settings. Sixty percent of the institutions were found in sizeable cities in 1960.[34]

In Canada a very different distribution pattern had developed, as pointed out in Chapter nine. The majority of the schools were located in the Western provinces. For example, 37 of the 54 institutions (69% of Canadian colleges) were located in Manitoba, Saskatchewan, Alberta, and British Columbia. Only three schools were in Quebec primarily because the province was predominantly Roman Catholic. There were only six schools between the four Atlantic provinces of Newfoundland, New Brunswick, Nova Scotia, and Prince Edward Island. The chief contrast was between Ontario and the three prairie provinces of Manitoba, Saskatchewan, and Alberta. While Ontario had twice the population of these three provinces, it had only 25 percent as many Bible schools.[35] This was largely due to the large number of denominational institutions that were started by the various ethnic groups in Western Canada to perpetuate cultural as well as religious values.

In classifying institutions as either "denominational" or "interdenominational," there was also a very clear pattern.[36] Of the 248 schools, 164 institutions, or 64 percent, were denominational. They enrolled 63 percent of all the students.[37] The reason for the larger number of denominational institutions was because many denominations assumed responsibility for organizing and maintaining schools to train their own candidates for church and church-related ministries. While these schools did not exclude students from other denominations, their primary mission was to serve the sponsoring denomination. On the other hand, the largest Bible institutes and colleges in both the United States and Canada were interdenominational, some of international reputation, such as Moody Bible Institute, Bible Institute of Los Angeles, and Prairie Bible Institute.

Among the denominational institutions, the Church of Christ/Christian Church sponsored the largest number of North American schools (37 or 14.9%); the Baptist groups were second (36 or 14.5%), and the Pentecostal groups were third (25 or 10%). Other denominational groups worth noting were the Wesleyans (21 schools), the Mennonites (13 schools, mostly in Canada), the Lutherans (eight schools), and the Christian and Missionary Alliance (five schools).[38]

The number of day students enrolled in the Bible institutes and colleges of the United States and Canada approximated 25,000 for the 1959-1960 academic year, but only 217 of the 248 respondent institutions reported their enrollment. Of the 23, 584 students that were reported, 2, 868 were part time. In the 170 reporting schools from the U. S., there were 20,167 students or 85.5 percent. In the 47 Canadian schools reporting, there were 3,417 daytime students or 14.5 percent.[39]

Ninety-two institutions reported evening school programs, which accounted for another 9,058 students. The combined enrollment for day school registrations and evening division enrollments totalled 32,642 students. S. A. Witmer purported that if estimates were included for non-reporting schools, the total would have been approximately 35,000 students involved in some type of Bible college education.[40]

The average day school enrollment for the 217 reporting institutions was 108.7, with the United States schools having an average enrollment of 118.6 in comparison to 72.7 for Canadian schools. In the Canadian context, however, Prairie Bible Institute, Briercrest Bible Institute, and Toronto Bible College accounted for 31.2 percent of all the students in Bible institutes and colleges.[41]

By 1960 the Bible college movement had started to carve out a legitimate place in North American higher education. Approximately 250 schools were classified as Bible institutes or Bible colleges. They had a combined enrollment of about

35,000 students. Major academic progress had been made in upgrading the quality of students, faculty, facilities, and programs. The curricula of many schools had been expanded to include three or four years of study, often resulting in a college degree. And a recognized accrediting association had been formed to provide standardization and accountability for participating schools. The remarks made by Enock C. Dryness, vice president and registrar of Wheaton College at the tenth annual meeting of the Accrediting Association of Bible Colleges captured the progress that had been made in Bible college education:

> I offer my congratulations for the tremendous progress which has been made during the past ten years. Not only is this true of the schools that are members of the Accrediting Association, but also of those who have not yet taken the step. With the establishment of the Accrediting Association of Bible Colleges, the Bible school movement has really come of age and achieved its rightful place in higher education.[42]

The Bible college movement had made significant progress in becoming a legitimate option within the higher education community. However, there were bigger challenges that Bible college leaders would have to face as they attempted to define the role of the Bible college in relationship to Christian liberal arts colleges, theological seminaries, and even the larger university community. There were also critical enrollment and financial issues to be encountered, and most of all, questions to be answered in regard to institutional mission.

CHAPTER ELEVEN

THE CHANGING YEARS:
1960-PRESENT

The period from 1960 to the present is characterized by several significant developments within the Bible college movement, some of which actually began in the 1940s. First, Bible colleges have continued to increase their academic standards and pursue outside recognition. Second, consistent with these educational advancements, Bible college leaders have attempted to identify their institutions with the larger higher educational community. This identification is evident by baccalaureate degree offerings, expanded general education requirements, and insistence on faculty having graduate degrees (in many cases an earned doctorate) in their particular academic disciplines. Because of these changes, Bible colleges have had to redefine their purpose more clearly in relationship to Christian liberal arts colleges and theological seminaries. Finally, like other colleges and universities in the 1970s and 1980s, Bible colleges are being forced to reevaluate their traditional roles to determine if changes in mission, programs, and even recruitment strategies are necessary to survive current struggles with declining enrollments, rising costs, and financial hardships.

Recognizing these critical issues that are confronting Bible colleges, this chapter answers the following questions: How have the changing expectations of educational agencies, the church, and society affected the Bible college movement from 1960 to the present? How have Bible colleges changed since

1960 in regard to their mission statements, academic programs, curricula, and student populations?

ACADEMIC RECOGNITION AND THE SEARCH FOR IDENTITY

The process toward academic recognition that began in the late 1940s and 1950s, has actually increased in the past three decades particularly through the influence of the Accrediting Association of Bible Colleges. The association received official approval from the U. S. Department of Education as a professional accrediting agency in 1948. Eighteen institutions were initially granted accreditation. In each successive five-year period from 1950 through 1994, an average of ten colleges was accredited. The number of new colleges being accredited remained steady until the late 1980s when 18 new institutions were granted recognition.[1] Starting in the late 1960s, American AABC institutions have also sought accreditation from regional associations (an option not available to Canadian colleges since regional accreditation does not exist).[2]

While most Bible college educators and church leaders have viewed accreditation and degree-granting authority as very positive, some pastors, alumni, and other financial supporters of AABC colleges have viewed these developments with suspicion. Some critics view such academic changes as the cause for drifting away from original Bible college missions. One chief academic officer expressed it this way:

> ". . . a Bible college is a Bible institute on its way to becoming a liberal arts college." . . . there is a precedent within the Bible college movement of schools beginning with a highly concentrated focus on Christian ministry, but with time, as their programs expand and they achieve degree-granting status and regional accreditation, they to some extent move away from their focus on biblical studies and ministry courses. They drop the word "Bible" from their name and in some cases become Christian liberal arts colleges.[3]

These statements imply that a change in degree-granting status or academic recognition automatically reflects a change in institutional mission. Although there may be examples to support this theory, there are also notable exceptions. For example, Moody Bible Institute has offered degrees since 1966 and held accreditation with AABC since 1951 and the North Central Association of Colleges and Schools since 1989. Yet, it has shown no indication of change in its mission or the purpose of its academic programs. Philadelphia College of Bible received accreditation with AABC in 1950 and with Middle States Association of Colleges and Schools in 1967. It still retains active involvement in the Bible college movement. These examples suggest that a college's decision to seek regional accreditation need not suggest a change in institutional mission.

In 1995 AABC reported that 28 percent of its colleges were accredited by a regional associations.[4] A number of examples can be cited of institutions that have achieved regional accreditation and still have remained firmly committed to a Bible college approach to education. There are, however, just as many illustrations of the opposite perspective. Of the 28 colleges that have withdrawn from the Accrediting Association of Bible Colleges since 1950, 18 of them did so within ten years of obtaining accreditation with their respective regional associations.[5]

In the case of Messiah Bible College, the decision to adopt a liberal arts college model preceded regional accreditation. The school changed its name to Messiah College in 1951 and withdrew from AABC in 1957. Accreditation with the Middle States Association of Colleges and Schools followed in 1963.[6] Regional accreditation only confirmed a strategic decision that had already been made by the leadership of the institution. Other colleges have followed a similar course. Cleveland Bible College became Malone College in 1957, Providence Bible College became Barrington College in 1959, and the Bible Institute of Los Angeles was renamed Biola College in 1949 and eventually Biola University. Of the original 30 members of the Accrediting Association of Bible Colleges (collegiate and intermediate), only 12 exist today as Bible colleges. Eight have since evolved into universities, four have become liberal arts colleges, three have merged with other institutions, and three have closed.[7]

The increase in voluntary withdrawals from AABC began in 1959. Southern California Bible College in Costa Mesa, California, became Southern California College in 1959 and then withdrew from AABC that same year. In the 1960s, five colleges withdrew from AABC:

1. Central Wesleyan College (Central, South Carolina, 1963);
2. Lee College (Cleveland, Tennessee, 1968);
3. Barrington College (Barrington, Rhode Island, 1968);
4. Bartersville Wesleyan College (Oklahoma City, Oklahoma, 1969); and
5. Nyack College (Nyack, New York, 1969).

Two colleges left the association in the 1970s: Grand Rapids Baptist College (Grand Rapids, Michigan; 1975) and Azusa Pacific College (now called Azusa Pacific University, Azusa, California, 1975).[8]

In the 1980s and early 1990s, 13 more colleges withdrew from the association. Biola College withdrew in 1987 when it became Biola University. Mid-South Bible College (Memphis, Tennessee) became Crichton College in 1987 and withdrew in 1989. Criswell Center for Biblical Studies (Dallas, Texas) became Criswell College in 1990 and withdrew the same year. Fort Wayne Bible College (Fort Wayne, Indiana) withdrew in 1991 and became Summit Christian College. It later merged with Taylor University (Upland, Indiana) and became the Fort Wayne Branch of that institution. Other colleges that withdrew from AABC include:

1. North Central Bible College (Minneapolis, Minnesota, 1991);
2. Simpson College (San Francisco, California; 1991);
3. Pacific Christian College (Fullerton, California, 1992);
4. Bethany College of the Assemblies of God (Santa Cruz, California, 1992);
5. William Tyndale College (Farmington Hills, Michigan, 1993);
6. Atlanta Christian College (Atlanta, Georgia, 1994);
7. Trinity College (Miami, Florida, 1994);

8. Colorado Christian University (Denver, Colorado, 1994); and

9. Northwest College (Kirkland, Washington, 1995).[9]

The majority of these schools are now considered Christian liberal arts colleges rather than Bible colleges.

By the early 1990s, the trend had become so common that Joseph Aldrich, president of Multnomah Bible College, called the move toward the liberal arts curriculum "a first-round temptation" for all Bible colleges.[10] Robert Kallgren of then Columbia Bible College (Columbia, South Carolina), called for immediate "self-assessment and strategic planning on the part of institutional presidents to help their schools adapt to "future considerations."[11]

In reality, the Accrediting Association of Bible Colleges had already begun to struggle with the issue. Throughout the 1980s, The *AABC Newsletter* published several articles that addressed the issue of whether member institutions should be allowed to expand their mission statements and to offers programs other than those leading to church-related ministries.[12] It was not surprising that the membership voted to expand the AABC mission statement to allow institutions the freedom to offer programs to prepare students for various types of employment. This change was really accommodating member colleges that had already broadened their mission statements and programs. This modification of policy allowed some colleges a more open attitude toward the recruitment of students with nonreligious vocational goals.[13]

President of Miami Christian College, Kenneth Gangel, described this shift in attitude by distinguishing between "traditional" and "progressive" Bible colleges:

The traditional Bible college is marked by an exclusive commitment to vocational Christian ministry; a single and simple curriculum; and an emphasis on terminal training; and complete separation from secular education. The progressive Bible college, by contrast, retains a primary commitment to vocational Christian ministry without exclusively restricting itself to professional ministerial programs. It defines "ministry" more broadly, offering a wider range of majors under that umbrella.[14]

Gangel listed the characteristics of the "progressive" Bible college as a willingness to pursue joint partnerships with public institutions, state, and regional projects; a desire to seek licensure where applicable; a serious commitment to holistic, Christocentric, and bibliocentric education; and a pursuit of the highest possible level of accreditation.[15]

A CHANGING STUDENT PROFILE

The broadening of academic programs within the more "progressive" Bible colleges also have had an impact on the numbers and percentages of students enrolled in various academic programs. Timothy Millard's recent study on "Changes in the Missions of Colleges Accredited by the American Association of Bible Colleges as Indicated by their Education Programs, Recruiting Practices, and Future Plans" demonstrated a significant change over the past 35 years in this particular area. He reported that "the majority of AABC colleges have accommodated, if not welcomed, a new type of student into their schools, the student with nonreligious or, at least, ambiguous goals."[16] He contended that this change in student profile did not just happen but was quite consistent with the changes in mission statements and programs to attract students who were interested in pursuing fields other than vocational Christian ministry.[17]

More significant, however, is that 69 percent of the AABC colleges in the study reported that the total percentage of students enrolled in church-related vocational majors had "decreased" while the percentage of students in non-church-related educational majors or undergraduate programs had "increased." While many students at Bible colleges were still enrolled in church-related vocational majors, a larger percentage were in programs designed specifically to meet nonreligious vocational goals or for students who did not wish to complete their formal education at a Bible college.[18]

SEMINARY EDUCATION

Just as the Bible college movement was forced to define itself in relationship to Christian liberal arts colleges and universities, a similar response was needed with regard to theological seminaries. During the formative years of the movement, Bible schools served as an alternative to seminary education. The emphasis was on practical training and solid biblical instruction. As the Bible schools started to develop into degree-granting colleges, however, academic administrators and church leaders started to see the need for seminary education that would not compete with, but rather complement, the undergraduate training received in a Bible college. Furthermore, growing out of the fundamentalist-modernist controversy of the 1920s was the development of many evangelical seminaries that had the same commitment to biblical authority as the Bible colleges. These developments forced Bible college leaders to address the relationship between their schools and theological seminaries and to explain the apparent duplication of efforts between the two types of institution.

In attempting to define their relationship with theological seminaries, Bible college leaders expressed several different perspectives. First, there was a small group who did not see the need for aspiring pastors and missionaries to receive seminary training. In some cases, they were even opposed to this type of advanced training, claiming that it was far too academic and lacked emphasis on practical training. They felt an undergraduate education in a Bible college was quite adequate and did not need to be duplicated at the graduate level. In the minds of this particular group, the terminal training of the Bible college was all that was needed to work with a church or mission organization. It was not until very recently that certain evangelical groups started to recognize the value of seminary training.

The second most common perspective among Bible college leaders was that seminary training was desirable but was often a reflection of the related denomination or church body. Consistent with this view was the development of a pre-seminary major in conjunction with existing college programs in Bible and theology. The pre-seminary program became preparatory for those who would choose to pursue a master's degree at a theological seminary. The existing church-related programs continued to serve as terminal programs for those planning to pursue a church-related vocation after graduation.[19]

Third, another approach that was widely adopted at a number of the Bible colleges was for institutions to broaden their programs to include graduate education. Some institutions actually evolved into free-standing seminaries and discontinued undergraduate training. For example, Bethany Bible Training School in Oak Brook, Illinois, developed into Bethany Theological Seminary. With this approach, seminary training was viewed as essential preparation for ministry.[20] More commonly, however, particularly among denominational institutions, a seminary was established and the undergraduate program moved from a Bible college to a liberal arts college model. For example, the Free Church Bible College and Seminary became the denominational college and seminary of the Evangelical Free Church of America under the name of Trinity College and Trinity Evangelical Divinity School (1961). Later it was renamed Trinity International University. Biola College became Biola University; established Talbot Theological Seminary (1983) by merging the appropriate undergraduate departments with the seminary. Nyack Missionary College became Nyack College and established a graduate school (1960) which became the Alliance Theological Seminary (1974). Finally, Gordon Theological College became Gordon College in the late 1950s and established Gordon Theological Seminary (1970).[21] The leaders of the educational institutions mentioned saw the need for both undergraduate and graduate training; however, in the process, they left the Bible college ranks.

A fourth approach common among both American and Canadian Bible colleges was when undergraduate institutions continued as Bible colleges while offering graduate programs in order to more thoroughly train men and women for church-related ministries. In 1995 the Accrediting Association of Bible Colleges reported that 26 percent of the member institutions were offering course work beyond the bachelor's degree.[22] Two American examples can be cited: Columbia Bible College (Columbia, South Carolina) established Columbia Graduate School of Bible and Missions in 1936 and Lincoln Christian College started Lincoln Christian Seminary in 1951. Other Bible colleges, such as Moody Bible Institute, Philadelphia College of Bible, and Lancaster Bible College have also established graduate divisions in recent years. Because there were few evangelical seminaries in Canada before 1960, Bible colleges took the lead in establishing graduate theological institutions. For example, Canadian Bible College established Canadian Theological Seminary in 1970; Winnipeg Bible College started Winnipeg Theological Seminary (now called Providence College and Theological Seminary) in 1972; Ontario Bible College founded Ontario Theological Seminary in 1976; and Briercrest Bible College created Briercrest Biblical Seminary in 1983. These seminaries are now among the largest in Canada.

The importance of seminary education has been reflected in the affairs of the Accrediting Association of Bible College. The focus of AABC historically has been undergraduate education while the Association of Theological Schools (ATS) has provided accreditation for graduate theological education in North America. During the time period between 1960 and 1976, ATS required seminaries to admit students who had earned a bachelor's degree from a regionally accredited college or seminary. If more than 15 percent of their students did not meet this requirement, the institutions actually received a discrepancy notation in the annual list published by ATS.[23]

This created problems for a number of the evangelical seminaries that accepted a large number of Bible college graduates. It also created tension between AABC and ATS, both of whom held membership with the U. S. Council on Postsecondary Education. The tension was resolved, however, when ATS revised its policy in 1976 to read that "Admission to theological studies shall be based upon graduation with an appropriate bachelor's degree from a college or university holding membership in the Association of Universities and

Colleges in Canada (AUCC) or accredited by an association holding membership in the Council on Postsecondary Education."[24] This new policy benefited AABC colleges in the United States, but it still did not benefit Canadian institutions since AUCC did not include Bible colleges in its purview.

THREE PARADIGMS FOR BIBLE COLLEGE EDUCATION

The Bible college movement has gone through significant changes during the last half of the twentieth century. The changes have been corporate as well as on individual college campuses. Viewed as a whole, the movement has tended to blend into the larger framework of Christian higher education. These institutions have accepted a certain degree of standardization, such as accreditation and upgraded admissions standards, and have evolved into degree-granting colleges. They have expanded the number of courses they offer and have diversified their programs. They have also welcomed a new type of student—one who does not always have church-related vocational goals. These changes have worked to make the historical distinction between Bible colleges and other evangelical colleges or universities more ambiguous.

A small number of Bible colleges have not changed their mission at all and are opposed to developing any "non-church related educational programs." Conversely, a larger number of Bible colleges have introduced non-church related educational programs in their institutions and plan to continue developing them in the future. These two groups fit Gangel's (1980) terminology when he distinguished between "traditional" and "progressive" Bible colleges.

Gary Millard, in attempting to identify how AABC colleges have responded to the preceding religious and educational developments in the later part of this century, also adopted the terminology of Gangel—"traditional" and "progressive." Millard concluded that the larger percentage of the institutions fit into the "progressive" category, while a smaller percentage match the "traditional" model. However, he also observed a third category—"evolving" Bible colleges—institutions having already adopted another model, the Christian liberal arts or comprehensive university model. According to Millard, they are in the process of transforming into broader, more complex institutions.[25]

Traditional Bible Colleges

Colleges in this particular category reportedly did not offer any non-church related educational majors nor did they have plans to add such programs in the near future. Their mission statements were generally limited to providing instruction for lay, professional, and preprofessional vocational ministry and reflected little change since 1950. Although the overall enrollment pattern for these institutions showed little change, there was often a difference between those students in church-related vocational programs versus those in lay-ministry programs. The percentage of those in vocational majors was frequently down while the percentage of those in lay-ministry programs or pre-seminary programs was up.[26]

It should be noted that this does not mean "traditional" Bible colleges do not offer programs for students with nonreligious goals or that they do not have such students in attendance; however, as a matter of policy, they have resisted recruiting students with nonreligious vocational goals by providing them with instruction that is directly related to their chosen career interests. About half of these schools, though, did offer undergraduate transfer programs. Millard suggested that many of the institutions in this category see themselves as playing a Christian "junior college" or spiritual foundation function.[27]

From these findings, Millard concluded that "traditional" Bible colleges: (1) have changed the least since 1950; (2) are unique in their resistance toward offering additional programs that are not church-related; and (3) have intentionally decided not to recruit students with "non-religious vocational goals by providing them with instruction that is directly related to their chosen career interests." Using non-church related educational programs as a sole criterion, about one-third of AABC institutions fit into the category of a "traditional" Bible college.[28]

Evolving Bible Colleges

In distinct contrast to the "traditional" Bible colleges, these types of institutions not only offer non-church-related educational majors, but plan on offering more in the future. These institutions have already identified themselves as a "Christian liberal arts college" or a "Christian university" or have indicated that "becoming a Christian liberal arts college or Christian university" expresses the future goal of their institution.[29]

Mission statements of colleges in this category tended to be broader and more abstract than the mission and goal statements of other Bible colleges. Not surprisingly, the majority of the institutions in the "evolving" Bible college grouping reported that their curricula had become more "academic" than "professional" or at least tended to be "more academic" in emphasis.[30]

Finally, the 1950-1994 enrollment patterns of colleges in this group demonstrated that the percentage of total enrollment in church-related vocational majors was down and the percentage of total enrollment in non-church related educational majors or undergraduate transfer programs was up.

Based on the above findings, Millard concluded that "evolving" Bible colleges have changed the most since 1950, will continue to expand their programs and majors, and represent institutions most likely to withdraw from the Accrediting Association of Bible Colleges in the future. "Evolving" Bible colleges accounted for about 15 percent of the institutions participating in the study.[31]

Progressive Bible Colleges

According to Millard's study, the largest percentage of (AABC) Bible colleges fit into this category. "Progressive" Bible colleges have "broadened" their mission statements, or if the mission statements have remained essentially the same, they have modified their programs to accommodate students with nonreligious vocational goals." Furthermore, they indicated an intention to continue to develop "more" non-church related educational majors.[32]

The vision of these institutions is to remain a Bible college but to define "ministry" more broadly so as to include other programs beyond the traditional ministries for pastors, missionaries, and evangelists. Part of this vision is to expand offerings to include a broader range of programs including those designed for students with nonreligious vocational goals. Not surprising, the total enrollment in "church-related vocational majors had decreased" while the percentage of total enrollment in "non-church related educational majors or undergraduate transfer programs had increased.[33]

Although "progressive" Bible colleges were similar to "evolving" Bible colleges, the leaders of these institutions reported that they would not seek "becoming a Christian liberal arts college or Christian university" at any time in the future. They do, however, seek to define a new role for their institutions, perhaps a modified one that is similar to that of other Christian colleges that do not specialize solely in training for vocational Christian ministry. "Progressive" Bible colleges included 55 to 65 percent of the colleges in the study.[34]

After examining these three models, there is little doubt that Bible colleges in North America have changed. The more critical questions relate to degree of change. Some have been completely transformed while others have evolved only subtly. "Traditional" Bible colleges have not changed their mission statements at all and intend to remain steadfast in their opposition to programs outside of church-related ministry. Conversely, "progressive" Bible colleges have not only introduced non-church related programs but plan to continue this pattern in the future. "Evolving" Bible colleges have adopted a very different paradigm and are in the process of becoming more comprehensive institutions.

Given the significant changes that have taken place within the Bible college movement, particularly since 1960, and knowing that there will certainly be further modifications, the final chapter of this book will look at these three paradigms and consider ways that Bible colleges, individually and corporately, can respond to the inevitable challenges that will confront the movement.

CHAPTER TWELVE

CRITICAL ISSUES
AND FUTURE DIRECTIONS

North American Bible colleges have survived longer than their critics would have thought possible, and they have endured for more decades than many of their early premillennialist leaders hoped would have been necessary. More than one-hundred years after the first Bible school was started, there are an estimated 500 Bible institutes and Bible colleges in the United States and Canada, some of which still bear a resemblance to their forbears. For example, the current curriculum for Bible colleges accredited by AABC still includes a core of biblical and theological studies, along with general studies (liberal arts) and professional studies. This is supplemented with practical Christian ministry assignments through which students apply what has been learned in the classroom. Furthermore, the ethos of the Bible college can still be described as evangelical, disciplined, devotional, and focused on spiritual formation.

Most of the AABC Bible colleges offer programs in biblical studies, pastoral ministry, Christian education, and music. Many also provide programs in elementary and perhaps secondary education, youth ministries, urban ministries, and business administration. A few even offer specialized programs in such areas as deaf ministries, social work, aviation, and other technology-oriented fields.

Increasing numbers of Bible colleges have qualified for various forms of accreditation or have university recognized education. Many of the longer-standing institutions now hold membership with the Accrediting Association of Bible Colleges and possibly with one of the regional accrediting associations. Urged on by these associations and by prevailing educational norms, Bible college educators have expanded their programs, incorporated more liberal arts subjects into the curriculum, and graduated increasing numbers of students with standard bachelor of arts and bachelor of science degrees. Some of the larger Bible colleges have even established their own seminaries or graduate divisions. Their library holdings have expanded. Their administrators have received appropriate training for their specific tasks. Their faculty members have earned graduate degrees and claimed time off for conducting research and attending professional meetings in their fields. In short, Bible colleges have become more recognized within the larger academic community.

In spite of these successes, Bible colleges face a somewhat ambiguous future. Struggles with limited financial resources, smaller student bodies, and meager endowments continue to make them more vulnerable than other types of church-related institutions. With the growth of Christian liberal arts colleges and universities and the increasing role of evangelical seminaries, some have questioned whether Bible colleges continue to play a vital educational role. What conclusions should be drawn about their future impact and future identity? While this self assessment may be viewed by some as negative, it could be very positive. It may be time for Bible colleges to carefully evaluate their mission, their programs, and their contributions to the church and society.

In 1980 Kenneth Gangel predicted that increasing numbers of Bible colleges would shift from a "traditional" model with an exclusive commitment to vocational ministry and an emphasis on terminal ministry training to a "progressive" model where the commitment would be to vocational training with a broader definition of ministry.[1] More recently, Robert C. Kallgren stated, "If Bible colleges do not face the future, these hardy little institutions may just disappear."[2] This prediction has become a reality as some schools have been forced to close, merge with other institutions, or make significant changes in order to survive.

As Bible colleges prepare to move into the twenty-first century, what are the critical issues that they must face? What is the future direction of the Bible college movement? What must these institutions do if they are to continue to be relevant?

CRITICAL ISSUES FOR BIBLE COLLEGES

In response to these critical questions that have been raised about the future direction of Bible colleges in North America, the author of this book offers the following recommendations for consideration. Much like Amos, he is "neither a prophet nor a prophet's son" (Amos 7:14). He will not look into his "crystal ball" and make bold predictions about the future of this educational and religious movement, but he can speak from twenty years of experience in Bible college education.

Institutional mission

A Bible college needs to have a clearly defined vision as it looks to the future. Vision is the essential element of an effective ministry, but it must grow out of the institutional mission. Peter Drucker, *Managing the Non-Profit Organization, Principles and Practices*, contended that "Non-profit organizations exist for the sake of their mission. It is the first task of the leader to make sure that everybody sees the mission, hears the mission, and lives the mission."[3] The mission should be the "raison d'etre," the driving force behind every decision that is made. An institution must choose the particular educational paradigm it will adopt: emphasis placed on exclusively church-related vocational training or inclusion of education for other service-oriented careers. This is not to suggest that one model is better than another. There may be a place for different types of Bible colleges in Christian higher education, but mission-related issues must be addressed.

Commitment to biblical/theological studies at the core of the curriculum. Regardless of the educational model that a college adopts, it is imperative that the Bible remain at the very center of all academic programs. Above all, Bible colleges must remain committed to a concentrated and careful study of the Word of God. A distinguishing quality of the Bible college, in contrast to the Christian liberal arts college or university, is the heavy concentration of courses in biblical/theological studies. The Bible is fundamental to the teaching and preparation for life and ministry.

There is always the danger of forsaking a Bible-centered philosophy of education. The history of higher education in North America bears this out. Holding to the full authority of Scripture can never be taken for granted. The board, administration, faculty, and staff of Bible colleges must affirm and reaffirm their total confidence in the Bible by their professional and personal lives.

On many occasions schools have drifted because academics became all important. Surely the goal must be academic excellence, but always coupled with an unswerving commitment to the Scriptures. The two must be wed together if we are to assure academic integrity along with orthodoxy.

Commitment to integrating faith. Students must be taught how to integrate their faith and learning with the way they live their lives. This starts by affirming that the Bible is at the center of all academic programs. The Scriptures are not only the core of the curriculum, but they must be related to the subject matter of all other courses. Knowing that all truth has its ultimate source in God, it must be pursued with honest, open, and thoughtful inquiry. This type of integration takes place through classroom instruction and through practical leadership and outreach opportunities. Students need to be encouraged to make sound judgments in matters of life and conduct. They need to be taught to think, act, and even react from a biblical world and life view.

Making connections between faith, living, and learning is a primary purpose of a Bible college education. Faculty, staff, and students make these necessary connections by establishing and maintaining relationships. The result is more than academic process; it is more than sharpening professional skills; it is more than getting a degree that will lead to a better job. It is learning how to relate one's faith in practical terms to others so that there can be a conscious influence for Christ in the world.

Commitment to academic excellence. As was pointed out at the beginning of this chapter, more Bible colleges have received recognition with different accrediting bodies or have negotiated for transfer credit with universities. Through the influence of prevailing educational norms, Bible colleges have expanded their programs, added more course offerings, and graduated more students with standard bachelor's degrees. More Bible college faculty are engaging in research and writing and making key contributions to the larger academic community. Library holdings are expanding for Bible colleges, and these institutions are also beginning to take advantage of new instructional technology. These types of academic advancements should be perceived as positive. Bible colleges can be academically respectable and still foster a heart for Christian service.

Educational flexibility

Bible colleges must remain educationally flexible in order to relate to the needs of a contemporary culture. The founding of the early Bible schools was in response to perceived needs of both church and society. For example, biblical training for the laity, more foreign missionaries, and evangelism in urban centers were the perceived needs to which Bible school founders responded. Throughout its history, the Bible college movement has adjusted its curricula to meet the needs of the time. The same cultural sensitivity must prevail. While holding a grip on the prominence and authority of the Bible, our colleges need to keep their training programs current with today's needs just as their leaders did in the past.

Improved academic delivery systems

Recognizing the need for educational flexibility, Bible colleges must always be looking for new and improved ways to provide quality education. Institutions must be looking for new groups of students, new geographic centers and even new curricula to complement the present student bodies and educational programs. The employment needs and opportunities of society in general, and the church and Christian organizations in particular, are becoming more varied, which will also necessitate adding to or modifying the present programs. If institutions are going to attract more and different students, they must develop new academic delivery systems such as instructional technology, distance education, and other forms of continuing education to attract nontraditional students.

With regard to technology, Bible colleges have traditionally provided instruction through oral communication and the printed media, but it must be realized that today's generation wants to be educated increasingly for media experience and interaction. Computers and other forms of media learning, such as the Internet are here to stay. Bible colleges need to be proactive in relationship to instructional technology rather than being forced to catch up. Technology provides an opportunity for teaching eternal values to those who are part of this information age.

Strengthened enrollment management efforts

It is imperative that Bible colleges develop a more comprehensive approach to enrollment management given the fact that institutional budgets are so largely student-driven. Successful management begins at the point of initial contact with a prospective student and continues until graduation. An assertive approach to recruitment and retention must be directed that provides a steady supply of qualified students to ensure institutional growth and vitality. Involved in this strategy are recruitment, financial aid, academic advising, academic assistance, orientation, student services, and a comprehensive approach to retention that utilizes all faculty and staff.

Strengthened commitment to quality student service

The quality of life for students in process of maturation is important for fostering growth and development to full potential for the Lord's service. This type of growth can take place through classroom instruction, chapel services, student ministries, and a wide variety of co-curricular activities. But student development also grows out of the informal interactions of all members of the academic community. Bible colleges have the responsibility for the development of complete, holistic students—the physical, mental, emotional, social, and spiritual dimensions of their lives.

Students should be provided with the highest quality experience possible while attending college. This involves both attending to needs and enriching lives. Students are important!

Appropriate response to a changing student population

The world of North American higher education is changing in respect to the student population, not only in terms of size but also composition. This demographic revolution consists of rising and falling numbers of younger and older students, male and female students, and various racial and ethnic groups. With more internationals, more racial and ethnic minorities, more women, and an older student population, various approaches to theological education must be developed. The focus of the early Bible schools was on students who were not being equipped for service through traditional education. Today's Bible colleges must also demonstrate the same kind of sensitivity and commitment to training, especially nontraditional students.

Factored into this demographic sensitivity is the need for greater attention being given to the laity who are involved in a wide array of valuable ministries within the contemporary church. The early Bible schools provided training for men and women, regardless of their age. In most cases they were not preparing large numbers of clergy and other religious professionals, but rather they were equipping laity for the work of the ministry. Perhaps Bible colleges need to return to some of these early values.

Increased participation in graduate education

When the early Bible schools were formed, they were a terminal type of training school for those who were not attending degree-granting colleges, universities, or seminaries. The training received in the Bible college was often considered adequate for those pursuing a church-related vocation. The expectations of today's churches and parachurch organizations, however, have changed. A seminary degree or some type of graduate training is often expected of pastors and church leaders. Bible college education is becoming less terminal and more foundational for career preparation.

THE ACCREDITING ASSOCIATION OF BIBLE COLLEGES REVISITED

Just as Bible colleges are being forced to examine a number of critical issues related to their future viability, the same is true for the movement's major accrediting body, the Accrediting Association of Bible Colleges. This year marks the Fiftieth Anniversary of AABC. After a half century of providing standardization and accountability for North American Bible colleges, the following questions must be asked: What is the future of the Accrediting Association of Bible Colleges? Can AABC remain a healthy and vital force for Bible colleges as we move into the twenty-first century?

Concerns

There are particular concerns that the Accrediting Association of Bible Colleges must address as the organization looks to the future. First, there is the problem of declining membership. Twenty-eight colleges have voluntarily left the association over the past forty years. More alarming, 16 (or more than half) of those institutions have withdrawn within the last decade. Although the membership count has remained stable because of new institutions, the total student enrollment and the corresponding income to AABC has declined.

Second, there is the apparent competition between the regional accrediting associations and AABC. According to the

1995-1996 *AABC Directory*, 25 of the member schools now have regional accreditation. If one excludes Canadian institutions (since regional accreditation is not available), 36 percent of the American AABC colleges have membership with one of the six regional accrediting bodies. As Bible colleges achieve regional accreditation, their need for AABC is reduced. Of the 28 colleges that have withdrawn from AABC, 18 did so within ten years of obtaining regional accreditation.[4] In his plenary address at the 1996 conference, AABC President Robert E. Picirilli reminded the delegates that regional accreditation "has become as much of a problem for AABC as a blessing for our institutions."[5]

Third, there is the ongoing tension surrounding the definition question—what constitutes a Bible college? Some desire to define a Bible college more narrowly. Colleges of this persuasion have adopted a more "traditional" paradigm. The more common "progressive" model allows for a broader approach to academic programming. Finally, as the smaller contingent of "evolving" colleges move toward a comprehensive liberal arts college or university, it likely means a further exodus from AABC. Some who favor the more traditional approach feel that not taking a stronger stand on the issue simply dilutes the distinctives of the Bible college. Others who favor a broader approach are just as convinced that this narrowness is holding the association back. The fact remains, however, that there are differences of opinion within AABC ranks about the defining essence of a Bible college.

Recommendations

In view of the uncertain future of the Accrediting Association of Bible colleges, the following are presented for consideration and possible implementation.

First, *a broader, more flexible definition of a Bible college* may be in order. The definition of a Bible college is not recorded in Scripture nor has it been handed down from heaven. The early Bible training schools, the Bible institutes, and now the Bible colleges have always been in a state of change in relationship to curricula and programming. This is inevitable given that these institutions have attempted to respond to the changing needs of the church, higher education, and society at large over the past 115 years.

We may need to be reminded that the early Bible schools were founded primarily to train the laity rather than the professional religious workers. These formative institutions taught primarily Bible along with a few practical ministry skills. General education was not part of the curriculum. Graduate-level education was not an expectation of most churches and missionary organizations when it came to staff, and so the Bible schools were able to serve as terminal institutions for theological education. The needs and expectations of evangelical church leaders have changed, but the same could be said of the laity who also assume significant ministry roles in today's contemporary church. Simply put, the needs of the church do change and require different types of training. Is it possible that God has called some Bible colleges to a different mission than others? Does every Bible college have to be defined exactly the same way in terms of professional programs and number of courses in Bible or theology? Why can't different educational paradigms be present in the same association if each institution is committed to thorough biblical instruction and is equally committed to preparing students for life and service? Shouldn't there be more flexibility relative to how broad or how narrow we choose to define the Bible college?

Second, *a reexamination of AABC membership requirements and standards* may be needed. Knowing that the association has lost a significant number of schools as they have evolved into more comprehensive institutions, is it possible that some of these schools would have stayed or would consider returning if a little more latitude is given in terms of the Bible college definition? What would be the possibility of several different categories of membership, allowing for those who define the Bible college more narrowly or more broadly.

There are also several hundred Bible institutes and colleges in the United States and Canada that will probably never be able to meet present AABC criteria because of limited resources and small student bodies. Yet they are providing clear biblical instruction and maintain some type of ministry focus. Is it possible for AABC to develop a nonmember affiliate status much like the Coalition of Christian Colleges and Universities has done in allowing into association Christian institutions that did not fit the traditional Christian liberal arts model? Colleges in affiliate status would be permitted to take advantage of academic publications, conferences, and other professional development opportunities. Why couldn't AABC provide similar professional stimulation and interaction for the many smaller Bible schools and colleges? This would not have to involve a lowering of accreditation standards.

Third, and perhaps most importantly, there is a need for *unity and tolerance within the Accrediting Association of Bible Colleges*. As the discussions continue in terms of definition, membership requirements, and even the future direction of AABC, there will be a wide variety of perspectives. As these views are exchanged, it must be done in an open, nonthreatening atmosphere where there is a respect for diversity. There needs to be a strong demonstration of unity within the Bible college ranks, particularly in regard to AABC's evangelical theological statement, a core of biblical and theological studies, and a shared purpose of educating students for service-oriented ministries. But there also needs to be respect, mutual understanding, and appreciation for how different institutions and individuals carry out the work of Bible-centered higher education. Randall Bell, executive director of the Accrediting Association of Bible Colleges, stated it most accurately,

> We live in a day and age of high expectations and low commitment. If the Bible college movement is going to be a strong force in theological education, member schools of AABC must become a more united community in affirming and implementing the mission of training students for the church of Jesus Christ.[6]

AFFIRMATION OF CORE VALUES

As we move closer to the twenty-first century, there are many challenges that face the Bible college movement as well as the Accrediting Association of Bible Colleges. Will it be possible for Bible college education to remain distinctive and yet varied? Is it possible for Bible colleges to teach an increasing number of liberal arts and professional courses and still maintain a strong core of biblical studies? Is it possible to gain broader academic recognition and still be firmly tied to a rich evangelical heritage? Can an institution be academically respectable and still foster a heart for Christian service?

The answers to these questions will help to determine the future direction of Bible colleges. It must be remembered, however, that Bible colleges will change. They have to change if they are going to remain relevant. This has been the pattern of this educational and religious movement for the past 115 years as it has adjusted its curricula and programs to meet the needs of a changing church and a changing society. The same type of sensitivity to time and culture must continue. Bible colleges must remain flexible in order to respond to current needs, and more specifically as we move into the next millennium.

Yes, change is inevitable within Christian higher education. In fact, it may even be good. There are, however, two core values that need to be affirmed if the Bible college movement is going to be true to itself. These are distinctives that should not be compromised. They must not be open for negotiation.

First, there must be *an affirmation to solid biblical instruction*. Clear, faithful teaching of God's word must continue to be a hallmark of the Bible college. Knowing that we live in a postmodern world where truth is perceived to be highly relative, today's college students more than even before need to be biblically literate. They need to know the Bible and know how to relate it to their world. If there were ever a time when Bible-centered education was needed, it is now. Regardless of the professional programs that an institution offers, Bible must be at the core of the curriculum. Robert Picirilli stated convincingly, "More than ever they (students) need the Bible, and Bible colleges can give them that better than anyone. Surely at least this is part of our distinctive mission."[7]

There is a second core value that is equally important. There must be *an affirmation to equip students for service in the church and society*. This is the primary reason why the Bible college movement was called into existence. Bible colleges have provided trained workers, professionals and laity, for over one-hundred years. Their alumni are a major force within North American churches and parachurch ministries and around the world. The last thing Bible colleges want is for that pattern to change.

Yet the needs of the contemporary church and related ministries may be changing. Although there will always be the need for workers in traditional pastoral and cross-cultural ministries, there are a wider variety of ministry opportunities available today. Bible colleges need to respond to such opportunities by offering the appropriate programs where possible. There is also a greater need for qualified lay people who are equipped to serve in ministries in the church as well as in marketplace vocations. Why shouldn't the Bible college be involved in this type of training? Every Bible college must be committed to equipping students for service in Christ's church in whatever form that takes.

The spiritual needs of the world, in depth and scope, are greater now than ever before. The issue is not whether there is a need for equipping Christians for service, but rather, how will the need be met most effectively. Although academic models such as the theological seminary play a vital role, the Bible college must continue to carry out the critical ministry of equipping students for His service.

APPENDICES

APPENDIX I

CURRENT AABC ACCREDITED COLLEGES
(FALL 1996)

Alaska Bible College (AK)
American Baptist College (TN)
Appalachian Bible College (WV)
Arizona College of the Bible (AZ)
Arlington Baptist College (TX)
Baptist Bible College (MO)
Baptist Bible College of Pennsylvania (PA)
Barclay College (KS)
Bethany Bible College (NB)
Boise Bible College (ID)
Briercrest Bible College (SK)
Calvay Bible College (MO)
Canadian Bible College (SK)
Catherine Booth Bible College (MB)
Central Bible College (MO)
Central Christian College of the Bible (MO)
Cincinnati Bible College (OH)
Circleville Bible College (OH)
Clear Creek Baptist Bible College (KY)
Colegio Biblico Pentecostal (PR)
Columbia Bible College (BC)
Columbia International University (SC)
Crown College (MN)
Dallas Christian College (TX)
East Coast Bible College (NC)
Eastern Pentecostal Bible College (ON)
Emmanuel Bible College (ON)
Emmaus Bible College (IA)
Eugene Bible College (OR)
Faith Baptist Bible College (IA)
Florida Christian College (FL)
Free Will Baptist Bible College (TN)
God's Bible School and College (OH)
Grace Bible College (MI)
Grace University (NE)
Great Lakes Christian College (MI)
Heritage Baptist College (ON)
Hobe Sound Bible College (FL)

International Bible College (AL)
John Wesley College (NC)
Johnson Bible College (TN)
Kentucky Christian College (KY)
Kentucky Mountain Bible College (KY)
L.I.F.E. Bible College (CA)
Lancaster Bible College (PA)
Lincoln Christian College (IL)
Magnolia Bible College (MS)
Manhattan Christian College (KS)
Mid-America Bible College (OK)
Minnesota Bible College (MN)
Moody Bible Institute (IL)
Multnomah Bible College (OR)
Nazarene Bible College (CO)
Nebraska Christian College (NE)
North American Baptist College (AB)
Northwest Baptist Theological College (BC)
Oak Hills Bible College (SW)
Ontario Bible College (ON)
Ozark Christian College (MO)
Philadelphia College of Bible (PA)
Piedmont Bible College (NC)
Practical Bible College (NY)
Providence College (MB)
Puget Sound Christian College (WA)
Reformed Bible College (MI)
Roanoke Bible College (NC)
Rocky Mountain College (AB)
St. Louis Christian College (MO)
San Jose Christian College (CA)
Southeastern Baptist College (MS)
Southeastern Bible College (AL)
Southeastern College of the Assemblies of God (FL)
Southwestern Assemblies of God University (TX)
Southwestern College (AZ)
Steinbach Bible College (MB)
Tennessee Temple University (TN)
Toccoa Falls College (GA)
Trinity Bible College (ND)
Trinity College of Florida (FL)
Valley Forge Christian College (PA)
Washington Bible College (MD)
Wesley College (MS
Western Pentecostal Bible College (BC)

APPENDIX II

HISTORY OF THE AABC MEMBERSHIP:
INCEPTION TO PRESENT (1947-1997)
(as of 1/2/97)

Because of the variance in terminology in the following table of colleges, an explanation is in order.

In the early years of the association, there were two levels of accreditation with two sets of criteria. The "Intermediate" level was to accommodate schools where secondary school education was not readily available. Some of these schools "had a high proportion of non-high school graduates. Also, faculty qualifications and library resources were in some cases detrimental to the achieving of 'collegiate level' status" (Mostert, *AABC Story*, 55, 57-59).

In the fall of 1953, a committee was appointed to "study the advisability of reorganizing the Intermediate Division into 'Associate Membership.' Delegates attending the 8th Annual Meeting approved the action." Thus 'Associate' membership was ratified at this meeting. The former dual approach to standards was done away and decisions about a college's status started to be based on degree of conformity to one set of criteria (Mostert, 58-59). (For a more indepth discussion of this issue, see Mostert, 38, 42-43, 47-48, 52, 55, 57-59.)

In 1974 the designation "Candidate for Accreditation" came into usage, replacing the term "Associate" membership. While "Associate" status could be held by a college for an indefinite period of time, five consecutive years was the limit that a college could remain in candidate status. The new terminology came to designate "pre-accredited status granted to those colleges that show promise of achieving accreditation within four years" (*1995-96 Manual*, 5).

Applicant status is a "pre-membership status granted to those colleges that meet the association's Conditions of Eligibility and that possess such qualitites as may provide a basis for achieving candidate status within four years" (*1995-96 Manual*, 5).

Colleges marked with an asterisk (*) are current AABC members that were charter accredited colleges. Colleges that attended the 1947 organizing meeting but did not immediately pursue membership are shown by ‡.

Alaska Bible College, Glennallen, AK
Applicant 1974; Candidate 1977; Accredited 1982-present

Aldersgate College, Moose Jaw, SK
Applicant 1980; Candidate 1981-85; Applicant 1992-95 (closed)

Allentown Bible Institute, Allentown, PA
Accredited (Collegiate level) 1952-54
Name changed to Eastern Pilgrim College (1954)

American Baptist College, Nashville, TN
Associate 1962; Accredited 1971-present
Name changed from American Baptist College of the Bible (1964)

Appalachian Bible College, Bradley, WV
Associate 1960; Accredited 1967-present

Arizona College of the Bible, Phoenix, AZ
Applicant 1977; Candidate 1978; Accredited 1981-present

Arlington Baptist College, Arlington, TX
Applicant 1975; Candidate 1977; Accredited 1981-present
Name changed from Bible Baptist Seminary (1974)

Atlanta Bible Institute, Atlanta, GA
Intermediate 1948-1952

Atlanta Christian College, East Point, GA
Associate 1960; Accredited 1965-94 (voluntary withdrawal)

Atlantic Baptist College, Moncton, NB
Applicant 1984-87

Azusa College, Azusa, CA
Accredited (Collegiate level) 1948-75

Baptist Bible College, Springfield, MO
Applicant 1974; Candidate 1975; Accredited 1978-present

Baptist Bible College-East, Boston, MA
Applicant 1984-86

Baptist Bible College of Indianapolis, Indianapolis, IN
Applicant 1992-present

Baptist Bible College of Pennsylvania, Clarks Summit, PA
Accredited 1968-present
Original name: Baptist Bible Seminary

Baptist Bible Institute of Cleveland, Cleveland, OH
Accredited (Intermediate level) 1948-53

Barclay College, Haviland, KS
Intermediate 1949; Associate 1954; Candidate 1974; Accredited 1975-present
Name changed from Friends Bible College (1990)

Barrington College, Providence, RI
Accredited (Collegiate level) 1948-68 (voluntary withdrawal)
Name changed from Providence-Barrington Bible College (1959)
Original Name: Providence Bible Institute, Providence, RI

Bartlesville Wesleyan College, Bartlesville, OK
Associate 1965-69
Name changed from Central Pilgrim College (1968)

Bay Ridge Christian College, Kendleton, TX
Applicant 1980-84, 1987-89; Candidate 1989-91 (status withdrawn); Applicant 1992-present

Berean Bible College, Calgary, AB
Applicant 1978-83
Name changed to Foothills Christian College (1983)

Berean Bible School, Allentown, PA
Associate 1958-68
Name changed to Pinebrook Jr. College, East Stroudsburg, PA

Berkshire Christian College, Lenox, MA
Accredited 1959-86 (closed)

Bethany Bible College, Santa Cruz, CA
Intermediate 1948; Associate 1954; Accredited 1959-90
Original Name: Glad Tidings Bible Institute, San Francisco, CA
New Name: Bethany College of the Assemblies of God, Scotts Valley, CA (1990)

Bethany Bible College, Sussex, NB
Applicant 1979; Candidate 1982; Accredited 1987-present

Bethany Bible Institute, Hepburn, SK
Applicant 1979; Candidate 1983-86; Candidate 1996-present

Bethany College of the Assemblies of God, Scotts Valley, CA
Intermediate 1948; Associate 1954; Accredited 1959-92 (voluntary withdrawal)
Original Name: Glad Tidings Bible Institute, San Francisco, CA
Previous Name: Bethany Bible College, Santa Cruz, CA (1980)

Bethesda Christian University, Anaheim, CA
Applicant 1992-present
Moved from Whittier to Anaheim (1995)

Bible Baptist Seminary, Arlington, TX
Name changed to Arlington Baptist College (1974)

Bible Institute of Los Angeles, Los Angeles, CA
Accredited (Collegiate level) 1948-54
Name changed to Biola Bible College (1955)

Big Sky Bible College, Lewistown, MT
Applicant 1975; Candidate 1977-84
Name changed from Montana Institute of the Bible (1980)

Biola Bible College, Los Angeles, CA
Accredited (Collegiate level) 1948-86
Name changed from Bible Institute of Los Angeles (1955) (later Biola)

Boise Bible College, Boise, ID
Applicant 1977; Candidate 1982; Accredited 1988-present

Briercrest Bible College, Caronport, SK
Applicant 1972; Associate/Candidate 1973; Accredited 1976-present

Buffalo Bible Institute, Buffalo, NY
Intermediate 1948; Associate 1954; Accredited 1958-59

California Christian College, Fresno, CA
Applicant 1974-75; 1979-81

California Lutheran Bible School, Anaheim, CA
Applicant 1980-82
Name changed to Lutheran Bible Institute of California

California Union University, Norwalk, CA
Applicant 1992-95 (status withdrawn)

Calvary Bible College, Kansas City, MO
Intermediate 1948; Accredited (Collegiate level) 1954-present
Name changed from Kansas City Bible College 1961

Canadian Bible College, Regina, SK
Associate 1960; Accredited 1961-present

‡Carver Bible Institute, Kansas City, MO

Catherine Booth Bible College, Winnipeg, MB
Applicant 1984; Candidate 1987; Accredited 1991-present

Central Baptist Bible College, Toronto, ON
Applicant 1986-89

Central Baptist College, Conway, AR
Associate; Candidate 1973; Accredited 1977-95 (voluntary withdrawal)

*Central Bible College, Springfield, MO
Accredited (Collegiate level) 1948-present
See Great Lakes Bible Institute, Zion, IL

Central Christian College of the Bible, Moberly, MO
Applicant 1977; Candidate 1980; Accredited 1982-present

Central Florida Bible College, Orlando, FL
Applicant 1979; Candidate 1980-85
Name changed to Florida Christian College, Kissimmee, FL (1985)

Central Indian Bible College, Mobridge, SD
Applicant 1988; Candidate 1992-96 (voluntary withdrawal)

Central Pentecostal College, Saskatoon, SK
Applicant 1988-92; Candidate 1992-present

Central Pilgrim College, Bartlesville, OK
Associate 1965-67
Name changed to Bartlesville Wesleyan College

Central Wesleyan College, Central, SC
Accredited 1955-63
Name changed from Wesleyan Methodist College (1958)

Chicago Evangelistic Institute, Chicago, IL
Accredited (Collegiate level) 1948-51

Moved to University Park, IA (1951); name changed to Vennard
College (1959)

Christian Training Institute, Edmonton, AB
Associate 1963-67
Name changed to North American Baptist College (1967)

Cincinnati Bible College, Cincinnati, OH
Accredited 1966-present

Circleville Bible College, Circleville, OH
Associate; Candidate 1973; Accredited 1976-present

Clear Creek Baptist Bible College, Pineville, KY
Applicant 1979; Candidate 1981; Accredited 1986-present

Cleveland Bible College, Cleveland, OH
Accredited (Collegiate level) 1953-54

Colegio Biblico Pentecostal De Puerto Rico, Saint Just, PR
Applicant 1980-83, 1985; Candidate 1986; Accredited 1990-present

Colegio Pentecostal Mizpa, Rio Piedras, PR
Applicant 1992-present

College of Biblical Studies, Houston, TX
Applicant 1992-present
Name changed from Houston Bible Institute (1996)

Colorado Christian University, Lakewood, CO
Associate 1969; Accredited 1974-94 (voluntary withdrawal)
Merger between Western Bible College, Denver, CO, and Rockmont
College, Longmont, CO, to form Colorado Christian College (1985)
Name changed from Colorado Christian College (1988)

Columbia Bible College, Abbotsford, BC
Applicant 1984; Candidate 1985; Accredited 1991-present

Columbia Bible College, Columbia, SC
Accredited (Collegiate level) 1948-95
Corporate name, Columbia International University, instituted (1995)

Columbia International University, Columbia, SC
Accredited (Collegiate level) 1948-present
See Columbia Bible College, Columbia, SC (1995)

Crichton College, Memphis, TN
Associate 1968; Accredited 1971-89 (voluntary withdrawal)
Name changed from Mid-South Bible College

Criswell Center for Biblical Studies, Dallas, TX
Applicant 1974; Candidate 1977; Accredited 1979-89
Name changed to The Criswell College (1989)

(The) Criswell College, Dallas, TX
Applicant 1974; Candidate 1977; Accredited 1979-90 (voluntary
    withdrawal)
Name changed from Criswell Center for Biblical Studies (1989)

Crown College, St. Bonifacius, MN
Accredited (Collegiate level) 1949; Accredited 1950-present
Original name: Saint Paul Bible Institute; changed to St. Paul Bible
    College (1958); name changed from Saint Paul Bible College (1991)

Dallas Bible College, Dallas, TX
Associate 1967; Accredited 1971-85
Name changed to Woodcrest College, Lindale, TX (1985)

Dallas Christian College, Dallas, TX
Applicant 1974; Candidate 1976; Accredited 1978-present

Denver Baptist Bible College, Broomfield, CO
Applicant 1974-78; Candidate 1978-83, 1985-86
Moved from Denver (1975)
Merged with Faith Baptist College (1986)

‡Denver Bible College, Denver, CO
Accredited (Intermediate level) 1948-49
Name changed to Rockmont College (1949)

Detroit Bible College, Detroit, MI
Accredited (Collegiate level) 1954-81
Name changed to William Tyndale College, Farmington Hills, MI
    (1981)
Moved from Detroit to Southfield (1976) and then to Farmington
    Hills (1978)

East Coast Bible College, Charlotte, NC
Applicant 1979; Candidate 1980; Accredited 1985-present

Eastern Bible Institute, Green Lane, PA
Intermediate 1949; Associate 1954-62

Name changed to Northeast Bible Institute (also known as Northeast
Bible College)

Eastern Christian College, Bel Air, MD
Applicant 1994-95 (voluntary withdrawal)
Became Branch Campus of Lincoln Christian College (1996)

Eastern Pentecostal Bible College, Peterborough, ON
Applicant 1983; Candidate 1986; Accredited 1989-present

Eastern Pilgrim College, Allentown, PA
Accredited (Collegiate level) 1954-70
Original Name: Allentown Bible Institute (1952-54)
New Name: Penn Wesleyan College (1970)

Elm Springs Bible College, Elm Springs, AR
Applicant 1996-present

Emmanuel Bible College, Kitchener, ON
Applicant 1975; Candidate 1979; Accredited 1982-present

**Emmanuel College School of Christian Ministries, Franklin Springs,
GA**
Applicant 1974; Candidate 1977; Accredited 1979-93 (voluntary
withdrawal)

Emmaus Bible College, Dubuque, IA
Intermediate 1948; Associate 1954-63; Applicant 1979; Candidate
1982; Accredited 1986-present
Original name: Emmaus Bible School; name changed to Emmaus
Bible College and moved from Oak Park, IL (1984)

Eugene Bible College, Eugene, OR
Applicant 1974; Candidate 1980; Accredited 1983-present
Merged with Open Bible College (1986)

Faith Baptist Bible College, Ankeny, IA
Associate 1964; Accredited 1969-present

Florida Baptist College, Lakeland, FL
Applicant 1975-76

Florida Bible College, Miramar, FL
Applicant 1981; Candidate 1984; Accredited 1989-96 (accreditation
withdrawn)
Moved from Kissimmee (1996); closed (1996).

Florida Christian College, Kissimmee, FL
Applicant 1979; Candidate 1980; Accredited 1985-present
Name changed from Central Florida Bible College, Orlando, FL
(1985)

Foothills Christian College, Calgary, AB
Applicant 1983-85 (closed)

Fort Wayne Bible College, Fort Wayne, IN
Accredited (Collegiate level) 1948-89
Name changed to Summit Christian College

‡Frankfort Holiness College, IN

Free Will Baptist Bible College, Nashville, TN
Accredited 1958-present

Friends Bible College, Haviland, KS
Intermediate 1949; Associate 1954; Candidate 1974; Accredited 1975-
90
Name changed to Barclay College (1990)

Glad Tidings Bible Institute, San Francisco, CA
Intermediate 1948-54
Name changed to Bethany Bible College, Santa Cruz, CA

Glen Cove Bible College, Glen Cove, ME
Applicant 1974-76

God's Bible School and College, Cincinnati, OH
Applicant 1979; Candidate 1982; Accredited 1986-present
Name changed from God's Bible College (1994)

Grace Bible College, Grand Rapids, MI
Accredited 1964-present

*Grace University, Omaha, NE
Accredited (Collegiate level) 1948-present
Name changed from Grace College of the Bible (1995)

Graham Bible College, Bristol, TN
Applicant 1977-85

‡Grand Rapids Baptist Bible College, Grand Rapids, MI
Accredited 1964-75
See Grand Rapids School of the Bible & Music

Grand Rapids School of the Bible & Music, Grand Rapids, MI
  Applicant 1988-93 (voluntary withdrawal)
  Moved from Comstock Park, MI (1991); merged with Grand Rapids
    Baptist College and Seminary (1993)

Great Lakes Bible Institute, Zion, IL
  Accredited (Intermediate level) 1949-54
  Merged with Central Bible Institute, Springfield, MO (1955)

Great Lakes Christian College, Lansing, MI
  Associate; Candidate 1973; Accredited 1977-present
  Name changed from Great Lakes Bible College (1992)

Gulf Coast Bible College, Houston, TX
  Associate 1966; Accredited 1968-85
  Name changed to Mid-America Bible College and moved to Okla-
    homa City, OK (1985)

Heritage Baptist College, Cambridge, ON
  Applicant 1986; Candidate 1991; Accredited 1996-present
  Name changed from London Baptist College (1993)
  Moved from London to Cambridge (1996)

Heritage Bible College, Dunn, NC
  Applicant 1974-75, 1994-present

Hillcrest Christian College, Medicine Hat, AB
  Applicant 1979; Candidate 1983; Accredited 1989-92
  Name changed from Hillcrest Bible Institute
  Merged with Mountain View Bible College, Didsbury, AB and
    renamed Rocky Mountain Bible College, Calgary, AB (1992)

Hobe Sound Bible College, Hobe Sound, FL
  Applicant 1974-76, 1980; Candidate 1981; Accredited 1986-present

Houston Bible Institute, Houston, TX
  Applicant 1992-present
  Name changed to College of Biblical Studies—Houston, Houston, TX
    (1996)

Independent Baptist College, Dallas, TX
  Applicant 1981-83, 1987-90 (voluntary withdrawal)

Intermountain Bible College, Grand Junction, CO
  Applicant 1980-84

International Bible College, Florence, AL
Applicant 1981; Candidate 1984; Accredited 1988-present

International Bible College, San Antonio, TX
Applicant 1979-82; 1984-86; 1992-95; Candidate 1995-present

International College, Honolulu, HI
Applicant 1974-83

Jimmy Swaggart Bible College, Baton Rouge, LA
Applicant 1986-88

John Wesley College, High Point, NC
Applicant 1974; Candidate 1976; Accredited 1982-present
Name changed from People's Bible Institute (1982)

Johnson Bible College, Knoxville, TN
Associate 1952-56 (voluntary withdrawal); Accredited 1970-present

Kansas City Bible College, Kansas City, MO
Intermediate 1948; Accredited (Collegiate level) 1954-60
Name changed to Calvary Bible College (1961)

Kansas City College & Bible School, Overland Park, KS
Applicant 1985-89

Kentucky Christian College, Grayson, KY
Associate 1961; Accredited 1962-present

Kentucky Mountain Bible College, Vancleve, KY
Intermediate 1948; Associate 1954-57; Applicant 1987; Candidate
    1989; Accredited 1994-present
Name changed from Kentucky Mountain Bible Institute (1990)

Kernersville Wesleyan College, Kernersville, NC
Associate 1961-70
Name changed from Southern Pilgrim College

L.I.F.E. Bible College, San Dimas, CA
Applicant 1974; Candidate 1976; Accredited 1980-present

Lancaster Bible College, Lancaster, PA
Associate 1959; Accredited 1964-present

Latin American Bible College, LaPuente, CA
Applicant 1981-85

Lee College, Cleveland, TN
Accredited 1959-68

Life Christian University, Gardena, CA
Applicant 1996-present

Lincoln Christian College, Lincoln, IL
Accredited (Collegiate level) 1954-present
Name changed from Lincoln Bible Institute (1961)

London Baptist Bible College, London, ON
Applicant 1986; Candidate 1991-93
Name changed to Heritage Baptist College (1993)

London College of Bible & Missions, London, ON
Associate 1956; Accredited 1959-67
Merged with Toronto Bible College to become Ontario Bible College
    (1968)

Luther Rice Bible College, Jacksonville, FL
Applicant 1981-85

Lutheran Bible Institute of California, Anaheim, CA
Applicant 1981-83
Name changed from California Lutheran Bible School

Lutheran Bible Institute of Seattle, Issaquah, WA
Applicant 1974; Candidate 1975; Accredited 1978-88

Magnolia Bible College, Kosciusko, MS
Applicant 1979-83, 1984; Applicant 1985; Candidate 1986; Accredited
    1989-present

Malone College, Cleveland, OH
Accredited (Collegiate level) 1948-57

*Manhattan Christian College, Manhattan, KS
Accredited (Collegiate level) 1948-present
Name changed from Manhattan Bible College

Manna Bible Institute, Philadelphia, PA
Applicant 1976; Candidate 1981-86; Candidate 1987-90 (status
    withdrawn)

Maranatha Baptist Bible College, Watertown, WI
Applicant 1986-87

‡Martinsville Bible College, Martinsville, VA

Mennonite Brethren Bible College, Winnipeg, MB
Accredited (Collegiate level) 1950-71

Messiah Bible College, Grantham, PA
Accredited (Collegiate level) 1948-57

Metropolitan Bible Institute, North Bergen, NJ
Intermediate 1948-49

Mexican Baptist Bible Institute, San Antonio, TX
Applicant 1979-80

Miami Bible College, Miami, FL
Associate 1969-72 (voluntary withdrawal)
Name changed to Miami Christian College (1974)

Miami Christian College, Miami, FL
Associate 1969-72; Candidate 1974; Accredited 1975-94
Name changed from Miami Bible College (1974)
Merged and renamed Trinity College at Miami (1994); became branch
    campus of Trinity College, Deerfield, IL (1994)

Mid-America Bible College, Oklahoma City, OK
Associate 1966; Candidate 1967; Accredited 1968-present
Name changed from Gulf Coast Bible College, Houston, TX (1985)

Mid-South Bible College, Memphis, TN
Associate 1968; Accredited 1971-86
Name changed to Crichton College

Mid-South Christian College, Senatobia, MS
Applicant 1979-83; 1985-86

Midwest Bible College, St. Louis, MO
Accredited 1959-60

Midwest Christian College, Oklahoma City, OK
Candidate 1974; Accredited 1979-85

Midwestern Baptist College, Pontiac, MI
Applicant 1974-76

*Minnesota Bible College, Rochester, MN
Accredited (Collegiate level) 1948-present

Montana Institute of the Bible, Lewistown, MT
 Applicant 1975; Candidate 1977-80
 Name changed to Big Sky Bible College (1980)

‡Moody Bible Institute, Chicago, IL
 Accredited 1951-present

Mountain View Bible College, Didsbury, AB
 Applicant 1976; Candidate 1981-86
 See Rocky Mountain College, Calgary, AB

Multnomah Bible College, Portland, OR
 Intermediate 1948; Accredited (Collegiate level) 1953-present
 Name changed from Multnomah School of the Bible (1993)

‡National Bible Institute, New York, NY

Nazarene Bible College, Colorado Springs, CO
 Candidate 1974; Accredited 1976-present
 Accredited branch campus: Emmanuel Bible College, Pasadena, CA
  (1991-present)
 Accredited branch campus: Instituto Teologico Nazareno, Baldwin
  Park, CA (1991-96) (closed)
 Accredited branch campus: Nazarene Indian Bible College, Albu-
  querque, NM (1988-present)

Nazarene Indian Bible College, Albuquerque, NM
 Applicant 1983-88 (voluntary withdrawal)
 See Nazarene Bible College, Colorado Springs, CO

Nazarene Spanish-American Bible College, San Antonio, TX
 Applicant 1979-80

Nebraska Christian College, Norfolk, NE
 Applicant 1979; Candidate 1981; Accredited 1985-present

New England Bible Institute, Framingham, MA
 Intermediate 1949; Associate 1954-56

North American Baptist College, Edmonton, AB
 Associate 1963; Candidate 1963; Accredited 1969-present
 Name changed from Christian Training Institute (1967)

North Central Bible College, Minneapolis, MN
 Intermediate 1949; Associate 1954; Accredited 1964-91 (voluntary
  withdrawal)

Northeast Bible College, Green Lane, PA
  Associate 1948; Accredited 1967-1977
  Original Name: Eastern Bible Institute, Green Lane, PA
  New Name: Valley Forge Christian College, Phoenixville, PA (1977)

Northeast Bible Institute
  See Eastern Bible Institute, Green Lane, PA; see also Northeast Bible
    College, Green Lane, PA

Northeastern Bible College, Essex Fells, NJ
  Associate 1956; Accredited 1958-90 (accreditation withdrawn)
  College closed 1990; record custodian: (201) 226-1074

Northwest Baptist Theological College, Langley, BC
  Applicant 1983; Candidate 1985; Accredited 1989-present
  Name changed from Northwest Baptist Bible College

Northwest Bible College, Kirkland, WA
  Accredited (Collegiate level) 1952-61
  Name changed to Northwest College of the Assemblies of God
  See Northwest College

Northwest Bible College, Edmonton, AB
  Applicant 1992-present

Northwest Bible College, Minot, ND
  Associate 1966; Accredited 1974-87 (closed)

Northwest College, Kirkland, WA
  Accredited (Collegiate level) 1952-95 (voluntary withdrawal)
  Name changed from Northwest Bible College
  Also known as Northwest College of the Assemblies of God

Northwestern College, Roseville, MN
  Applicant 1980-82

‡Northwestern Schools, Minneapolis, MN

Nyack Missionary College, Nyack, NY
  Accredited (Collegiate level) 1948-69

Oak Hills Bible College, Bemidji, MN
  Applicant 1985; Candidate 1987; Accredited 1990-present
  Name changed from Oak Hills Bible Institute (1989)

Okanagan Bible Institute, Kelowna, BC
  Applicant 1982-88 (voluntary withdrawal)

Omaha Baptist Bible College, Omaha NE
Associate 1964-66

Ontario Bible College, North York, ON
Associate 1956; Accredited 1959-present
Result of merger between London College of Bible & Missions,
    London, ON, and Toronto Bible College, Toronto, ON (1968)

Open Bible College, Des Moines, IA
Associate; Candidate 1962; Accredited 1977-86
Merged with Eugene Bible College (1986)

Owasso Bible College, Owasso, MI
Accredited (Collegiate level) 1950-61

Ozark Christian College, Joplin, MO
Applicant 1982; Candidate 1985; Accredited 1988-present
Name changed from Ozark Bible College

Pacific Bible College, Azusa, CA
Accredited (Collegiate level) 1948-1956

Pacific Bible Institute, Fresno, CA
Accredited (Collegiate level) 1949-1954

Pacific Christian College, Fullerton, CA
Accredited 1963-92 (voluntary withdrawal)
Name changed from Pacific Bible Seminary

Patten Bible College, Oakland, CA
Applicant 1974; Candidate 1976-1977

Penn Wesleyan College, Allentown, PA
Accredited 1952-1970
Name changed from Eastern Pilgrim College (1970)
New Name: United Wesleyan College, Allentown, PA (1972)

Philadelphia College of Bible, Langhorne, PA
Accredited (Collegiate level) 1949-present

Piedmont Bible College, Winston-Salem, NC
Associate 1955; Accredited 1956-present

‡Pilgrim Bible College, Kernersville, NC

Pillsbury Baptist Bible College, Owatonna, MN
Applicant 1996-present

Pinebrook Junior College, Coopersburg, PA
Candidate 1989-92 (closed)
Original Name: Berean Bible School, Allentown, PA
Previous Location: East Stroudsburg, PA

Practical Bible College, Bible School Park, NY
Applicant 1979; Candidate 1983; Accredited 1985-present
Name changed from Practical Bible Training School (1993)

Prairie Bible College, Three Hills, AB
Applicant 1989; Candidate 1994-present
Name changed from Prairie Bible Institute

Providence-Barrington Bible College, Providence, RI
Accredited (Collegiate level) 1948-1958
Original Name: Providence Bible Institute
New Name: Barrington College (1959)

Providence Bible Institute, Providence, RI
Accredited (Collegiate level) 1948-1958
New Name: Providence-Barrington Bible College (1954)

Providence College, Otterburne, MB
Associate 1965; Accredited 1973-present
Name changed from Winnipeg Bible College (1991)
Moved from Winnipeg to Otterburne (1970)

Puget Sound Christian College, Edmonds, WA
Applicant 1974; Candidate 1975; Accredited 1979-present
Name changed from Puget Sound College of the Bible (1984)

Reformed Bible College, Grand Rapids, MI
Intermediate 1951; Associate 1954; Accredited 1964-present

Rio Grande Bible Institute, Edinburg, TX
Applicant 1989; Candidate 1994-present
Also known as Rio Grande Bible Institute and Language School

Roanoke Bible College, Elizabeth City, NC
Applicant 1974; Candidate 1976; Accredited 1979-present

Rockmont College, Longmont, CO
Accredited (Collegiate level) 1949; Associate 1958-70
Original Name: Denver Bible Institute, Denver, CO (1949)
Merged with Western Bible College to form Colorado Christian
   College (1985)

Rocky Mountain College, Calgary, AB
Candidate 1983; Accredited 1989-present
Merger: Mountain View Bible College and Hillcrest Christian
   College (1992)

Rosedale Bible Institute, Irwin, OH
Applicant 1992-present

Saint Louis Christian College, Florissant, MO
Candidate 1974; Accredited 1977-present

Saint Paul Bible College, St. Bonifacius, MN
Collegiate; Candidate 1949; Accredited 1950-91
See Crown College (1991)

Salem Bible College, Salem, OR
Applicant 1996-present

San Jose Christian College, San Jose, CA
Associate 1964; Accredited 1969-present
Name changed from San Jose Bible College (1989)

Shasta Bible College, Redding, CA
Applicant 1984-1985

Simpson College, Redding, CA
Accredited (Collegiate level) 1952-91 (voluntary withdrawal)
Moved from San Francisco, CA (1989)
Previous Name: Simpson Bible College

Simpson Bible Institute, Seattle, WA
Accredited (Collegiate level) 1948-49

Southeastern Baptist College, Laurel, MS
Applicant 1980; Candidate 1983; Accredited 1988-present

Southeastern Bible College, Birmingham, AL
Accredited 1962-present

Southeastern College of the Assemblies of God, Lakeland, FL
Intermediate 1948; Accredited 1954-present
Name changed from Southeastern Bible College

Southern Arizona Bible College, Hereford, AZ
Applicant 1983-1986

Southern Bible College, Houston, TX
Associate 1968; Accredited 1973-84 (closed)

Southern California Bible College, Costa Mesa, CA
Accredited (Collegiate level) 1948-1959

Southern Pilgrim College, Kernersville, NC
Associate 1961-1969
New Name: Kernersville Wesleyan College, Kernersville, NC

Southwestern Assemblies of God College, Waxahachie, TX
Accredited (Collegiate level) 1948-95
Original Name: Southwestern Bible Institute, Waxahachie, TX
See Southwestern Assemblies of God University

*Southwestern Assemblies of God University, Waxahachie, TX
Accredited (Collegiate level) 1948-present
Original Name: Southwestern Bible Institute, Waxahachie, TX
Name changed to Southwestern Assemblies of God College
Name changed to Southwestern Assemblies of God University (1995)

Southwestern College, Phoenix, AZ
Associate; Candidate 1972; Accredited 1977-present
Also known as Southwestern Conservative Baptist Bible College

Spurgeon Baptist Bible College, Mulberry, FL
Applicant 1976; Candidate 1981-1986

Steinbach Bible College, Steinbach, MB
Applicant 1979-82, 1984; Candidate 1987; Accredited 1991-present

Summit Christian College, Fort Wayne, IN
Accredited (Collegiate level) 1948-91 (voluntary withdrawal)
Original Name: Fort Wayne Bible College
Merged with Taylor University (1991)

‡Temple Missionary Training School, Fort Wayne, IN

Tennessee Temple University, Chattanooga, TN
   Applicant 1979; Candidate 1980; Accredited 1984-present

Texas Bible College, San Antonio, TX
   Applicant 1989-92 (voluntary withdrawal)

Toccoa Falls College, Toccoa Falls, GA
   Candidate 1953; Accredited 1957-present
   Name changed from Toccoa Falls Bible Institute (1975)

Toronto Bible College, Toronto, ON
   Accredited 1966-67
   Merged with London College of Bible & Missions, London, ON
      (1968) to form Ontario Bible College (1968)

Tri-State Bible College, South Point, OH
   Applicant 1976-85; 1996-present

Trinity Baptist College, Jacksonville, FL
   Applicant 1977-1978

Trinity Bible College, Ellendale, ND
   Applicant 1975; Candidate 1977; Accredited 1980-present

Trinity College of Florida, New Port Richey, FL
   Applicant 1985; Candidate 1990; Accredited 1996-present
   Moved from Holiday, Florida (19??)

Trinity College at Miami, Miami, FL
   Candidate 1969; Accredited 1975-94
   See Miami Christian College

United Wesleyan College, Allentown, PA
   Accredited 1972-91 (closed as of December 31, 1990)
   Original Name: Allentown Bible Institute (1952-54)
   Second Name: Eastern Pilgrim College (1954-70)
   Previous Name: Penn Wesleyan College (1970-72)

Valley Forge Christian College, Phoenixville, PA
   Associate 1948; Candidate 1961; Accredited 1967-present
   Name changed from Northeast Bible College, Green Lane, PA (1977)

Vancouver Bible Institute, Surrey, BC
   Associate 1972; Accredited 1975-1978 (closed)

*Vennard College, University Park, IA
  Accredited (Collegiate level) 1948-95
  Original Name: Chicago Evangelistic Institute, Chicago, IL
  Closed December 31, 1995; reopened fall 1996

Washington Bible College, Lanham, MD
  Associate 1956; Candidate 1957; Accredited 1962-present

Wesley College, Florence, MS
  Applicant 1974; Candidate 1977; Accredited 1979-present
  Name changed from Westminster College and Bible Institute (1976)

Wesleyan Methodist College, Central, SC
  Accredited (Collegiate level) 1955-58
  Name changed to Central Wesleyan College (1958)

West Coast Christian College School of Christian Ministries, Fresno, CA
  Candidate 1974; Accredited 1976-92 (voluntary withdrawal)
  Name changed from Pacific Northwest Bible Institute

Western Baptist College, Salem, OR
  Intermediate 1952; Associate 1954; Accredited 1959-96 (voluntary withdrawal)
  Name changed from Western Baptist Bible College

Western Bible College, Denver, CO
  Associate 1969; Accredited 1974-1985
  Merged with Rockmont College to form Colorado Christian University, Lakewood, CO (1985)

Western Christian College, Dauphin, MB
  Applicant 1996-present

Western Pentecostal Bible College, Clayburn, BC
  Applicant 1976; Candidate 1978; Accredited 1980-present

Westminster College, Florence, MS
  Applicant 1974-1976
  Name changed to Wesley College

Whitworth Bible College, Brookhaven, MS
  Applicant 1981-1982

William Tyndale College, Farmington Hills, MI
  Accredited 1954-93 (voluntary withdrawal)

Moved from Southfield (1978)
Name changed from Detroit Bible College, Detroit, MI (1981)

Winnipeg Bible College, Otterburne, MB
Associate 1965; Accredited 1973-91
Name changed to Providence College (1991)

Woodcrest College, Lindale, TX
Associate 1967; Accredited 1971-86 (closed)
Name changed from Dallas Bible College, Dallas, TX (1985)

Zarephath Bible Institute, Zarephath, NJ
Applicant 1994-present

Zion Bible Institute, Barrington, RI
Applicant 1995-96

NOTES

CHAPTER ONE - INTRODUCTION: A STORY THAT DEMANDS TELLING

[1] *AABC Directory*, 1995-96; annual report data of accredited and candidate colleges, November 1, 1994, reported in 48th annual meeting program book, 24-25.

[2] Lenice F. Reed, "The Bible Institute in America," (Unpublished M.A. thesis, Wheaton College, Illinois, 1947), 1-2.

[3] S. A. Witmer, *The Bible College Story: Education with Dimension* (New York: Channel Press, Inc. 1962), 18.

[4] *AABC Brochure*, 1995.

[5] John Mostert, *Bible College Distinctives* (Wheaton, Illinois: American Association of Bible Colleges, 1969), 5-6.

[6] George Sweeting, "Understanding America's Bible School Movement," *Moody Monthly* (March 1984), 100.

[7] *Ibid.*

[8] C. A. Beard, "Written History as an Act of Faith," *American Historical Review*, XLIX (1934), 219-231.

[9] Louis R. Gottschalk, *Understanding History: A Primer of History Method* (New York: The University of Chicago Press, 1964), 9.

CHAPTER TWO - NORTH AMERICAN PROTESTANTISM: *1882-1920*

[1] Sydney E. Ahlstrom, *A Religious History of the American People* (New Haven and London: Yale University Press, 1972), 823-824.

[2] *Ibid.*, 824.

[3] Arthur M. Schlesinger, Sr., *A Critical Period in American Religion, 1875-1900* (Philadelphia: Fortress Press, 1967), 1.

[4] Robert T. Handy, *The History of the Churches in the United States and Canada* New York: Oxford University Press, 1977), 344.

[5] *Ibid*, 352.

[6] John Webster Grant, *The Church in the Canadian Era* (Burlington, Ontario: Welch Publishing Company Inc., 1988), 60.

[7] Louis Gaspar, *The Fundamentalist Movement* (Paris: Milton and Company, 1963), 8.

[8] George W. Dollar, "The Early Days of American Fundamentalism," *Bibliotheca Sacra*, CXXIII, #490 (April 1966), 115.

[9] Gaspar, 8.

[10] Stewart G. Cole, *The History of Fundamentalism* (Westmont, Connecticut: Greenwood Press, Publishers, 1931), 17.

[11] Samuel Eliot Morrison, Henry Steele Commanger, and William E. Leuchtenberg, *The Growth of the American Republic*, Vol. II (sixth edition: New York: Oxford University Press, 1969), 108.

[12] Winthrop S. Hudson, *Religion in America* (New York: Charles Scribner's Sons, 1965), 208.

13 Edward J. Pfeffer, "The Reception of Darwinism in the United States, 1859-1880," (Unpublished Ph.D. dissertation, Brown University, 1957), 1.

14 *Ibid.*, 7.

15 Richard Hofstadter, *Social Darwinism in American Thought* (Boston: Beacon Press, 1964), 29.

16 Pfeifer, 182.

17 D. C. Masters, *Protestant Church Colleges in Canada: A History* (Toronto: University of Toronto Press, 1966), 91.

18 Hofstadter, 14.

19 C. Greg Singer, *A Theological Interpretation of American History* (Nutley, New Jersey: The Craig Press, 1969), 93.

20 Hofstadter, 3.

21 Singer, 126-127.

22 Hofstadter, 30.

23 Charles Hodge, *What Is Darwinism?* (New York: Scribner Armstrong and Co., 1874), 3.

24 Hofstadter, 26.

25 Hodge, 7.

26 William C. McLoughlin, *Modern Revivalism: Charles Grandison Finney to Billy Graham* (New York: Oxford University Press, 1950), 274.

27 *Ibid.*, 275.

28 Gamaliel Bradford, *D. L. Moody: A Worker in Souls* (New York: Harper and Brothers, 1928), 64.

29 Hofstadter, 3.

30 Kenneth S. Latourette, *The Nineteenth Century Outside Europe*, Vol. III of *Christianity in a Revolutionary Age* (Grand Rapids, Michigan: Zondervan Publishing House, 1969), 152.

31 Gaspar, 8.

32 The fountainhead of modern rationalism is generally recognized to be Immanual Kant (1724-1814). The famous Konigsberg professor, stood at the "turning point of his age" in that he brought his century, the Age of Enlightenment, "to understand itself" [Gaspar, 8]. Kant postulated through his *Critique of Judgment* and *Critique of Practical Reason* that there are two realms of reality, the "noumena," which is beyond time and space, and the "phenomena." Truth, for Kant, resulted from an interplay between impulses from the phenomenal world and the innate categories with the mind. [Karl Barth, *Protestant Thought from Rosseau to Ritschl* (New York: Simon and Schuster, 1969), 150.] The noumenal world is unknowable to man because he cannot perceive such impulses except through an innate categorical imperative, moral conscience. By moral duty man can exercise his rational ability to discover God. The Bible, a book which is part of the phenomenal world, is only a subjective record of man's religious experience and may be understood by reason and sensation. Kant's emphasis on a subjective approach to relativism provided a seedbed for the subsequent germination of biblical criticism, which rejected any type of literal approach to the Scriptures.

It was during this period in Germany that reason was brought to bear on the study of the Scriptures with the techniques of literary and historical criticism. George Park Fisher, a church historian of the late nineteenth century, described the influence of German thought on higher criticism as follows:

. . . in the whole expanse of biblical and historical criticism, traditional assumptions and opinions are combated, now the text of the Bible attacked, now the genuineness of biblical books contested, now the foundations of received views respecting the church, and the history of doctrines taken away. Zeal for exploration in all these directions was kindled in all German universities [George Park Fisher, *History of Christian Doctrine* (New York: Charles Scribner's Sons, 1896), 497].

It was Johann Gottfried Eichhorn (1752-1827) who coined the term, "higher criticism," in his *Einleitung in das Alte Testament*, and for this and his critical studies, he has been called the "Father of Higher Criticism" [Miner Brodhead Stearns, "The Development of European Protestant Theology After 1700" (Unpublished Th.D. dissertation, Dallas Theological Seminary, 1964), 84].

In the field of Old Testament critical studies, Julius Wellhausen (1844-1918) is perhaps the most widely known German scholar for his views on the development of the religion of Israel. He popularized the thesis that Israel's religion evolved from a primitive faith centering in a tribal deity to a belief in Yahweh as a God of righteousness. [Otto Pfleiderer, *The Development of Theology in Germany Since Kant* (New York: MacMillan and Co., 1890), 163-174]. With this presupposition he sought to arrange the documents of the Old Testament according to the creative period of the prophets, which was believed to be pivotal.

In the field of New Testament critical studies, the publication of David Strauss' *Leben Jesu* (1835) provided a major impulse for the inception of an epoch. The teacher of Strauss, Ferdinand C. Baur (1792-1860), the central figure in the newer Tubingen school, published in the same year, *Die Sogenannten Pastoralbrief des Apostles Paulus*, which denied Pauline authorship of the pastoral epistles. The effect of these two writings upon the conservative school of Protestant Christianity is stated by James Orr in 1910:

Three quarters of a century ago an able and determined assault was made upon the Gospels, first by Strauss, in his *Life of Christ*, then by what is known as the Tubingen School of Criticism (under Baur). The result of this assault was in Strauss' case, to resolve the whole content of the Gospels into myth, and, in the hands of Baur and his followers, to carry down most of the literature of the New Testament to the second century, and to discredit its historical worth [James Orr, *The Faith of a Modern Christian* (New York: Nodder and Stoughton, n.d.), 42].

The result of Kantian idealism was that the Bible was viewed as subjective revelation of man's evolving religious experience, not the objective Word of God. Nontraditional views of the Scriptures were taught from classrooms of the major German universities and were imbibed by many young North American theologues and then brought to the pulpits of their native land. Religious historian G. G. Atkins wrote, "By 1890 disturbing rumors were abroad. The work of a long generation of German scholars, whose conclusions challenged or recast the inherited conceptions of the Bible, reached America, indirectly through Scotland, or imported directly in the mental baggage of young theological students who had studied abroad. These young scholars found it easy to get their learning through customs but hard to find a pulpit to show it in. The best of them became the teachers of a new generation."

33 Gaius Glen Atkins, *Religion in Our Times* (New York: Round Table Press, Inc., 1932), 90.

34 Frances P. Weisenberger, *Ordeal of Faith: The Crisis of Church-Going America* (New York: Philosophical Library, Inc., 1959), 80.

35 Milton R. Rudnick, *Fundamentalism and the Missouri Synod* (St. Louis: Concordia Publishing House, 1966), 33-34.

36 Weisenberger, 99-100.

37 Rudnick, 33.

38 J. T. McNeill, *The Presbyterian Church in Canada: 1875-1925*, 207-209; cited by Grant, 63.

39 For a detailed account of the Workman case, see George A. Boyle, "Higher Criticism and the Struggle for Academic Freedom in Canadian Methodism," (Unpublished Th.D. thesis, Victoria University, 1965).

40 John Webster Grant, *The Church in the Canadian Era* (Burlington, Ontario: Welch Publishing Company Inc., 1988), 63.

41 Handy, 361.

42 Ernest R. Sandeen, *The Roots of Fundamentalism, British and American Millenarianism, 1800-1930* (Chicago: The University of Chicago Press, 1970), 183.

43 Frank E. Gaebelein, *Christian Education in a Democracy* (New York: Oxford University Press, 1951), 167.

44 Harold Allen Durfee, "The Theologies of the American Social Gospel: A Study of the Theological and Philosophical Presuppositions of the American Social Gospel," (Unpublished Ph.D. dissertation, Columbia University, 1951), 1.

45 John Dillenberger and Claude Welch, *Protestant Christianity* (New York: Charles Scribner's Sons, 1954), 182.

46 Friedrich Schleiermacher, *The Christian Faith*, Vol. I (New York: Harper and Row, Publishers, 1963), 17.

47 Dillenberger and Welch, 199.

48 Albrecht Ritschl, *The Christian Doctrine of Justification and Reconciliation* (Clifton, New Jersey: Reference Book Publishers, Inc., 1966), 608.

49 Dillenberger and Welch, 200.

50 C. Howard Hopkins, *The Rise of the Social Gospel in American Protestantism, 1865-1915* (New Haven: Yale University Press, 1940), 14-23.

51 *Ibid.*, 20-21.

52 *Ibid.*, 4.

53 Horace Bushnell, *Christian Nurture* (London: Richard D. Dickinson, 1899), 10, 118, 176, 21. Washington Gladden (1836-1918) was a Congregationalist minister who was the early leader of the social gospel movement through his work, *Applied Christianity, Moral Aspects of Social Questions* (1860). Cf. Jacob Henry Dorn, *Washington Gladden: Prophet of the Social Gospel* (Columbus: Ohio University Press, 1967).

54 Walter Rauschenbusch, *A Theology of the Social Gospel* (New York: The MacMillan Company, 1922), 97-99, 243-247; *Christianizing the Social Order* (New York: The MacMillan Company, 1912), 93; and *The Social Principles of Jesus* (New York: Association Press, 1927), 52.

55 Hofstadter, 105-107.

56 Rudnick, 13.

57 Robert T. Handy, *The Social Gospel Movement in America, 1870-1920* (New York: Oxford University Press, 1966), 15.

58 Mark A. Noll, *A History of Christianity in the United States and Canada* (Grand Rapids: Wm. B. Eerdmans Publishing Company, 1992), 275-281.

59 Robert T. Handy, *A History*, 361-363.

60 Noll, 281.

61 Robert E. Wenger, "Social Thought in American Fundamentalism, 1918-1933," (Unpublished Ph.D. dissertation, University of Nebraska, 1973), 216-217.

62 *Ibid.*, 218.

63 William R. Moody, *The Life of Dwight L. Moody* (New York: Fleming H. Revell Company, 1900), 170.

64 *Ibid.*

65 James M. Gray, "Progressive Poverty," *Moody Monthly*, XXXII (February, 1932), 279-280.

66 Dollar, 116.

67 Rudnick, 24-32.

68 Carroll Edwin Harrington, "The Fundamentalist Movement in America, 1870-1920," (Unpublished Ph.D. dissertation, University of California, 1959), ii.

CHAPTER THREE - NORTH AMERICAN HIGHER EDUCATION: *1882-1920*

1 Walter P. Metzger, *Academic Freedom in the Age of the University* (New York: Columbia University Press, 1955), 1.

2 Laurence R. Veysey, *The Emergence of the American University* (Chicago: The University of Chicago Press, 1965), 8.

3 Frederick Rudolph, *The American College and University* (New York: Vintage Books, 1962), 241.

4 Myron F. Wicke, *The Church-Related College* (Washington, DC: Center for Applied Research in Education, Inc., 1964), 2.

5 Clarence P. Shedd, *The Church Follows Its Students* (New Haven: Yale University Press, 1938), 1-2.

6 Frances C. Rosecrance, *The American Colleges and Its Teachers* (New York: The MacMillan Company, 1962), 30.

7 Elwood P. Cubberley, *The History of Education* (Cambridge: Riverside, 1946), 703.

8 Clarence H. Benson, *A Popular History of Christian Education* (Chicago: Moody Press, 1943), 107.

9 Samuel E. Morrison, *The Founding of Harvard College* (Cambridge: Harvard University Press, 1935), 432-433.

10 *Ibid.*, 333-337.

11 "Charter of William and Mary," (1693, cited by Richard Hofstadter and Wilson Smith, *American Higher Education, A Documentary History* (Chicago: The University of Chicago Press, 1961), 33-39.

12 "Thomas Clapp Defends the Ideal of the Sectarian College," (1754), cited by Hofstadter and Smith, 111-117. George Sweeting, "Understanding America's Bible School Movement," *Moody Monthly*, March 1984, 101.

13 "New York Gazette" or "Weekly Post-Boy" (June 1754), cited by Hofstadter and Smith, 109-111.

14 "Charter of Rhode Island College" (1764), cited by Hofstadter and Smith, 134-136. Sweeting, "Understanding America's Bible School Movement," 101.

15 John S. Brubacher and Willis Rudy, *Higher Education in Transition* (New York: Harper and Brothers, 1958), 71.

16 S. A. Witmer, *Education with Dimension* (New York: Channel Press, Inc., 1962), 28.

17 A. Gregor, *Commonwealth Universities Yearbook 1993* (London: ACU, 1993), 340.

18 Peter Rae, "Clearly Canadian: Church-Related Higher Education," (Unpublished paper presented at With Heart and Mind Conference in May, 1995), 3.

19 Robin S. Harris, *A History of Higher Education in Canada: 1663-1960* (Toronto: University of Toronto Press, 1976), 3-12, and D. C. Masters, *Protestant Church Colleges in Canada* (Toronto: University of Toronto Press, 1966), 17-88.

20 Michael Skolnik and Glen Jones, "A Comparative Analysis of Arrangements for State Coordination of Higher Education in Canada and the United States," *Journal of Higher Education* (1962), 1069.

21 Rae, 4.

22 Harris, 27.

23 Masters, 32.

24 Christopher Jencks and David Riesman, *The Academic Revolution* (Chicago: The University of Chicago Press, 1968), 312.

25 Oscar and Mary F. Handlin, *The American College and American Culture* (New York: McGraw-Hill Book Company, 1970), 44.

26 *Ibid.*

27 Varnum L. Collins, *Princeton* (New York: Oxford University Press, 1914), 222-223.

28 Masters, 89.

29 *Ibid.*

30 *Ibid.*, 92.

31 Hofstadter and Smith, 595.

32 Rudolph, 252.

33 Hofstadter and Smith, 477.

34 *Ibid.*, 568.

35 Metzger, 106.

36 "Antebellum" refers to American colleges started between 1800 and 1860 with denominational affiliation.

37 Metzger, 4-5.

38 Hofstadter and Smith, 697.

39 Veysey, 56.

40 Gregor, 340.

41 Glen Jones, "The Canadian Idea of the University," (Unpublished paper presented at the St. John's College Conference on the University, 1994), 14.

42 Rae, 5.

43 Jones, 15.

44 Rae, 5.

45 Skolnik and Jones, 87-89.

46 Veysey, 25.

47 Noah Porter, *Two Sermons* (New Haven: Yale University Press, 1876), 25, cited by Veysey, 25-26.

48 Masters, 77.

49 Cubberley, 705.

50 Metzger, 4.

51 George M. Marsden and Bradley J. Longfield, *The Secularization of the Academy* (New York: Oxford University Press,1992), 12.

52 *Ibid.*, 31.

53 Masters, 209.

54 Rudolph, 76-77.

55 *Ibid.*, 77-78.

56 Guy E. Snavely, *The Church and the Four-Year College* (New York: Harper and Brothers, 1955), 5.

57 *Ibid.*

58 George P. Schmidt, *The Old-Time College President* (New York: Columbia University, 1930), 184-186.

59 *Ibid.*, 187-188.

60 Jencks and Riesman, 322.

61 *Ibid.*, 322-323.

62 *Ibid.*, 324.

63 *Ibid.*

64 *Ibid.*, 315.

CHAPTER FOUR - THE RISE OF THE BIBLE SCHOOL: *1882-1920*

[1] Elwood P. Cubberley, *The History of Education* (Cambridge: Riverside, 1946), 667-672.

[2] Frank E. Gaebelein, *Christian Education in a Democracy* (New York: Oxford University Press, 1951), 167-168.

[3] Peter Rae, "Clearly Canadian: Church-Related Higher Education," (Unpublished paper presented at With Heart and Mind Conference in May, 1995), 11.

[4] George A. Rawlyk, *The Canadian Protestant Experience, 1760-1990* (Burlington, Ontario: Welch Publishing Company, 1990), 298.

[5] George W. Dollar, "The Early Days of American Fundamentalism," *Bibliotheca Sacra*, CXXIII, #490 (April 1966), 115.

[6] The first period was from 1725-1750; the second from 1795-1835; while the fourth period was from 1945 to perhaps 1970. It is more difficult to set a date for the end of the fourth period. William G. McLoughlin, *Modern Revivalism: Charles Grandison Finney to Billy Graham* (New York: Oxford University Press, 1954), 8.

[7] The term "modern revivalism" is used by McLoughlin to describe "professional mass evangelism." *Ibid.*, 11, 166.

[8] Mark A. Noll, *A History of Christianity in the United States and Canada* (Grand Rapids: Wm. B. Eerdmans Publishing Co., 1992), 127.

[9] John Webster Grant, *The Church in the Canadian Era* (Burlington, Ontario: Welch Publishing Company, 1988), 74-75.

[10] McLoughlin, 168.

[11] John David Hannah, "James Martin Gray: His Life and Work," (Unpublished Th.D. dissertation, Dallas Theological Seminary, 1974), 38-62.

[12] James F. Findlay, Jr., *Dwight L. Moody, American Evangelist, 1837-1899* (Chicago: The University of Chicago Press, 1969), 164-226.

[13] Noll, 278.

[14] Ernest R. Sandeen, *The Roots of Fundamentalism, British and American Millenarianism, 1800-1930* (Chicago: The University of Chicago Press, 1970), 196.

[15] Hannah, 41.

[16] Dollar, "The Early Days of American Fundamentalism," 121.

[17] Sandeen, 133-134.

[18] Milton R. Rudnick, *Fundamentalism and the Missouri Synod* (St. Louis: Concordia Publishing House, 1966), 29.

[19] James H. Brookes, "Introductory," *The Truth*, I (1875), 4-5; cited by Hannah, 57.

[20] A. J. Gordon, "Editorial," *The Watchword*, I (October 1878), 1; cited by Hannah, 58.

[21] *After Fifty Years: A Record of God's Working Through the Christian and Missionary Alliance* (Harrisburg, Pennsylvania: Christian Publications, 1939), 18.

[22] Sandeen, *The Roots of Fundamentalism*, 208-220.

23 Gene Getz, *MBI, The Story of the Moody Bible Institute* (Chicago: Moody Press, 1969), 254-264.

24 Leslie K. Tarr, *Shields of Canada* (Grand Rapids: Barker Book House, 1967), 108-110.

25 Hannah, 59.

26 Stewart H. Cole, *The History of Fundamentalism* (Westmont, Connecticut: Greenwood Press, Publishers, 1931), 45.

27 Frank E. Gaebelein, *History of the Scofield Reference Bible* (New York: Oxford University Press, 1969), 52. See also *Scofield Reference Bible* (New York: Oxford University Press, 1967), v-viii. The first edition was completed and published in 1909 by Oxford University Press. The 1909 copyright was renewed in 1917, 1937, 1945; the work was revised in 1967.

28 Sandeen, 183.

29 Getz, 23.

30 *Record of Christian Work* (February 1886), 5-6; *Chicago Tribune* (23 January 1886); 3, and *Chicago Inter-Ocean* (23 January 1886), 7.

31 T. B. Madsen, "The Origin of the Bible Institute," *The Evangelical Beacon,* XVI (19 November 1946), 6.

32 A. B. Simpson, "Editorial," *The Gospel in All Lands* (March 1880), 55; and A. J. Gordon, "The Missionary Training Schools—Do Baptists Need Them?" *Baptist Quarterly Review* XII (January 1890), 77.

33 Charles Ray, *The Life of Charles Haddon Spurgeon* (London: Passmore and Alabaster, 1902), 221-225.

34 Ernest B. Gordon, *Adoniram Judson Gordon: A Bibliography* (New York: Fleming H. Revell, 1896), 247.

35 William S. McBirnie, Jr., "A Study of the Bible Institute Movement," (Unpublished D.R.E. dissertation, Southwestern Baptist Theological Seminary, 1953), 19; and Getz, 24.

36 S. A. Witmer, *Education with Dimension* (Manhasset, New York: Channel Press, Inc., 1962), 34; and C. B. Eavey, *History of Christian Education* (Chicago: Moody Press, 1964), 338.

37 The institute was relocated in Nyack in 1897 and was renamed several times before receiving its present name, Nyack College. Eavey, 338-339.

38 The institute was incorporated in 1891. In 1916 it merged with Don O. Shelton's National Bible Institute, which was established in 1907. The name was later changed to Shelton College and eventually moved to Cape May, New Jersey. Osborn's Union Missionary Training Institute does not show up in much of the historical data, apparently it was small in size and was merged with and absorbed by the larger National Bible Institute. Hannah, 53.

39 Getz, 29-46.

40 Nathan R. Wood, *A School of Christ* (Boston: Halliday Lithograph Corporation, 1953), 11-12.

41 *Ibid.*

42 *Johnson Bible College Catalog, 1995-1996,* 1-2.

43 John G. Stackhouse, *Canadian Evangelicalism in the Twentieth Century* (Toronto: University of Toronto Press, 1993), 51-70.

44 Witmer, 37-38.

45 *Ibid.*, 39.

46 Hubert Reynhout, Jr., "A Comparative Study of the Bible Institute Curriculums," (Unpublished M. A. thesis, University of Michigan, 1947), 43-47.

47 Much of the information in this table comes from Hubert Reynhout, Jr., "A
Comparative Study of Bible Institute Curriculums," and S. A. Witmer,
Education with Dimension.

48 Madsen, 6.

49 Virginia Lieson Brereton, *Training God's Army: The American Bible
School, 1880-1940* (Indianapolis: Indiana University Press, 1990), 63.

50 *Ibid.*, 64.

51 A. T. Pierson, *The Crisis of Missions* (New York: Robert Carter and
Brothers, 1886), 327; cited by Brererton, 59.

52 "Mr. Moody's New Plan," cited by Wilbur M. Smith, *An Annotated
Bibliography of D. L. Moody* (Chicago: Moody Press, 1948), 78.

53 Findlay, 327.

54 Brereton, 59.

55 Findlay, 333.

56 Brererton, 59.

57 *Ibid.*, 59-60.

58 Renald E. Showers, "The History of Philadelphia College of Bible,"
(Unpublished Th.M. thesis, Dallas Theological Seminary, 1959), 62.

59 Brereton, 60.

60 A. B. Simpson, "The Training and Sending Forth of Workers," *Christian
and Missionary Alliance* XVIII (30 April 1897), 419.

61 *Ibid.*

62 Brereton, 63.

63 Getz, 37.

CHAPTER FIVE – EARLY BIBLE SCHOOL LEADERS

1 A. E. Thompson, *The Life of A. B. Simpson* (Harrisburg, Pennsylvania:
Christian Publications, Inc., 1960), 3.

2 A. W. Tozer, *Wingspread: Albert B. Simpson—A Study of Spiritual Attitude*
(Harrisburg, Pennsylvania: Christian Publications, Inc., 1943), 12.

3 Thompson, 9.

4 *Ibid.*, 15.

5 *Ibid.*, 27-28.

6 *Ibid.*, 31.

7 *Ibid.*, 43.

8 Tozer, 40.

9 *Ibid.*, 44.

10 A. B. Simpson, "The Macedonian Cry," *Christian Alliance and Foreign
Missionary Weekly*, 31 August 1894, 198.

11 Thompson, 85.

12 A. B. Simpson, "Editorial," *Christian Alliance and Foreign Missionary
Weekly*, 5 January, 1894, 49.

13 John H. Cable, *A History of the Missionary Training Institute: The Pioneer School of America* (Harrisburg, Pennsylvania: Christian Publications, Inc., 1933), 17.

14 Thompson, 105-106.

15 *After Fifty Years: A Record of God's Working Through The Christian and Missionary Alliance* (Harrisburg, Pennsylvania: Christian Publications, Inc., 1937), 18.

16 C. Donald McKaig, "The Educational Philosophy of Dr. A. B. Simpson, Founder of the Christian and Missionary Alliance," (Unpublished Ph.D. dissertation, New York University, 1948), 23-24.

17 Tozer, 142-143.

18 James F. Findlay, Jr., *Dwight L. Moody, American Evangelist, 1837-1899* (Chicago: The University of Chicago Press, 1969), 61.

19 Donald A. Wells, "D. L. Moody and His Schools: An Historical Analysis of an Educational Ministry," (Unpublished Ph.D. dissertation, Boston University, 1972), 57.

20 William R. Moody, *The Life of D. L. Moody* (New York: Fleming H. Revell, 1900), 15.

21 Wells, 58.

22 Findlay, 106.

23 *Ibid.*, 78.

24 Wells, 60.

25 J. C. Pollock, *Moody: A Biographical Sketch of the Pacesetter in Modern Mass Evangelism* (New York: The MacMillan Company, 1963), 171.

26 William R. Moody, 263-264.

27 *Ibid.*, 336.

28 *Ibid.*, p, 443.

29 Gene A. Getz, *MBI: The Story of Moody Bible Institute* (Chicago: Moody Press, 1969), 26-69.

30 Ernest B. Gordon, *Adoniram Judson Gordon: A Bibliography* (New York: Fleming H. Revell Company, 1896), 19.

31 *The Clarendon Light*, January 1895, 2.

32 *Ibid.*

33 George G. Houghton, "The Contributions of A. J. Gordon to American Christianity," (Unpublished Th.D. dissertation, Dallas Theological Seminary, 1970), 6.

34 Ernest B. Gordon, 355.

35 *Ibid.*, 251-259.

36 A. T. Pierson, *The Missionary Review of the World* IV (January 1891), 62.

37 Houghton, 2.

38 *Ibid.*, 173.

39 Virginia L. Brereton, *Training God's Army: The American Bible School, 1880-1940* (Indianapolis: Indiana University Press, 1990), 51.

40 William A. BeVier, "A Biographical Sketch of C. I. Scofield," (Unpublished M. A. thesis, Southern Methodist University, 1960), 3.

41 Charles G. Trumbull, *The Life of C. I. Scofield* (New York: Oxford University Press, 1920), 6.

[42] *Ibid.*, 8.

[43] *Ibid.*, 16-22.

[44] BeVier, 23.

[45] Trumbull, 27-31.

[46] *Ibid.*, 51.

[47] BeVier, 39-40.

[48] The work of the Bible was aided by the labors of several consulting editors. They were: A. C. Gaebelein; James M. Gray, President, Moody Bible Institute; Arthur T. Pierson, author and editor; William Erdman, Presbyterian minister and author; W. F. Moorehead, president, Xenia Theological Seminary; and Elmore Harris, president, Toronto Bible Institute. Arno C. Gaebelein, *The History of the Scofield Reference Bible* (New York: Our Hope Publications, 1943), 45-47, 57-58. William L. Pettingill, co-founder of Philadelphia School of Bible, was added for the 1917 edition. Each of these individuals was involved in the Bible institute movement, either as an administrator, teacher, or guest lecturer.

[49] *The Central American Bulletin* (Dallas: The Central American Mission 1956).

[50] Ronald E. Showers, "The History of Philadelphia College of Bible," (Unpublished Th.M thesis, Dallas Theological Seminary, 1959), 23-24.

[51] Trumbull, 64-65.

[52] *Ibid.*, 65.

[53] *Ibid.*, 105.

[54] BeVier, 94.

[55] Roger Martin, *R. A. Torrey, Apostle of Certainty* (Murfreesboro, Tennessee: Sword of the Lord Publishers, 1976), 7.

[56] *Ibid.*, 25-28.

[57] *Ibid.*, 36-40.

[58] *Ibid.*, 59-62.

[59] *Ibid.*, 85-90.

[60] Ernest R. Sandeen, *The Roots of Fundamentalism, British and American Millenarianism, 1800-1930* (Chicago: The University of Chicago Press, 1970), 196,

[61] Martin, 222-232.

[62] "To the Memory of Dr. Harris," *The Canadian Baptist* (January 4, 1912), 4.

[63] Ian S. Rennie, "Gratitude for the Past," *Recorder* (Spring, 1984), 6.

[64] *Ibid.*, 8.

[65] Rennie, 8.

[66] John G. Stackhouse, Jr., *Canadian Evangelicalism in the Twentieth Century* (Toronto: University of Toronto Press, 1993), 36.

[67] L. Thomas Smith, Jr., *Above Every Other Desire: A Centennial History of Johnson Bible College* (Kimberlin Heights, Tennessee: Johnson Bible College, 1993), 20.

[68] *Ibid.*, 21.

[69] *Ibid.*, 21-22.

[70] *Ibid.*, 26-27.

71 *Ibid.*, 44.

72 *Ibid.*, 57.

73 William R. Moody, 344-345.

74 "Left Unfinished," *Serving-and-Waiting,* October, 1921, 1.

CHAPTER SIX - COMMON THEOLOGICAL THEMES

1 Virginia L. Brereton, *Training God's Army: The American Bible School, 1882-1940* (Bloomington, Indiana University Press, 1990), 1.

2 Donald George Tinder, "Fundamentalist Baptists in Northern and Western United States, 1920-1950," (Unpublished Ph.D. dissertation, Yale University, 1969), 38.

3 Brereton, 2.

4 Horace Bushnell, *Christian Nurture* (London: Richard D. Dickinson, 1899), 10.

5 *Ibid.*, 21.

6 Brereton, 2.

7 Mark A. Noll, *A History of Christianity in the United States and Canada* (Grand Rapids, Michigan: William B. Eerdmans Publishing Company, 1992), 371.

8 Thomas F. Henstock, "A History and Interpretation of the Curriculum of Central Bible Institute," (Unpublished M.A. thesis, Central Bible Institute, 1964), 52.

9 *Bible Institute of Los Angeles Bulletin* (October, 1920), pp, 23-33; cited by Brereton, 87.

10 Timothy P. Weber, *Living in the Shadow of the Second Coming: American Premillennialism, 875-1982* (Grand Rapids, Michigan: Academie Books, 1983), 13.

11 *Ibid.*, 15-16.

12 George E. Ladd, *The Blessed Hope* (Grand Rapids, Michigan: Eerdmans, 1956), 35-40.

13 Ernest R. Sandeen, *The Roots of Fundamentalism: British and American Millenarianism, 1800-1930* (Chicago: The University of Chicago Press, 1970), 81-90.

14 Cyrus I. Scofield, *Scofield Reference Bible* (New York: Oxford University Press, 1909), 5.

15 Cyrus I. Scofield, *Rightly Dividing the Word of Truth* (New York: Fleming H. Revell, 1888), 18.

16 Sandeen, *The Roots of Fundamentalism*, 132.

17 Gene A. Getz, *MBI: The Story of Moody Bible Institute* (Chicago: Moody Press, 1969), 161.

18 Noll, 378.

19 *Ibid.*

20 *Ibid.*, 379.

21 J. C. Pollock, *The Keswick Story: The Authorized History of the Keswick Convention* (London: Hodder and Stoughton, 1964).

22 Brereton, 5.

[23] A. T. Pierson, "The Message: Its Practical Application," *The Keswick Convention* (1895), 92-93.

[24] Brereton, 7.

[25] Dr. & Mrs. Howard Taylor, *J. Hudson Taylor: A Biography* (Chicago: Moody Press, 1965).

[26] Brereton, 8.

[27] Charles H. Brackett, "The History of Azusa College and the Friends," (Unpublished M.A. thesis, University of Southern California, 1967), 55.

[28] Noll, 386.

[29] *Ibid.*

[30] Robert T. Handy, *A History of the Churches in the United States and Canada* (New York: Oxford University Press, 1977), 298

[31] *Ibid.*

[32] Noll, 387.

[33] Brereton, 13.

[34] For example, the Central Bible Institute, founded by the Assemblies of God in 1922, was one of the earliest and most stable Pentecostal schools. Yet its academic standards remained low until the 1940s when administrators started to move toward accreditation. Students were not required to have a high school education until 1948, and the school offered no degrees until the following year. *Ibid.*

CHAPTER SEVEN - THE FAITH MISSION MOVEMENT

[1] John R. Mott, "The Beginning of the Student Volunteer Movement," *Record of Christian Work*, 10 September 1911, 1.

[2] Albert B. Simpson, "Editorial," *The Gospel in All Lands*, January 1881, 40.

[3] Harold R. Cook, *Highlights of Christian Missions* (Chicago: Moody Press, 1967), 64-66.

[4] William W. Sweet, *The Story of Religion in America* (New York: Harper and Brothers, 1939), 251-252.

[5] Robert D. Linder, "Introduction: The Christian Centuries," *Eerdman's Handbook to the History of Christianity* (Grand Rapids, Michigan: Eerdmans, 1977), xxii.

[6] Ruth A. Tucker, *From Jerusalem to Irian Jaya, A Biographical History of Christian Missions* (Grand Rapids, Michigan: Academie Books, 1983), 229.

[7] *Ibid.*

[8] Cook, 65-66.

[9] Tucker, 289.

[10] *Ibid*, 173-180.

[11] *Ibid.*, 180.

[12] Timothy P. Weber, *Living in the Shadow of the Second Coming: American Premillennialism, 1875-1982* (Grand Rapids, Michigan: Academie Books, 1983), 75.

[13] J. Herbet Kane, *Faith Mighty Faith: A Handbook of the Interdenominational Foreign Mission Association* (New York: Interdenominatioal Foreign Mission Association, 1956), 111.

[14] *Ibid.*

[15] J. Herbert Kane, *Understanding Christian Missions* (Grand Rapids, Michigan: Baker Book House, 1974), 157.

[16] Tucker, 290.

[17] Kane, *Faith Mighty Faith*, ii.

[18] Cook, 65.

[19] Kane, *Understanding Christian Missions*, 159.

[20] C. B. Eavey, *History of Christian Education* (Chicago: Moody Press, 1964), 336-337.

[21] Cook, 67; Kane, *Understanding Christian Missions*, 161; Tucker, 289.

[22] Cook, 67.

[23] Kane, *Understanding Christian Missions*, 161.

[24] Clifford E. Larsen, "An Analysis of the General Conceptions Underlying Bible Institute Courses on How to Teach the Bible," (Unpublished Ph.D. dissertation, University of Southern California, 1955), 80-81.

[25] David Rambo, "The Role of the Bible College Movement in Missions," *AABC Newsletter*, XXVIII (September 1984), 1.

[26] S. A. Witmer, *Education with Dimension* (New York: Channel Press, 1962), 35.

[27] Kane, *Understanding Christian Missions*, 161.

[28] Tucker, 289.

[29] *Missionary Training Institute Catalog, 1922-1923* (Nyack, New York: Missionary Training Institute, 1922), 8.

[30] Tucker, 295-297.

[31] *Ibid.*, 300-301.

[32] *Moody Bible Institute Monthly*, XXIII (May 1923), 433.

[33] A. J. Gordon, "Short Cut Methods," 1.

[34] "The Gordon Missionary Training School," *The Watchword*, XVII (June 1895), 87.

[35] "Student Volunteers," *Hypernikon* (Boston: Gordon Bible and Missionary College, 1920), 71.

[36] Kane, *Understanding Christian Missions*, 161-162.

[37] *Ibid.*, 162.

[38] Clifton J. Phillips, "The Student Volunteer Movement," *The Missionary Enterprise in China and America*, John K. Fairbank, ed. (Cambridge: Harvard University Press, 1974), 103.

[39] Gene A. Getz, *MBI: The Story of the Moody Bible Institute* (Chicago: Moody Press, 1969), 167.

[40] "Student Volunteers," *Hypernikon* (1920), 71.

[41] W. C. Stevens, "Notes from Nyack," *Alliance Weekly*, 13 April 1912, 27.

[42] *Ibid.*

CHAPTER EIGHT - PROTESTANT FUNDAMENTALISM: 1918-1930

1 H. Richard Niebuhr, "Fundamentalism," *Encyclopedia of the Social Sciences*, 15 volumes (New York: MacMillan Company, 1931), VI, 526-527.

2 Stewart G. Cole, *The History of Fundamentalism* (New York: Harper and Row, 1931); Norman F. Furniss, *The Fundamentalist Controversy, 1918-1931* (New Haven: Yale University Press, 1954).

3 Cole, 34, 98, 103-108, 129, 223; Furniss, 13, 16, 50, 72, 119-122, 130-133.

4 Ernest R. Sandeen, *The Roots of Fundamentalism: British and American Millenarianism, 1800-1930* (Chicago: The University of Chicago Press, 1970); *The Origins of Fundamentalism: Toward an Historical Interpretation* (Philadelphia: Fortress Press, 1968).

5 LeRoy Moore, Jr., "Another Look at Fundamentalism: A Response to Ernest R. Sandeen," *Church History* XXXVII (June 1968), 195-202.

6 George M. Marsden, "Defining Fundamentalism," *Christian Scholar's Review* I (Winter 1971), 141-151.

7 Ernest R. Sandeen, "Defining Fundamentalism: A Reply to Professor Marsden," *Christian Scholar's Review* (Spring, 1971, 227-232.

8 Timothy P. Weber, *Living in the Shadow of the Second Coming: American Premillennialism, 1875-1982* (Grand Rapids, Michigan: Academie Books, 1983), 32-33.

9 *Ibid.*, 33.

10 Robert T. Handy, *A History of the Churches in the United States and Canada* (New York: Oxford University Press, 1977), 294; and Mark A. Noll, *A History of Christianity in the United States and Canada* (Grand Rapids, Michigan: William B. Eerdmans Publishing Company, 1992), 381.

11 Handy, 381-384; Noll, 381.

12 Noll, 381-382.

13 George M. Marsden, *Fundamentalism and American Culture: The Shaping of Twentieth Century Evangelicalism, 1875-1925* (New York: Oxford University Press, 1980), 141-195.

14 Noll, 382-383.

15 Bruce Shelley, "William Bell Riley: A Champion of Fundamentalism," *Conservative Baptist* (Summer 1976), 3.

16 Willard B. Gatewood, Jr., *Controversy in the Twenties: Fundamentalism, Modernism, and Evolution* (Nashville, Broadman Press), 18.

17 Noll, 383-384.

18 Handy, 384.

19 Noll, 384.

20 *Ibid.*, 385.

21 *Ibid.*

22 Robert E. Wenger, "Social Thought in American Fundamentalism, 1918-1933," (Unpublished Ph.D. dissertation, University of Nebraska, 1973), 57-75.

23 Handy, 385.

24 *Ibid.*

25 John G. Stackhouse, Jr., *Canadian Evangelicalism in the Twentieth Century* (University of Toronto Press, 1993), 23-34.

26 Handy, 389-390.

27 Stackhouse, 33-34.

28 *Ibid.*, 35-45.

29 Handy, 390.

30 Stackhouse, 42-45.

31 Noll, 385.

32 Martin E. Marty, *Modern American Religion,* 2 volumes (Chicago: University of Chicago Press, 1986); cited by Noll, 385.

33 Noll, 385.

34 *Ibid.*, 385-386.

35 Virginia Brereton, *Training God's Army: The American Bible School, 1880-1940* (Indianapolis: Indiana University Press, 1990), 33.

36 *Ibid.*

37 *Ibid.*, 34-35.

38 *Ibid.*, 35.

39 *Ibid.*

40 Edward Dobson Edward Hinson, *The Fundamentalist Phenomenon: A Resurgence of Conservative Christianity* (Garden City, New York: Double-Day and Company, 1981), 110.

41 *Ibid.*, 113-128.

42 Sandeen, *Roots of Fundamentalism*, 183.

43 Marsden, *Fundamentalism and American Culture*, 128.

44 Dollar, *A History of Fundamentalism in America*, 188.

CHAPTER NINE – THE MOVEMENT IN CANADA

1 "101 Reasons to Prepare for Life and Ministry in Canada: Annual College Guide," *Faith Alive* (November 1985), 31-54.

2 Bruce L Guenther, "The Origin of the Bible School Movement in Western Canada: Towards an Ethnic Interpretation," (Paper Presented at the Canadian Society of Church History, Carleton University, June 1993), 135.

3 Ben Harder, "The Bible Institute-College Movement in Canada," *Journal of the Canadian Church Historical Society* 22 (April 1980), 29. Harder's article was the first to appear in an academic journal that specifically addressed the topic of the Canadian Bible college movement.

4 George A. Rawlyk, *Canadian Baptists and Higher Education* (Kingston, Ontario: McGill-Queen's Academic Press, 1988), 298.

5 Guenther, 156.

6 *Ibid.*, 158. Guenther noted that the first Bible school in Canada was the Union Missionary Training Institute in Niagara Falls (1885); the second was the Christian Institute in Toronto (1888); and the third was the Toronto Missionary Training School (1893). All three schools closed within a few years. The Toronto Bible Training School had the backing of a much broader constituency and still exists as Ontario Bible College.

7 Brain A. McKenzie, "A History of the Toronto Bible College (1894-1968): A Study in Canadian Fundamentalism," (Unpublished Ph.D. dissertation, University of Toronto, 1992), 2.

8 Ian S. Rennie, "Gratitude for the Past," *Recorder* (Spring 1984), 8.

9 John G. Stackhouse, Jr., *Canadian Evangelicalism in the Twentieth Century* (University of Toronto Press, 1993), 55.

10 Harder, 38-43.

11 Guenther, 136-137.

12 Stackhouse, 84-85. Moody Bible Institute in Chicago has consistently been the largest Bible college in the world.

13 Robert Burkinshaw, "Evangelical Bible Colleges in Twentieth Century Canada," (Paper presented at a conference on "Aspects of the Canadian Evangelical Experience," Queen's University, May 1995), 1.

14 Stackhouse, 75.

15 For the early history of Winnipeg Bible College, see "Minute Book of Winnipeg Bible Training School" (6 September 1926-23 April 1931), Providence College and Theological Seminary, Otterburne, Manitoba; Edward Hildebrandt, "A History of the Winnipeg Bible Institute," (Unpublished Th.M. thesis, Dallas Theological Seminary, 1965).

16 D. Bruce Hindmarsh, "The Winnipeg Fundamentalist Newtwork, 1910-1940: The Roots of Transdenominational Evangelicalism in Manitoba and Saskatchewan," (Paper presented at a conference on "Aspects of the Canadian Evangelical Experience," Queen's University, May 1995), 22-25.

17 Guenther, 138.

18 *Ibid.*

19 The first Bible school in Western Canada was probably the Holiness Bible School, located first in Crystal City, MB (1909-1911). After several relocations, it eventually merged with a Free Methodist School (former Aldersgate College) in Moose Jaw, SK. *Ibid*, 146.

20 *Herbert Bible School Prospectus (1955-56)*, 5.

21 Guenther, 149-155.

22 *Ibid.*, 150.

23 *Ibid.*

24 Frank Epp, *Mennonites in Canada, 1786-1920, The History of Separate People* Vol. I (Toronto: MacMillan of Canada, 1974), 237-240.

25 The three sponsoring conferences are the Evangelical Mennonite Conference, the Evangelical Mennonite Mission Conference, and the Chortitzer Mennonite Conference. *Steinbach Bible College Catalogue, 1996*, 4.

26 Rudy A. Regeher, "A Century of Private Schools," *Call to Faithfulness: Essays in Canadian Mennonite Studies*, Henry Poetcker and Rudy A. Regehr (eds.) (Winnipeg: Canadian Mennonite Bible College, 1972), 113.

27 Guenther, 152.

28 *Ibid.*

29 *Ibid.*, 153.

30 The Pentecostal Assemblies of Canada is the Canadian counterpart to the Assemblies of God in the United States.

31 *Canadian Bible College Catalogue, 1996*, 2.

32 John M. Badertscher, Gordon Harland, and Roland E. Miller, *Religious Studies in Manitoba and Saskatchewan: A State-of-the-Art Review, The Study of Religion in Canada,* Vol. 4 (Waterloo: Wilfred Laurier University Press for the Canadian Corporation for Studies in Religion, 1993), 140-141.

33 New Brunswick Legislature, "An Act to Incorporate the New Brunswick Bible Institute. . . ." 1947.

34 *Ibid.*

35 Vancouver Bible Training School, Council Minutes, 17 May 1918.

36 George A. Rawlyk, "Protestant Colleges in Canada: Past and Future," in George Marsden and Bradley Longfield, eds. *The Secularization of the Academy* (New York: Oxford University Press, 1992), 278-302.

37 John G. Stackhouse, Jr., "Women in Public Ministry in Twentieth-Century Canadian and American Evangelicalism: Five Models," *Studies in Religion* 17 (Fall 1988), 471-485.

38 G. D. Pries, *A Place Called Peniel: Winkler Bible Institute, 1925-1975* (Altona, Manitoba: Friesen & Sons, 1975), 73.

39 Burkinshaw, 5-6.

40 *Ibid.*, 6.

41 *Ibid.*, 5.

42 G. Ronald Neufeld and Allen Steven, *Stay in School Initiatives: A Summary of School Dropouts and Implications for Special Education* (Kingston: The Canadian Council for Exceptional Children, 1992), 2.

43 S. A. Witmer, "Report on Canadian Bible Institutes and Bible Colleges," (Report presented at the Conference of Christian Educators of Alberta, Saskatchewan, and Manitoba, May 31-June 2, 1960), 2.

44 W. E. Mann, *Sect, Cult, and Church in Alberta* (University of Toronto Press, 1955), 85.

45 *Ibid.*, 89.

46 Joel Carpenter, "Fundamentalist Institutions and the Rise of Evangelical Protestantism, 1929-1942," *Church History* (March 1980), 67.

CHAPTER TEN - THE GROWTH YEARS: 1930-1960

1 The number of Bible institutes and colleges started between 1882 and 1920 reported by Witmer is less than the figure reported by Reynholt in Chapter four. Reynholt's list was more comprehensive, including a number of early Bible schools that closed after only a few years of operation. S. A. Witmer, *The Bible College Story: Education With Dimension* (Manhasset, New York: Channel Press, Inc., 1962), 39.

2 *Ibid.*, 40.

3 *Ibid.*, 39.

4 *Ibid.*

5 Witmer's list of Canadian Bible schools was not as comprehensive as one compiled by Bruce Guenther and cited in Chapter nine. Guenther also included many small denominational schools that closed after short periods of time or merged with other institutions. *Ibid.*

6 *Ibid.*

7 The President's Committee on Education Beyond the High School, *Second Report to the President* (Washington, DC: US Government Printing Office, 1957), 1-2.

8 *Educational Attainment of Canadians* (Ottawa: Statistics Canada, 1991).

9 Witmer, 43.

10 John Mostert, *The AABC Story* (Fayetteville, Arkansas: American Association of Bible Colleges, 1986), 43.

11 William C. Ringenberg, *The Christian College: A History of Protestant Higher Education* (Grand Rapids, Michigan: William B. Eerdmans Publishing Company, 1984), 166.

12 *Ibid*, 167.

13 Witmer, 42-44.

14 Ringenberg, 167.

15 Witmer, 44.

16 John Mostert, *The AABC Story* (Fayetteville: Arkansas: American Association of Bible Colleges, 1986), 14.

17 Letter by Principal John McNicol of Toronto Bible College to Dr. Samuel Sutherland of the Bible Institute of Los Angeles, dated December 11, 1942.

18 Witmer, 45-46.

19 Mostert, 18.

20 *Ibid.*

21 *Ibid.*, 31.

22 *Ibid.*, 32.

23 The name was abbreviated in 1958 to the Accrediting Association of Bible Colleges. The name was changed again to the American Association of Bible Colleges in 1973. Finally, in 1994, the name was changed back to the Accrediting Association of Bible Colleges.

24 Mostert, 41.

25 Witmer, 46.

26 *Ibid.*

27 Mostert, 159.

28 Witmer, 46.

29 Ringenberg, 170.

30 Mostert, 54-55, 158.

31 *Ibid.*, 73-75.

32 The data did include evening divisions that were conducted in connection with day institutions.

33 Witmer, 49.

34 *Ibid.*

35 *Ibid.*, 49-50.

36 *Ibid.*, 51-52.

37 Witmer used the term "denominational" to refer to institutions that were under the control of a particular denomination in organization and accountability. "Interdenominational" institutions were independent of denominational control with board members selected irrespective of denominational affiliation.

38 Witmer, 53.

[39] *Ibid.*, 53-54.

[40] *Ibid.*, 54-55.

[41] *Ibid.*, 55.

[42] *Ibid.*

[43] Enock C. Dryness, "The Bible College and Accreditation," *Newsletter*, Vol. II, No. 2 (May 1958), 1.

CHAPTER ELEVEN – THE CHANGING YEARS OF THE BIBLE COLLEGE MOVEMENT: *1960-PRESENT*

[1] Timothy R. Millard, "Changes in the Missions of Colleges Accredited by the American Association of Bible Colleges as Indicated by their Educational Programs, Recruiting Practices, and Future Plans," (Unpublished Ed.D. dissertation, University of Virginia, 1994), 66.

[2] Millard developed a detailed list that showed the advancement of AABC member schools including their founding dates, dates they lengthened their programs, dates they began to offer bachelor's degrees, dates they received initial accreditation with AABC, and dates they received initial regional accreditation.

[3] Gary R. Moncher, "The Bible College and American Moral Culture," (Unpublished Ph.D. dissertation, University of California, Berkeley, 1987), 140.

[4] *Accrediting Association of Bible Colleges Directory: 1995-1996.*

[5] *AABC Directory: 1995-1996*, 142; Millard, 72-77.

[6] *Catalogue of Messiah College: 1995-1996*, 7.

[7] Millard, 78-80.

[8] *AABC Directory: 1995-1996*, 142.

[9] *Ibid.*

[10] Randall Balmer, "We Do Bible Better," *Christianity Today* 35 (16 September 1991), 25.

[11] Robert Kallgren, "Bible Colleges: Their Present Health and Possible Futures," (Unpublished Ed.D. dissertation, University of South Carolina, 1988), 145.

[12] Norman D. Rempel, "A Descriptive and Comparative Survey of General Education in the U.S. Bible College Curriculum," (Unpublished Ph.D. dissertation, University of Nebraska-Lincoln, 1992), 89-92.

[13] Millard, 91.

[14] Kenneth Gangel, "The Bible College: Past, Present, and Future," *Christianity Today* 24 (7 November, 1980), 34-36.

[15] *Ibid.*

[16] Millard, 178-181.

[17] *Ibid.*

[18] *Ibid.*

[19] *Ibid.*, 84.

[20] *Ibid.*, 85.

[21] *Ibid.*

22 *AABC Directory: 1995-1996.*

23 *Ibid.*, 86.

24 S. A. Witmer, "Let the Issue Be Faced," *AABC Newsletter* (4 August 1960); Mostert, 114-115.

25 Millard, 197-198.

26 *Ibid.*, 197-202.

27 *Ibid.*

28 *Ibid.*

29 *Ibid.*, 201-202.

30 *Ibid.*, 202-203.

31 *Ibid.*

32 *Ibid.*, 203-204.

33 *Ibid.*, 204-205.

34 *Ibid.*

CHAPTER TWELVE - CRITICAL ISSUES AND FUTURE DIRECTIONS

1 Kenneth Gangel, "The Bible College: Past, Present, and Future," *Christianity Today* (7 November, 1980), 36.

2 Robert C. Kallgren, "The Invisible Colleges," *Christianity Today* (16 September, 1991), 27.

3 Peter Drucker, *Managing the Non-Profit Organization, Principles and Practices* (New York: Harper Brothers, 1992), 3.

4 *The Accrediting Association of Bible Colleges Directory: 1995-1996*, 142; Timothy R. Millard, "Changes in the Missions of Colleges Accredited by the American Association of Bible Colleges as Indicated by their Educational Programs, Recruiting Practices, and Future Plans," (Unpublished Ed.D. dissertation, University of Virginia, 1994), 66.

5 Remarks taken from an address given by Robert E. Picirilli, president of the Accrediting Association of Bible Colleges, at the 1996 AABC conference in Fort Mill, South Carolina (15 February, 1996).

6 Telephone interview with Randall Bell, executive director of the Accrediting Association of Bible Colleges (27 September, 1996).

7 Address given by Picirilli at the 1996 AABC conference (15 February, 1996).